Baughman, Judith S.

Literary Masters Vol. 1
F. Scott Fitzgerald

LITERARY MASTERS

ISSN 1526-1530

LITERARY MASTERS

Volume 1

F. Scott Fitzgerald

Judith S. Baughman
University of South Carolina

with **Matthew J. Bruccoli**
University of South Carolina

A MANLY, INC. BOOK

GALE GROUP

Detroit
New York
San Francisco
London
Boston
Woodbridge, CT

F. SCOTT FITZGERALD

Matthew J. Bruccoli and Richard Layman, *Editorial Directors*

ADVISORY BOARD

For Elizabeth Smith Baughman,
reader and student

TABLE OF CONTENTS

F. SCOTT FITZGERALD

A NOTE TO THE READER

THE TELLER IN THE TALE

*by Alvin Kernan,
Senior Advisor in
the Humanities,
The Andrew W.
Mellon Foundation*

A few years ago it was fashionable to speak of "the death of the author" and to argue that "language writes, not the man." These postmodernist views were part of a philosophy that discounted the individuality of the writer in favor of a world of impersonal texts and systems, such as language, which furnish a "scriptor" with the only conceptions of reality he or she can have. In this view of things the author disappeared into a "mere grammatical subject"; the time and place were doing the writing, not the author.

This vast, gray, impersonal view has not prevailed, however, because it goes against the grain of what we all know and feel to be the actual case. Historically, our literature is not just a set of coded texts but living writings intertwined with the names of the men and women who wrote them. We cannot think of *The Canterbury Tales* without thinking of the sly but somewhat bumbling Geoffrey Chaucer, good-natured but sharply ironic, who introduces himself as one of the pilgrims in his own poem. And we try our best to see William Shakespeare, always a somewhat mysterious fellow, in the figure of the magician Prospero on his magic island in *The Tempest*. Charles Dickens, as a frightened boy sent to work in the blacking factory in industrialized London, hangs about his novels in the same way that Ernest Hemingway in his macho pose and his death by suicide is always present when we turn the pages of *A Farewell to Arms* or the "Up in Michigan" stories. As in the last example, the lives of the poets often throw dark shadows back on their works. The alcoholic F. Scott Fitzgerald ends his life trying desperately to write another novel as good as his early *The Great Gatsby*. Flannery O'Connor sits in her small house in Georgia, suffering from a disease—lupus—that ravages her immune system, and records experiences of Americans who are as vulnerable to the world as is her own body.

The teller not only writes the tale, but, in doing so, he or she becomes a part of it, and our sense of the tale is not complete until the teller's presence is evoked. This is one reason why biographies and vignettes, collections of biographical information, and memories of the type found in these volumes about our writers are so interesting and so useful. More than useful, really. We have not fully read the tale until we can see the teller in it, who will, if we come to know him or her well enough, sensitize us to how the tale is told and what is likely to be in it. Every tale-teller has a distinctive way of telling—the style—and a particular subject matter. To know who is writing is, therefore, to know to look for things that would otherwise escape us. Theodore Dreiser, the American novelist, was a moody man, pessimistic about the possibilities of life, convinced that our fates are woven from a host of small details, the need for a winter coat in *Sister Carrie* or the bright attractiveness of an upper middle-class parlor in *An American Tragedy*. These ordinary details can in their bulk bore us and turn us away from the story if we are not aware that this is the Dreiserian signature, the way in which he renders the flatness of ordinary life and points to the fate that lies concealed in it.

Every author differs from every other in how and what he or she writes, but in the end they combine, if we see and know them well enough, to create a scene that is close to the center of literature, to its place and role in the world. Some writing careers portray this scene more powerfully than others do. Samuel Johnson, for example, was a personality so titanic as nearly to overwhelm his writings, physically grotesque, frequently nearly mad with depression, an impoverished hack most of his life, endlessly talking for victory and heroically facing the hard facts of human life. In Johnson's life, writing his great dictionary of the English language or his *Lives of the Poets* was his defense against the madness of emptiness and meaninglessness. That is to say, he wrote to preserve his sanity by giving order and meaning to the world and to the language through which we approach it.

Every teller of tales, when we come to know him or her, is engaged in something like this Johnsonian struggle to order and make sense of the world of random facts and experiences, to preserve some sense of things, people, and times that would otherwise be forgotten and lost forever in the past. Consider another writer, our own Southern novelist William Faulkner, a struggler who is not as successful as Johnson in his authorial task of imposing order on a messy and painful sense of the confusions of life. Faulkner's story is that of a mythical Mississippi county, Yoknapatawpha County, that he creates in an attempt to locate and order in time and space the confused and confusing memories of the

Southern past, such as the Civil War and slavery and primitive wilderness, with modern-day consciousness that cannot forget the past but also cannot reconcile it with its own immediate interests and thoughts. The strain shows in Faulkner's stories, in the absence of clear chronology, in the tangled syntax of his long sentences, in his frequent descent into stream-of-consciousness writing.

To include the tellers with their tales, which is what this series of the Gale Study Guides is designed to make possible for the common reader, is to see the heroic scene of literature itself, throughout the world, where men and women writers make and have made the most skillful use of the word-hoard of language and the freedom of fiction to preserve our collective past and to make sense out of things that in their multitude are always threatening to fly apart into chaos.

AUTHOR'S ACKNOWLEDGMENTS

My chief debt is to Professor Matthew J. Bruccoli, who wrote the chapters "Fitzgerald's Eras" and "Fitzgerald as Studied" for this book and vetted the rest. Professor Bruccoli improved my parts of this volume, as did Elizabeth Smith Baughman and Professor Ronald Baughman. The following graduate students in the Department of English at the University of South Carolina provided crucial research assistance: Dr. Park Bucker, Seth Clabough, Joseph Goeke, Lisa Kerr, and Gwen Macallister.

Many of the illustrations used in this book come from the Matthew J. and Arlyn Bruccoli Collection of F. Scott Fitzgerald, Thomas Cooper Library, University of South Carolina. I am especially grateful to the staff of the Special Collections Department: Dean George Terry, Dr. Patrick Scott, Jamie Hansen, Paul Schultz, Mary Anyomi, and Mark Herro.

J. S. B.

PUBLISHER'S ACKNOWLEDGMENTS AND PERMISSIONS

This book was produced by Bruccoli Clark Layman, Inc. R. Bland Lawson is the series editor and the in-house editor.

Production manager is Philip B. Dematteis.

Copyediting supervisor is Phyllis A. Avant. Senior copyeditor is Thom Harman. The copyediting staff includes Brenda Carol Blanton, James Denton, Worthy B. Evans, Melissa D. Hinton, William Tobias Mathes, and Jennifer S. Reid.

The index was prepared by Alex Snead, Cory McNair, and Jeff Miller.

Layout and graphics series leader is Karla Corley Brown. She was assisted by Zoe R. Cook and Janet E. Hill, graphics supervisor.

Photography editors are Charles Mims, Scott Nemzek, and Paul Talbot. Digital photographic copy work was performed by Joseph M. Bruccoli and Zoe R. Cook.

Systems manager is Marie L. Parker.

Typesetting supervisor is Kathleen M. Flanagan. The typesetting staff includes Kimberly Kelly, Mark J. McEwan, Patricia Flanagan Salisbury, and Alison Smith.

Following is a list of the copyright holders who have granted us permission to reproduce material in this volume of Gale Study Guides to Great Literature. Every effort has been made to trace copyright, but if omissions have been made, please let us know.

COPYRIGHTED MATERIAL IN *Literary Masterpieces, Vol. 1: F. Scott Fitzgerald* **WAS REPRODUCED FROM THE FOLLOWING SOURCES:**

Material from Fitzgerald's *Notebooks* (New York: Harcourt Brace Jovanovich/Bruccoli Clark, 1978), reprinted by permission of Harcourt Brace.

Material from *F. Scott Fitzgerald: A Life in Letters* (New York: Scribners, 1994), *Afternoon of an Author* (New York: Scribners, 1958),

The Romantic Egoists (New York: Scribners, 1974), *Dear Scott/Dear Max* (New York: Scribners, 1971), and *The Letters of F. Scott Fitzgerald* (New York: Scribners, 1963) reprinted by permission of Simon & Schuster and Harold Ober Associates.

Material from *The Crack-Up* (New York: New Directions, 1945)—including quotations from "The Crack-Up," "Pasting It Together," "Handle With Care," "My Lost City," "Early Success," and "Echoes of the Jazz Age"—reprinted by permission of New Directions and Harold Ober Associates.

Material from *As Ever, Scott Fitz* (Philadelphia & New York: J. B. Lippincott, 1972) reprinted by permission of J. B. Lippincott and Harold Ober Associates.

Material from *Correspondence of F. Scott Fitzgerald* (New York: Random House, 1980) reprinted by permission of Random House and Harold Ober Associates.

"Thousand-and-First Ship" and "My Very Very Dear Marie" from F. Scott Fitzgerald, *Poems: 1911–1940* (Bloomfield Hills, Mich. & Columbia, S.C.: Bruccoli Clark, 1981), by permission of Harold Ober Associates.

Fitzgerald's postcard to Scottie, 25 January 1928, courtesy of Matthew J. and Arlyn Bruccoli Collection of F. Scott Fitzgerald, University of South Carolina; by permission of Harold Ober Associates.

PHOTOGRAPHS AND ILLUSTRATIONS APPEARING IN *Literary Masterpieces, Vol. 1: F. Scott Fitzgerald,* **WERE RECEIVED FROM THE FOLLOWING SOURCES:**

Cover of *The Smart Set* courtesy of Matthew J. and Arlyn Bruccoli Collection of F. Scott Fitzgerald, University of South Carolina.

Dust jacket for *Tender Is the Night* (New York: Scribners, 1934), courtesy of Matthew J. and Arlyn Bruccoli Collection of F. Scott Fitzgerald, University of South Carolina.

Dust jacket for *This Side of Paradise* (New York: Scribners, 1920), courtesy of Matthew J. and Arlyn Bruccoli Collection of F. Scott Fitzgerald, University of South Carolina.

Dust jacket for *Flappers and Philosophers* (New York: Scribners, 1920), courtesy of Matthew J. and Arlyn Bruccoli Collection of F. Scott Fitzgerald, University of South Carolina.

F. Scott Fitzgerald's monthly expenses in 1923, courtesy of Matthew J. and Arlyn Bruccoli Collection of F. Scott Fitzgerald, University of South Carolina; reproduced by permission of Harold Ober Associates.

F. Scott Fitzgerald and John O'Hara, photograph by Belle O'Hara, courtesy of Matthew J. and Arlyn Bruccoli Collection of F. Scott Fitzgerald, University of South Carolina.

Photographs of the Fitzgeralds, Maxwell Perkins, Harold Ober, and Sheilah Graham courtesy of Matthew J. and Arlyn Bruccoli Collection of F. Scott Fitzgerald, University of South Carolina.

Final manuscript page of *The Great Gatsby,* Manuscripts Division, Princeton University Library; reproduced by permission of Harold Ober Associates and Princeton University.

Inscribed photograph of Ernest Hemingway, courtesy of the Matthew J. and Arlyn Bruccoli Collection of F. Scott Fitzgerald, University of South Carolina.

Illustration by F. R. Gruger from "The Rich Boy," *Red Book* (January 1926), courtesy of Matthew J. and Arlyn Bruccoli Collection of F. Scott Fitzgerald, University of South Carolina.

Page from F. Scott Fitzgerald's *Ledger,* reproduced by permission of Harold Ober Associates.

Fitzgerald's revised galley proof for *Tender Is the Night,* Manuscripts Division, Princeton University Library, reproduced by permission of Princeton University and Harold Ober Associates.

Fitzgerald's revised galley proof for *The Great Gatsby,* Manuscripts Division, Princeton University Library, reproduced by permission of Princeton University and Harold Ober Associates.

Final manuscript page for *The Great Gatsby,* Manuscripts Division, Princeton University Library, reproduced by permission of Princeton University and Harold Ober Associates.

Fitzgerald's revised galley proof for the conclusion of *The Great Gatsby,* Manuscripts Division, Princeton University Library, reproduced by permission of Princeton University and Harold Ober Associates.

Fitzgerald's revised coda to "The Swimmers" typescript (*The Saturday Evening Post,* 19 October 1929), courtesy of Matthew J. and Arlyn Bruccoli Collection of F. Scott Fitzgerald, University of South Carolina; reproduced by permission of Harold Ober Associates.

Fitzgerald's revised galley proof for *Tender Is the Night,* Manuscripts Division, Princeton University Library; reproduced by permission of Princeton University and Harold Ober Associates.

CHRONOLOGY[1]

1853: Edward Fitzgerald, father of F. Scott Fitzgerald, is born near Rockville, Maryland.

1858: Anthony D. Sayre, father of Zelda Sayre, is born in Tuskegee, Alabama.

1860: Mary (Mollie) McQuillan, mother of F. Scott Fitzgerald, is born in St. Paul, Minnesota.

Minnie Buckner Machen, mother of Zelda Sayre, is born in Eddyville, Kentucky.

June 1884: Anthony Sayre and Minnie Machen are married near Eddyville, Kentucky.

12 February 1890: Edward Fitzgerald and Mollie McQuillan are married in Washington, D.C.

24 September 1896: Francis Scott Key Fitzgerald is born at 481 Laurel Avenue, St. Paul.

April 1898: Edward Fitzgerald's St. Paul furniture factory fails, and he takes a salesman's job with Procter & Gamble in New York State. He and his family live alternately in Buffalo and Syracuse until July 1908.

24 July 1900: Zelda Sayre is born at South Street, Montgomery, Alabama.

21 July 1901: Annabel Fitzgerald, F. Scott Fitzgerald's sister, is born.

1907: Sayre family moves to 6 Pleasant Avenue, Montgomery, where Zelda lives until her marriage.

March 1908: Edward Fitzgerald loses his Procter & Gamble job.

July 1908: Fitzgerald family returns to St. Paul.

September 1908: F. Scott Fitzgerald becomes student at St. Paul Academy.

1909: Judge Anthony Sayre is appointed associate justice of the Alabama Supreme Court.

October 1909: "The Mystery of the Raymond Mortgage," a short story that is Fitzgerald's first appearance in print, is published in *The St. Paul Academy Now and Then*.

August 1911: Fitzgerald's first play, *The Girl from Lazy J,* is produced by the Elizabethan Dramatic Club in St. Paul.

September 1911: Fitzgerald becomes student at Newman School, Hackensack, New Jersey.

August 1912: Fitzgerald's second play, *The Captured Shadow,* is produced by the Elizabethan Dramatic Club in St. Paul.

November 1912: Fitzgerald meets Father Sigourney Fay and Anglo-Irish writer Shane Leslie.

August 1913: Fitzgerald's third play, *Coward,* is produced by the Elizabethan Dramatic Club in St. Paul.

September 1913: Fitzgerald enters Princeton University as a member of the Class of 1917; meets Edmund Wilson (Class of 1916), who will become a distinguished literary critic, and John Peale Bishop (Class of 1917), who will become a respected poet.

September 1914: Fitzgerald's fourth play, *Assorted Spirits,* is produced by the Elizabethan Dramatic Club in St. Paul.

December 1914: Fitzgerald's first Princeton Triangle Club show, *Fie! Fie! Fi-Fi!,* for which he wrote book and lyrics, is produced.

4 January 1915: In St. Paul, Fitzgerald meets Ginevra King, a Lake Forest, Illinois, debutante, with whom he becomes romantically involved.

April 1915: Fitzgerald's play *Shadow Laurels* is his first publication in *The Nassau Literary Magazine*.

June 1915: Fitzgerald's "The Ordeal," later rewritten as "Benediction," is his first short story to be published in *The Nassau Literary Magazine*.

28 November 1915: Fitzgerald drops out of Princeton for remainder of his junior year.

December 1915: *The Evil Eye*, Fitzgerald's second Princeton Triangle Club show, for which he wrote lyrics, is produced.

September 1916: Fitzgerald returns to Princeton as member of Class of 1918.

December 1916: *Safety First*, Fitzgerald's third Princeton Triangle Club show, for which he wrote lyrics, is produced.

26 October 1917: Fitzgerald receives commission as second lieutenant in U.S. infantry.

20 November 1917: Fitzgerald reports to Fort Leavenworth, Kansas; starts work on "The Romantic Egotist," a novel.

End of February 1918: On leave from army, Fitzgerald goes to Princeton, where he finishes first draft of "The Romantic Egotist"; sends novel to Shane Leslie, who in May submits it to Charles Scribner's Sons.

15 March 1918: Fitzgerald is stationed at Camp Zachary Taylor in Louisville, Kentucky.

April 1918: Fitzgerald is stationed at Camp Gordon, Georgia.

May 1918: Zelda Sayre graduates from Sidney Lanier High School, Montgomery, Alabama.

June 1918: Fitzgerald arrives at Camp Sheridan near Montgomery.

July 1918: Fitzgerald meets Zelda Sayre at a country-club dance in Montgomery.

August 1918: "The Romantic Egotist" is rejected by Scribners, which also declines revised typescript in October.

26 October 1918: Fitzgerald's regiment reports to Camp Mills, Long Island.

November 1918: Armistice is signed, and war ends before Fitzgerald's regiment can be sent overseas.

Late November 1918: Fitzgerald's unit returns to Camp Sheridan.

February 1919: Fitzgerald is discharged from army. Informally engaged to Zelda Sayre, he goes to New York, works for the Barron Collier advertising agency, and tries unsuccessfully to break into the magazine market.

Spring 1919: Fitzgerald visits Montgomery in April, May, and June in efforts to convince Zelda Sayre to marry him.

June 1919: Zelda Sayre breaks engagement.

July 1919: Fitzgerald quits advertising, goes on binge, and returns to St. Paul where he rewrites "The Romantic Egotist" while living with parents at 599 Summit Avenue.

September 1919: "Babes in the Woods," Fitzgerald's first story to be sold to a magazine, is published in *The Smart Set*.

16 September 1919: Maxwell Perkins of Scribners accepts Fitzgerald's rewritten novel, now titled *This Side of Paradise*.

November 1919: Fitzgerald becomes a client of Harold Ober at the Reynolds literary agency. The agency sells "Head and Shoulders" to *The Saturday Evening Post* for $400; the story, Fitzgerald's first appearance in the magazine, is published 21 February 1920.

November 1919–February 1920: "The Debutante" (November 1919), "Porcelain and Pink" (January 1920), "Benediction" (February 1920), and "Dalyrimple Goes Wrong" (February 1920) are published by *The Smart Set*.

Mid January 1920: Fitzgerald visits Zelda Sayre in Montgomery; their engagement is resumed.

March–May 1920: *The Saturday Evening Post* publishes "Myra Meets His Family" (20 March), "The Camel's Back" (24 April), "Bernice Bobs Her Hair" (1 May), "The Ice Palace" (22 May), and "The Offshore Pirate" (29 May).

26 March 1920: *This Side of Paradise* is published.

3 April 1920: Fitzgerald and Zelda Sayre marry at the rectory of St. Patrick's Cathedral in New York.

May 1920: The Fitzgeralds rent a house at Westport, Connecticut, where Fitzgerald works on *The Beautiful and Damned*.

July 1920: "May Day," Fitzgerald's naturalistic novelette, is published in *The Smart Set*.

10 September 1920: *Flappers and Philosophers,* Fitzgerald's first collection of short stories, is published.

October 1920: The Fitzgeralds rent an apartment on Fifty-ninth Street in New York City.

3 May 1921: First trip to Europe: the Fitzgeralds visit England, France, and Italy. They return to America in late July and move to St. Paul.

September 1921–March 1922: *Metropolitan Magazine* serializes *The Beautiful and Damned*.

26 October 1921: The Fitzgeralds' daughter, Scottie, is born.

4 March 1922: *The Beautiful and Damned* is published in book form.

2 April 1922: "Friend Husband's Latest," a tongue-in-cheek review of *The Beautiful and Damned* that is Zelda Fitzgerald's first commercial publication, appears in *The New York Tribune*.

June 1922: Fitzgerald's satirical novelette "The Diamond as Big as the Ritz" is published in *The Smart Set*.

22 September 1922: *Tales of the Jazz Age,* Fitzgerald's second collection of short stories, is published.

Mid October 1922: The Fitzgeralds rent a house at Great Neck, Long Island, and begin their friendship with Ring Lardner.

December 1922: "Winter Dreams," one of the *Gatsby* cluster stories, is published in *Metropolitan Magazine*.

27 April 1923: *The Vegetable,* Fitzgerald's satirical play, is published.

19 November 1923: *The Vegetable* fails at tryout in Atlantic City, New Jersey.

5 April 1924: Fitzgerald's humorous essay "How to Live on $36,000 a Year" is published in *The Saturday Evening Post*.

May 1924: Second trip to Europe: the Fitzgeralds visit Paris, then leave for the Riviera.

June 1924: The Fitzgeralds take up residence at Villa Marie, Valescure; "Absolution," a *Gatsby* cluster story, is published in *The American Mercury.*

Summer 1924: The Fitzgeralds meet American expatriates Gerald and Sara Murphy at Cap d'Antibes.

July 1924: Zelda Fitzgerald becomes involved with French naval aviator Edouard Jozan. "'The Sensible Thing,'" another *Gatsby* cluster story, is published in *Liberty.*

Summer–Fall 1924: Fitzgerald completes and revises first draft of *The Great Gatsby.*

ca. 10 October 1924: Fitzgerald writes to Perkins about a promising young American writer, "Ernest Hemmingway," whose work has been published in Paris.

Late October 1924: The Fitzgeralds live in Rome, where Fitzgerald revises *The Great Gatsby* galleys.

February 1925: The Fitzgeralds stay in Capri.

10 April 1925: *The Great Gatsby* is published.

Late April 1925: The Fitzgeralds return to Paris.

May 1925: Fitzgerald meets Ernest Hemingway at the Dingo bar, Montparnasse.

Summer 1925: Fitzgerald starts planning the Francis Melarky version of the novel that will evolve into *Tender Is the Night.*

August 1925: The Fitzgeralds spend a month at Cap d'Antibes, then go back to Paris.

January–February 1926: The novelette "The Rich Boy," a post-*Gatsby* cluster story, is published in two issues of *The Red Book Magazine.*

2 February 1926: Owen Davis's play version of *The Great Gatsby* opens on Broadway; it has a successful run of 113 performances and is the basis for the 1926 silent movie.

26 February 1926: *All the Sad Young Men*, Fitzgerald's third collection of short stories, is published.

Early March 1926: The Fitzgeralds rent a villa at Juan-les-Pins on the Riviera.

May 1926: "How to Waste Material: A Note on My Generation," an essay-review of Hemingway's *In Our Time* (1925), is published in *The Bookman.*

December 1926: The Fitzgeralds return to America.

January–February 1927: The Fitzgeralds spend two months in Hollywood where Fitzgerald works on "Lipstick" (unproduced) for United Artists; they meet actress Lois Moran.

March 1927: The Fitzgeralds move to Wilmington, Delaware, where they rent "Ellerslie." Zelda Fitzgerald starts ballet lessons.

April 1928: Third trip to Europe: the Fitzgeralds spend the summer and early fall in Paris.

28 April 1928: "The Scandal Detectives," the first of the eight-story Basil Duke Lee series, is published in *The Saturday Evening Post.*

Summer 1928: Zelda Fitzgerald intensifies ballet training as she works with Paris ballet teacher Lubov Egorova.

7 October 1928: The Fitzgeralds return to America and Ellerslie.

March 1929: Fourth trip to Europe: the Fitzgeralds live in Paris until June, spend the summer in Cannes, and return to Paris in October.

2 March 1929: "The Last of the Belles" is published in *The Saturday Evening Post.*

July 1929: Zelda Fitzgerald's "The Original Follies Girl" is published under byline "Zelda and F. Scott Fitzgerald" in *College Humor;* it is the first in a series of stories she writes for the magazine.

5 April 1930: "First Blood," the first of Fitzgerald's five-story Josephine Perry series, is published in *The Saturday Evening Post.*

23 April–11 May 1930: Suffering her first emotional breakdown, Zelda is hospitalized at Malmaison Clinic outside Paris; she discharges herself.

22 May 1930: Zelda Fitzgerald is hospitalized at Val-Mont Clinic in Glion, Switzerland.

5 June 1930: Zelda Fitzgerald becomes a patient at Prangins Clinic at Nyon, Switzerland.

Summer and Fall 1930: Fitzgerald commutes between Paris and Switzerland; in the fall he moves to Lausanne.

11 October 1930: "One Trip Abroad," the story of an American couple who deteriorate in Europe, is published in *The Saturday Evening Post*.

26 January 1931: Edward Fitzgerald dies. Fitzgerald travels alone to America for his father's interment.

February 1931: Fitzgerald returns to Europe and commutes between Paris and Switzerland.

21 February 1931: "Babylon Revisited," one of Fitzgerald's greatest stories, is published in *The Saturday Evening Post*.

15 August 1931: "Emotional Bankruptcy," an important Josephine Perry story, is published in *The Saturday Evening Post*.

15 September 1931: Zelda Fitzgerald is released from Prangins. Shortly thereafter the Fitzgeralds return permanently to America and rent a house in Montgomery.

November 1931: Fitzgerald's retrospective essay "Echoes of the Jazz Age" is published in *Scribner's Magazine*.

November–December 1931: Second Hollywood trip: Fitzgerald travels alone to Hollywood to work on *Red-Headed Woman* for Metro-Goldwyn-Mayer. His script is not used.

Early 1932: Fitzgerald plans the Dick Diver version of *Tender Is the Night*.

January 1932: The Fitzgeralds travel to St. Petersburg, Florida, where Zelda Fitzgerald suffers a second emotional collapse.

12 February 1932: Zelda Fitzgerald becomes a patient at Phipps Psychiatric Clinic, Johns Hopkins Hospital, Baltimore.

March 1932: While at the Phipps Clinic, Zelda Fitzgerald completes the first draft of her novel, *Save Me the Waltz*.

20 May 1932: Fitzgerald rents "La Paix" at Towson, Maryland, outside Baltimore, where he writes most of *Tender Is the Night*.

26 June 1932: Zelda Fitzgerald is discharged from Phipps and moves to "La Paix," where she lives with her family.

October 1932: "Crazy Sunday," a story about Hollywood, is published in *The American Mercury*.

7 October 1932: *Save Me the Waltz* is published.

26 June–1 July 1933: *Scandalabra,* Zelda Fitzgerald's play, is produced by Vagabond Junior Players in Baltimore.

11 October 1933: "Ring," Fitzgerald's memorial tribute to his friend Ring Lardner, is published in *The New Republic*.

December 1933: Fitzgerald rents a house in Baltimore.

January–April 1934: *Tender Is the Night* is serialized in four issues of *Scribner's Magazine*.

12 February 1934: Zelda Fitzgerald suffers her third breakdown and returns to the Phipps Clinic where she remains until she is transferred to Craig House, Beacon, New York, in March 1934.

29 March–30 April 1934: Zelda Fitzgerald's art is exhibited in New York at Cary Ross's gallery and at Algonquin Hotel.

12 April 1934: *Tender Is the Night* is published.

19 May 1934: Zelda Fitzgerald is transferred to Sheppard-Pratt Hospital in Towson, Maryland.

20 March 1935: *Taps at Reveille,* Fitzgerald's fourth and final story collection, is published.

Summer 1935: Fitzgerald lives at the Grove Park Inn, Asheville, North Carolina.

September 1935: Fitzgerald rents an apartment in Baltimore.

November–December 1935: Fitzgerald lives in Hendersonville, North Carolina, where he begins writing the essays later collected in *The Crack-Up* (1945); he returns to Baltimore at the end of December.

February–April 1936: *The Crack-Up* essays—"The Crack-Up" (February), "Pasting It Together" (March), and "Handle with Care" (April)— are published in *Esquire*.

8 April 1936: Zelda Fitzgerald is transferred to Highland Hospital in Asheville, North Carolina.

July 1936: Fitzgerald stays at the Grove Park Inn in Asheville.

August 1936: Hemingway's "The Snows of Kilimanjaro"—with its reference to "poor Scott Fitzgerald"—is published in *Esquire,* which includes in the same issue Fitzgerald's "Afternoon of an Author."

September 1936: Mollie McQuillan Fitzgerald dies in Washington, D.C. Scottie Fitzgerald enrolls at the Ethel Walker School in Connecticut.

January 1937: Fitzgerald moves to Tryon, North Carolina.

6 March 1937: "'Trouble,'" Fitzgerald's last story in *The Saturday Evening Post,* is published.

July 1937: Third Hollywood trip: Fitzgerald receives a six-month contract with M-G-M at $1,000 a week; he lives at the Garden of Allah, a hotel on Sunset Boulevard.

14 July 1937: Fitzgerald meets Sheilah Graham, with whom he becomes romantically involved.

July 1937–February 1938: Fitzgerald works on *Three Comrades* script; for this movie he earns his only screen credit, which he shares with E. E. Paramore.

October 1937: "Early Success," one of Fitzgerald's retrospective essays, is published in *American Cavalcade.*

December 1937: Fitzgerald's M-G-M contract is renewed for one year at $1,250 a week.

February 1938–January 1939: Fitzgerald works on M-G-M scripts for "Infidelity," Marie Antoinette, The Women, and Madame Curie. He receives no screen credits because his scripts are not used.

April 1938: Fitzgerald moves to a bungalow at Malibu Beach.

September 1938: Scottie Fitzgerald enters Vassar College.

November 1938: Fitzgerald moves to Encino, California.

December 1938: Fitzgerald's M-G-M contract is not renewed.

January 1939: Fitzgerald works briefly on David O. Selznick's *Gone With the Wind*.

10–12 February 1939: Fitzgerald and screenwriter Budd Schulberg go to Dartmouth College to work on a script for *Winter Carnival*; both are fired for drunkenness.

March 1939–October 1940: Fitzgerald takes freelance jobs at Twentieth Century-Fox, Universal, Goldwyn, and Paramount studios. His scripts are not produced.

Summer 1939: Fitzgerald plans a novel about Hollywood, *The Love of the Last Tycoon: A Western*.

July 1939: Fitzgerald breaks with his longtime agent, Harold Ober, when Ober refuses to resume his earlier practice of advancing money on unwritten or unsold stories.

September 1939: Fitzgerald unsuccessfully attempts to sell *Collier's* serial rights to his novel in progress.

December 1939: "The Lost Decade," a story about a man who has been drunk for ten years, is published in *Esquire*.

January 1940: "Pat Hobby's Christmas Wish," the first of a seventeen-story series about a Hollywood hack writer, is published in *Esquire*.

March–August 1940: Fitzgerald works on "Cosmopolitan," a screenplay based on his 1931 story "Babylon Revisited," for Lester Cowan. The screenplay is not produced.

Mid April 1940: Zelda Fitzgerald is discharged from Highland Hospital. For the rest of her life, she lives with her mother in Montgomery, though she occasionally returns to Highland Hospital.

May 1940: Fitzgerald moves to an apartment in Hollywood.

21 December 1940: Fitzgerald has a heart attack and dies at Sheilah Graham's apartment, 1443 North Hayworth Avenue, Hollywood.

27 December 1940: Fitzgerald is buried in Rockville Union Cemetery, Rockville, Maryland.

27 October 1941: *The Last Tycoon* (with *The Great Gatsby* and stories), edited by Edmund Wilson, is published by Scribners.

12 August 1945: *The Crack-Up*, edited by Wilson, is published by New Directions.

September 1945: *The Portable F. Scott Fitzgerald*, selected by Dorothy Parker and with an introduction by John O'Hara, is published by Viking.

November 1947: Zelda Fitzgerald returns to Highland Hospital.

10 March 1948: Zelda Fitzgerald dies in a fire at Highland Hospital.

17 March 1948: Zelda Fitzgerald is buried with Scott Fitzgerald at Rockville Union Cemetery.

18 November 1950: Scottie Fitzgerald Lanahan donates the Fitzgerald Papers to Princeton University.

7 November 1975: F. Scott and Zelda Fitzgerald are reinterred in the Fitzgerald family plot at St. Mary's Church, Rockville, Maryland.

18 June 1986: Scottie Fitzgerald Lanahan Smith dies; she is buried with her parents at St. Mary's Church, Rockville.

NOTE

1. Adapted from Matthew J. Bruccoli's *Some Sort of Epic Grandeur,* revised edition (New York: Carroll & Graf, 1993) and from Mary Jo Tate's *F. Scott Fitzgerald A to Z* (New York: Facts on File, 1998).

ABOUT F. SCOTT FITZGERALD

Born: 24 September 1896 in St. Paul, Minnesota
Died: 21 December 1940 in Hollywood, California
Married: Zelda Sayre, 3 April 1920
Education: Attended Princeton University

CHILDHOOD AND EDUCATION

Francis Scott Key Fitzgerald (he was a second cousin, three times removed, of the author of "The Star-Spangled Banner") was born in St. Paul, Minnesota, on 24 September 1896. His father, Edward Fitzgerald, a Marylander with sympathies for the Old South, was an unsuccessful businessman. His mother, Mary (Mollie) McQuillan Fitzgerald, was the mildly eccentric daughter of a wealthy St. Paul wholesale grocer. The family was Irish American and Roman Catholic. In a 1933 letter to writer John O'Hara, Fitzgerald reported: "I am half black Irish and half old American stock with the usual exaggerated ancestral pretensions. The black Irish half of the family had the money and looked down upon the Maryland side of the family who had, and really had, that certain series of reticences and obligations that go under the poor old shattered word 'breeding' (modern form 'inhibitions'). So being born in that atmosphere of crack, wisecrack and countercrack I developed a two cylinder inferiority complex. . . . I spent my youth in alternately crawling in front of the kitchen maids and insulting the great."[1]

Fitzgerald's ambivalent attitude toward his parents began in his early childhood. According to his *Ledger*—the autobiographical, financial, and publishing record he kept between 1919 and 1936—he entertained youthful fantasies that he was a child of mysterious origins: "Suspicion that he is a changeling," reads an autobiographical entry for January 1906.[2] In his 1936 essay "Author's House," he returned to this material, recalling "my first childish love of myself, my belief that I would never die like other people, and that I wasn't the son of my parents but a son of a king, a king who ruled the whole world."[3] Mollie and Edward Fitzgerald had lost two daughters, aged three and one, a few months before Scott's birth, which undoubtedly intensified their devotion to him. In "Author's House" Fitzgerald speculated that the deaths of his older sisters were instrumental in his choosing his career: ". . . I think that came first of all though I don't know how it worked exactly. I think I started then to be a writer."[4]

Fitzgerald was embarrassed by his mother's odd behavior and careless dress and by his father's apparent lack of purpose. In one of his earliest preserved letters, written when he was ten years old, he asked his mother for money but discouraged her from visiting him at an Ontario summer camp by insisting that she would not like the adult company, the "accomadations," or the food.[5] Although he admired his father's Southern manners and gentlemanly qualities, Fitzgerald was ashamed of Edward Fitzgerald's failures both as a wicker-furniture manufacturer in St. Paul and as a salesman for Procter & Gamble in upstate New York, where the family lived for about ten years. Fitzgerald later recalled that when his father was dismissed from his salesman's job in 1908, he "lost his essential drive, his immaculateness of purpose. He was a failure the rest of his days."[6]

Following their return to St. Paul in July 1908, the Fitzgerald family—which now included a daughter, Annabel—lived comfortably on the income from Mollie's inheritance. They rented a series of houses or apartments in the fashionable Summit Avenue area, and Scott became a member of upper-middle-class adolescent circles. He attended parties and dances with the children of the wealthy, but he remained acutely aware of his family's less certain economic and social position. Like the young protagonist of his eight retrospective Basil Duke Lee stories, written in 1928 and 1929, Fitzgerald sought popularity with his St. Paul friends, both boys and girls. Like Basil, he was only partially successful in his quest.

From 1908 through 1911 Scott attended the St. Paul Academy, a private day school, where he achieved his first publications, including his earliest known story, "The Mystery of the Raymond Mortgage."[7] A *Ledger* entry for January 1911 reads, "Became an inveterate author and a successful, not to say brilliant debater and writer."[8] At St. Paul Academy Fitzgerald played football and baseball but was both an unsuccessful athlete and an undisciplined student. His longing for recognition sometimes made him bossy and boastful. In September 1911 he was enrolled at the Newman School, a Roman Catholic prep school in Hackensack, New Jersey. His study habits did not improve during his two years at Newman as he sought football glory and published fiction, verse, and articles in the *Newman News*. During summer vacations Fitzgerald wrote and acted in plays that were produced by a St. Paul amateur theater group, the Elizabethan Dramatic Club.

Fitzgerald at Princeton University, ca. 1915

At the Newman School Fitzgerald encountered two of the strongest influences on his early years: the Anglo-Irish author Shane Leslie and Father Sigourney Fay. Leslie, a cousin of Winston Churchill and a Roman Catholic convert, struck young Fitzgerald as "the most romantic figure I had ever known. He had sat at the feet of Tolstoy, he had gone swimming with Rupert Brooke, he had been a young Englishman of the governing classes when the sense of being one must have been, as Compton McKenzie says, like the sense of being a Roman citizen."[9] Father—later Monsignor—Fay made the Roman Catholic Church seem romantic, and for a while Fitzgerald talked about entering the priesthood. Fay, who became the model for Monsignor Darcy in *This Side of Paradise* (1920), also was the dedicatee of the novel.

Despite his poor academic record, Fitzgerald managed to be admitted to the Princeton class of 1917, and the university had an enduring impact on him. Labeling Princeton in *This Side of Paradise* "the pleasantest country club in America,"[10] Fitzgerald later wrote that it preserved "much of what is fair, gracious, charming and honorable in American life."[11] At the university he sought distinction, first by going out for freshman football (he was promptly cut from the squad) and then by immersing himself in Princeton's literary life. He wrote the lyrics for three musical comedies performed by the Triangle Club, the university's theatrical group; he published in the humor magazine, *The Tiger;* and he contributed serious work to *The Nassau Literary Magazine*. Fitzgerald, who was unimpressed by his Princeton English professors, recalled in a 3 August 1940 letter to his daughter, Scottie: "[S]ome of the professors who were teaching poetry really

"There'd be an orchestra

Bingo! Bango!

Playing for us

To dance the tango

And people would clap

When we arose

At her sweet face

And my new clothes."

F. Scott Fitzgerald

From "Thousand-and-First Ship," in *Poems, 1911–1940*, edited by Matthew J. Bruccoli, with a foreword by James Dickey (Bloomfield Hills, Mich.: Bruccoli Clark, 1981), p. 122.

hated it and didn't know what it was about. I got in a series of endless scraps with them so that finally I dropped English altogether."[12]

Fitzgerald acknowledged, however, the tutelage of two undergraduates, both of whom remained his lifelong friends: Edmund Wilson, who later became a distinguished literary critic, and John Peale Bishop, who developed into a respected poet. Bishop encouraged his classmate's reading and, according to *This Side of Paradise,* introduced him to the works of Oscar Wilde and other authors:

So he [Amory Blaine, Fitzgerald's autobiographical protagonist] found "Dorian Gray" and the "Mystic and Sombre Dolores" and the "Belle Dame sans Merci"; for a month was keen on naught else. The world became pale and interesting, and he tried hard to look at Princeton through the satiated eyes of Oscar Wilde and Swinburne—or "Fingal O'Flahertie" and "Algernon Charles," as he called them in précieuse jest. He read enormously every night: Shaw, Chesterton, Barrie, Pinero, Yeats, Synge, Ernest Dowson, Arthur Symons, Keats, Sudermann, Robert Hugh Benson, the Savoy Operas—just a heterogeneous mixture, for he suddenly discovered that he had read nothing for years."[13]

Expressing an acute sense of his own destiny, Fitzgerald once startled Wilson by announcing, "I want to be one of the greatest writers who ever lived, don't you?"[14] The aspiring author became a prominent figure at Princeton through his writing; during his sophomore year he was elected secretary of the Triangle Club, and that same year he was elected to the socially prestigious Cottage Club.

Fitzgerald's grades at Princeton were poor, however, making him ineligible to perform in Triangle Club musicals or to assume the campus offices to which he had been elected; he was compelled to repeat his junior year. In his *Ledger* for 1915–1916 he wrote, "A year of terrible disappointments + the end of all college dreams. Everything bad in it was my own fault."[15] Later, in 1936, he reiterated, "To me college would never be the same. There were to be no badges of pride, no medals, after all. It seemed on one March afternoon that I had lost every single thing I wanted—. . . ."[16] For Fitzgerald, Princeton had represented a splendid opportunity for a middle-class boy with talent, intelligence, energy, and charm to seize the advantages—position, influence, eminence—that seemed to come almost automatically to young men of wealth and high social standing. He had squandered his opportunity. He recognized his own culpability in this regard, but he also sensed that his modest social and economic background might be a very real obstacle to the fulfillment of his dreams.

During his Princeton years, Fitzgerald had formed a romantic attachment with a beautiful and popular young debutante from Lake Forest, Illinois, Ginevra King, whom he escorted to proms, Princeton football games, and New York shows. By late 1916 Ginevra no longer regarded Fitzgerald as her primary suitor but instead encouraged the attentions of wealthier young men. During a visit to her home in August 1916, Fitzgerald overheard somebody say, "Poor boys shouldn't think of marrying rich girls," a remark that he recorded in his *Ledger.*[17] Through Princeton University and Ginevra King, Fitzgerald began to develop a vision of both the nature of his dreams and the difficulties he might have in fulfilling them.

MILITARY SERVICE, ZELDA SAYRE, AND EARLY SUCCESS

The entrance of the United States into World War I in 1917 provided Fitzgerald with an escape from his academic difficulties. He joined the infantry and was commissioned a second lieutenant in October. Expecting to die in battle, he used the three-month period when he was in training at Fort Leavenworth, Kansas, and on leave at Princeton's Cottage Club to write a novel, "The Romantic Egotist." Submitted to Charles Scribner's Sons in both its original and a slightly revised version, the novel was rejected twice during a two-month period in the fall of 1918.

While he was waiting for word about his novel, Second Lieutenant Fitzgerald—who to his lasting regret did not see combat because the war ended before his unit could be shipped overseas—underwent further training at Southern military bases, including Camp Sheridan near Montgomery, Alabama. There, during the late summer of 1918, he met and fell in love with Zelda Sayre, the eighteen-year-old daughter of an Alabama Supreme Court judge. She was a celebrated belle with a reputation for independence and unconventional behavior. In a Febru-

Dust jacket for Fitzgerald's first novel (1920), which made him a celebrity at age twenty-three (Matthew J. and Arlyn Bruccoli Collection of F. Scott Fitzgerald, Thomas Cooper Library, University of South Carolina)

ary 1920 letter Fitzgerald explained to a friend his attraction to the young woman: "I fell in love with her courage, her sincerity and her flaming self respect and its these things I'd believe in even if the whole world indulged in wild suspicions that she wasn't all that she should be."[18] Fitzgerald had to compete with many other young men for her attention. Beautiful, intelligent, and socially secure, Zelda was not wealthy, but she shared Fitzgerald's ambitions for glamour, success, and fame. By the time he was discharged from the army in February 1919, Scott Fitzgerald and Zelda Sayre were engaged.

Fitzgerald went to New York where, as he later recalled in "My Lost City," "in a haze of anxiety and unhappiness I passed the four most impressionable months of my life. New York had all the iridescence of the beginning of the world. . . . [but] I was haunted always by my other life . . . my shabby suits, my poverty, and love."[19] Some of his feelings of distress were reflected in his 1920 novelette, "May Day," in which artist Gordon Sterrett suffers confusion and failure in the New York City of May 1919. Fitzgerald took a copywriting job at a small salary with the Barron Collier advertising agency and collected 122 rejection slips for stories he was writing after work. He wanted Zelda Sayre to marry him immediately and made several trips to Montgomery to try to convince her to do so. But, like Rosalind Connage in *This Side of Paradise* and Jonquil Cary in Fitzgerald's 1923 story "'The Sensible Thing,'" she understood that they would be miserable without money. Restless, she attended parties, saw other men, and fretted over Fitzgerald's frequent letters to her: "Scott, you've been so sweet about writing—but I'm so damned tired of being told that you 'used to wonder why they kept princesses in towers'—you've written that verbatim, in your last six letters!"[20] When Zelda Sayre broke their engagement in June 1919, Fitzgerald quit his job, went on a bender, and returned to St. Paul, where he rewrote his novel.

Against all odds *This Side of Paradise* was accepted by editor Maxwell Perkins of Scribners in September 1919, beginning the warm lifelong professional and personal relationship between the writer and the editor. Fitzgerald later described his response to his improbable success: " . . . I'd taken a job repairing car roofs at the Northern Pacific shops. Then the postman rang, and that day I quit work and ran along the streets, stopping automobiles to tell friends and acquaintances about it—my novel *This Side of Paradise* was accepted for publication. That week the postman rang and rang, and I paid off my terrible small debts, bought a suit, and woke up every morning with a world of ineffable toploftiness and promise."[21] Also during the fall of 1919, Fitzgerald became a client of literary agent Harold Ober, who sold the young author's stories to *The Saturday Evening Post* and other large-circulation magazines; short fiction eventually brought him most of his income. In early 1920, with his future seemingly secure, Fitzgerald and Zelda Sayre resumed their engagement.

This Side of Paradise was published on 26 March 1920, and Fitzgerald married Zelda, who was not a Catholic, at the rectory of St. Patrick's Cathedral in New York City on 3 April. The novel, which sold out its first printing in three days, was a surprise success to everybody except Fitzgerald. Critical responses to the book were generally favorable: the literary editor of the *Chicago Daily News* headlined his review, "Whew! How That Boy Can Write!"[22] *This Side of Paradise* was among the first of the novels associated with the spirit of the 1920s. It portrayed the youth of America questing for meaningful self-definitions: the new woman attempting to liberate herself from conventional restraints, and the Ivy League collegian seeking his individual destiny, often through reference to books that influenced him. John O'Hara recalled in 1945, "A little matter of twenty-five years ago I, along with half a million other men and women between fifteen and

"Dear Pie-phyiognomy

We'll be back Fri night late or Sat. morning early. I have been elected President of Canada but am too busy as King of the World to take the job

'I love you', say I

'I know it', says Scotty

yrs.

(What was he the god of?)–> geo. Washington"

F. Scott Fitzgerald

Postcard to six-year-old Scottie Fitzgerald, postmarked from Quebec, 25 January 1928 (Matthew J. and Arlyn Bruccoli Collection of F. Scott Fitzgerald, Thomas Cooper Library, University of South Carolina).

thirty, fell in love with a book [*This Side of Paradise*]. It was the real thing, that love. . . . I took the book to bed with me, and I still do, which is more than I can say of any girl I knew in 1920."[23] For many young readers who in the prosperous 1920s would be the first members of their families able to afford college or university educations, *This Side of Paradise* seemed a guide to collegiate conduct. The book was the first American college novel with literary distinction.

It became a Scribners custom to follow a Fitzgerald novel with a collection of his short stories. In September 1920 Scribners published *Flappers and Philosophers*, which included "The Offshore Pirate," "The Ice Palace," and "Bernice Bobs Her Hair," all stories that seriously treat concerns of young people. At the top of his form Fitzgerald produced cleverly plotted stories that appealed to a diverse audience and that developed important ideas in a charming, witty, and often moving style. Although by the mid 1920s he lamented the necessity to write money-making short stories because they were hard work and drained time and energy away from novel writing, Fitzgerald always tried to imbue them with genuine feeling. In a 1935 letter to Harold Ober, he explained, ". . . all my stories are concieved like novels, require a special emotion, a special experience—so that my readers, if such there be, know that each time it'll be something new, not in form but in substance. . . ."[24]

With the publication of *This Side of Paradise* and of his stories in *The Saturday Evening Post*, Scott and Zelda Fitzgerald became celebrities. Newspapers published photographs of the handsome twenty-three-year-old author and his beautiful nineteen-year-old wife. Articles about and interviews with the Fitzgeralds throughout the boom years of the 1920s focused upon their glamour and their extravagant style of living. Their behavior, fueled by bootleg alcohol and youthful high spirits, was often flamboyant, sometimes outrageous; but, as Edmund Wilson later recalled, their appeal was genuine: "The remarkable thing about the Fitzgeralds was their capacity for carrying things off and carrying people away by their spontaneity, charm, and good looks. They had a genius for imaginative improvisations of which they were never quite deprived even in their later misfortunes."[25] Scott and Zelda spent money faster than he could earn it, and he was often in debt to Scribners and to Ober. In 1924, when the average income of an American family was less than $2,000 per year, Fitzgerald wrote a humorous article titled "How to Live on $36,000 a Year"[26]—and ruefully concluded that he and his family could not do so.

The Fitzgeralds' only child, Frances Scott (Scottie) Fitzgerald, was born on 26 October 1921, and in his *Ledger* Fitzgerald noted his wife's remarks as she came out from under the anesthesia: "Oh God, goofo I'm drunk. Mark Twain. Isn't she smart—she has the hiccups. I hope its beautiful and a fool—a beautiful little fool."[27] (Fitzgerald later gave this last sentence to Daisy Buchanan in *The Great Gatsby.*) As she was growing up, Scottie Fitzgerald was provided with capable nursemaids and governesses who helped shield her from the frequent confusions of the Fitzgeralds' lives. Her memories of her early years were of a "child's paradise which my parents created for me."[28] In the introduction to *The Romantic Egoists,* a collection of biographical material about the Fitzgeralds published in 1974, she wrote of herself and her parents:

The highs and lows of their short, dramatic lives have been examined under so many microscopes (including some pretty inaccurate ones) that I can't distinguish any longer between memories and what I read somewhere. I was much too young to do more than curtsey to Hemingway, Wolfe, Gertrude Stein, and other literary greats my parents came to know in Paris but seldom saw in later years; and, as is altogether too abundantly demonstrated on these pages, my childhood was that of a most pampered and petted doll. I remember being punished only once, for what misdemeanor I don't recall, and being sent to my room for the day without books or toys, a most cataclysmic deprivation! After a few hours my father tiptoed in to see how I was and caught me reading under the covers: a very popular French children's book called *Jean Qui Grogne Et Jean Qui Rit.* Instead of delivering the threatened spanking, he got so intrigued with the book's illustrations that I had to spend the rest of the afternoon reading it aloud to him in English. So much for the sort of reminiscences I would be able to contribute to literary scholarship.[29]

In 1922 Fitzgerald's second novel, *The Beautiful and Damned,* and his second collection of short stories, *Tales of the Jazz Age,* were published. The novel, a story of a destructive marriage and the deterioration of an attractive couple, sold well but did not advance the young writer's reputation or art. One problem with the novel was that Fitzgerald, who was trying to write in a naturalistic mode, could not fundamentally embrace the central tenet of literary naturalism: that people's actions and fates are determined by external forces rather than by the qualities of their own characters. Another—perhaps related—problem with the book was that he was unable to control its structure and point of view. The novel can, however, be read as a prophetic warning for the Fitzgeralds' own marriage. In a 14 June 1940 letter to Scottie, Fitzgerald commented on the clearly autobiographical elements in his portrayals of Anthony and Gloria Patch: "Gloria was a much more trivial and vulgar person than your mother. I can't really say there was any resemblance except in the beauty and certain terms of expression she used, and also I naturally used many circumstantial events of our early married life. However the emphases were entirely different. We had a much better time than Anthony and Gloria had."[30] Though *The Beautiful and Damned* is now the least praised of Fitzgerald's novels, the collection of stories that followed it—*Tales of the Jazz Age*—included two early masterpieces and a pair of novelettes, or long stories. One of these novellas is his most accomplished experiment with naturalistic material, "May Day," which merges the New York antisocialist riots and a Yale dance at a luxury hotel in May 1919; the other is his satiric fantasy, "The Diamond as Big as the Ritz," which examines the corrupting power of wealth.

During the summer and fall of 1922 Fitzgerald worked on his play, *The Vegetable,* a comedy-satire about a freight clerk who becomes president of the United States, causes massive confusion, and then happily becomes a postman. In October 1922, the Fitzgeralds moved to Great Neck, Long Island, a suburb of New York City, so that he could supervise the production of the play and work on his third novel. The play, which failed in tryout, never reached Broadway. Progress on the novel was stalled by Great Neck parties with the show-business people who lived there, by frequent excursions to New York, and by Fitzgerald's steady drinking. During a three-month period in early 1924, he went on the wagon and wrote ten stories that got him out of debt, but the most important benefits of his Great Neck residence were the development of his close friendship with writer

Fitzgerald, mid 1920s

Ring Lardner and his accumulation of material for his next novel, *The Great Gatsby.*

THE EXPATRIATE EXPERIENCE AND *THE GREAT GATSBY*

In the spring of 1924 the Fitzgeralds left Great Neck for Europe, settling on the French Riviera, where they hoped to live quietly and inexpensively while he worked on his third novel. During that summer and fall Fitzgerald immersed himself in writing; as he later recorded in his *Notebooks,* "I can never remember the times when I wrote anything—This Side of Paradise time or Beautiful and Damned or Gatsby time for instance. Lived in story."[31] While Fitzgerald was occupied with his novel, Zelda became romantically involved with Edouard Jozan, a French naval aviator. The Fitzgeralds' marriage survived this crisis, but as he recalled in his *Notebooks,* "That September 1924, I knew something had happened that could never be repaired."[32] His sense of betrayal clearly influenced his work in progress, the story of a man who loves a woman incapable of matching his commitment. In an August 1924 letter to his Newman School and Princeton classmate Ludlow Fowler, who became the model for Anson Hunter in "The Rich Boy," Fitzgerald wrote: "Thats the whole burden of this novel—the loss of those illusions that give such color to the world so that you don't care whether things are true or false as long as they partake of the magical glory."[33]

Another event of that Riviera summer had significant personal and literary consequences. At Cap d'Antibes the Fitzgeralds met Gerald and Sara Murphy, American expatriates who were known for their artistic tastes, elegant style of living, and hospitality. Although the Fitzgerald-Murphy relationship was strained by the Fitzgeralds' increasingly erratic behavior during succeeding Riviera summers, Gerald's September 1925 letter testifies to the real warmth of feeling between the couples: ". . . you two belong so irrevocably to that rare race of people who are *valuable.* . . . Scott will uncover for me values in Sara, just as Sara has known them in Zelda through her affection for Scott."[34] Fitzgerald later described Gerald Murphy as his model for successful social behavior,[35] and he used the Murphys as partial models for Dick and Nicole Diver in his most ambitious work, *Tender Is the Night.*

During the fall of 1924 Fitzgerald completed the working draft of *The Great Gatsby,* which was variously titled "Among Ash-Heaps and

Millionaires," "Gatsby," "Gold-Hatted Gatsby," "Trimalchio" (the name of the ostentatious party-giver in the *Satyricon* of Petronius, a first-century-A.D. Roman writer), "Trimalchio in West Egg," "The High-Bouncing Lover," and "On the Road to West Egg." He disliked the title *The Great Gatsby* and tried shortly before publication to have it changed to "Under the Red White and Blue." Both Fitzgerald and Maxwell Perkins felt that the novel could be improved through restructuring. Accordingly, during late 1924 and early 1925, while he and Zelda were living in Italy, Fitzgerald radically revised and rewrote *The Great Gatsby* in galley proofs.

The novel was published in April 1925 to a disappointing reception. Although the reviews were mostly favorable, praising Fitzgerald's style and ability to draw characters, very few early critics recognized the importance of *The Great Gatsby*. Sales for the novel were not good—fewer than twenty-four thousand copies in 1925, which brought Fitzgerald less than $7,000. He earned more for stage and movie rights to *The Great Gatsby* than he did from book sales. Fitzgerald's third story collection, *All the Sad Young Men,* appeared to good reviews and fair sales in February 1926. His best volume of short fiction, it included four major works thematically related to *The Great Gatsby:* the novelette "The Rich Boy" and the short stories "Winter Dreams," "Absolution," and "'The Sensible Thing.'"

Shortly after the publication of *Gatsby* in spring 1925, Scott and Zelda Fitzgerald rented an apartment in Paris, where his complex relationship with Ernest Hemingway began. At that time the twenty-five-year-old Hemingway, who had published two slender books with small Paris presses, was unknown outside the expatriate community. Fitzgerald—who at twenty-eight had produced three novels, one play, more than forty stories, and nearly thirty articles and reviews— enjoyed wide critical and popular success. Fitzgerald recognized Hemingway's genius and promoted his career, and it was largely through Fitzgerald's efforts that Hemingway joined Perkins's cadre at Scribners. The two writers spent much time together in Paris and, later, on the Riviera, but from the beginning of their relationship Fitzgerald was intimidated by Hemingway's commanding presence and his exaggerated reputation as an athlete and war hero. Both men were drinkers, but Hemingway could hold his liquor, whereas Fitzgerald would get drunk on comparatively small amounts of alcohol, thereby failing one of the younger writer's tests of manhood. Furthermore, Zelda Fitzgerald and Hemingway detested each other from the start: she labeled him a phony, and he called her insane, claiming that she deliberately interfered with her husband's work. As Hemingway's reputation ascended and Fitzgerald's collapsed in the 1930s, the friendship of the two writers became increasingly strained.

Although Fitzgerald spent much of his time between May 1924 and September 1931 in Europe, including more than four years in Paris or on the Riviera, he was not truly involved in the American expatriate literary life. Already an established author before his first extended stay in France, Fitzgerald had no interest in writing for the experimental small magazines or book publishers that then flourished in Paris, and he remained indifferent to the innovations in art and music that were under way. Hemingway introduced him to Gertrude Stein, the legendary expatriate American writer and patroness of the arts, who liked him and praised his novels. Fitzgerald also spent time with Sylvia Beach at her Shakespeare & Co. bookshop, which was a meeting place for American writers. He became acquainted with the Irish fiction writer James Joyce through Beach, and he befriended the young French novelist André Chamson. By and large, however, Fitzgerald remained a tourist in France, enjoying the bars and cabarets of Paris and the beauty of the Riviera, but fundamentally believing that residence in France—and Europe, in general—tended to corrupt Americans.

Between 1925 and 1930, Fitzgerald unsuccessfully worked on his fourth novel, for which he initially planned to use a French setting and to deal with matricide. But the material did not fundamentally engage him, and he was easily distracted by the social life in Paris and on the Riviera. In a September 1925 letter to John Peale Bishop, Fitzgerald described his situation: "There was no one at Antibes this summer except me, Zelda, the Valentino, the Murphy's, Mistinguet, Rex Ingram, Dos Passos, Alice Terry, the Mclieshes, Charlie Bracket, Maude Kahn, Esther Murphy, Marguerite Namara, E. Phillips Openhiem, Mannes the violinist, Floyd Dell, Max and Chrystal Eastman, ex-Premier Orlando, Ettienne de Beaumont—just a real place to rough it, an escape from all the world."[36] By the summer of 1926 Fitzgerald's alcoholic behavior was often outrageous: he disrupted the Murphys' parties; he engaged in drunken pranks with the American playwright Charles MacArthur; and he frequently quarreled with Zelda, whose antics had taken on a self-destructive cast. She once threw herself headfirst down stone stairs when Fitzgerald flirted with the dancer Isadora Duncan, and on another occasion she challenged Fitzgerald to dive from cliffs into the sea at night. In his *Ledger* for 1925–1926, he summarized the year as "Futile, shameful useless,"[37]

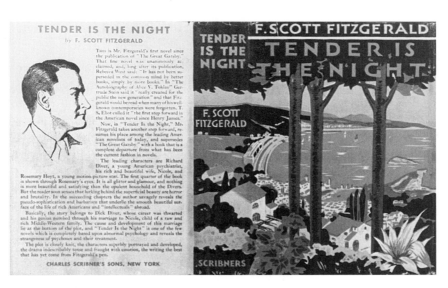

Dust jacket for Fitzgerald's 1934 novel, which is set primarily on the French Riviera (Matthew J. and Arlyn Bruccoli Collection of F. Scott Fitzgerald, Thomas Cooper Library, University of South Carolina)

and in December 1926 the couple left the Riviera for the United States.

The Fitzgeralds hoped to bring a degree of order to their lives in America. After an unsuccessful stay in Hollywood, they settled outside Wilmington, Delaware, in a rented mansion called "Ellerslie." While he struggled with his novel, Zelda at the age of twenty-eight began ballet lessons, which she continued when the Fitzgeralds returned to Paris in the spring of 1928. From October 1928 through February 1929, they were again at "Ellerslie" but in March went back to Paris and the Riviera. Wanting careers of her own, Zelda intensified her ballet training and began writing a series of short stories for *College Humor,* which the magazine published, under a joint byline, as by both Fitzgeralds. Fitzgerald remained stalled on his novel and distressed by the necessity to produce *The Saturday Evening Post* stories, though they were earning him the highest magazine prices of his career—$4,000 per story in 1929. Moreover, he was aware that his drunken behavior was damaging his personal and professional reputations. His *Ledger* summary for 1928–1929 reads: "<u>Ominous</u> No Real Progress in <u>any</u> way + <u>wrecked myself with dozens of people</u>."[38]

"Darling, Berne is such a funny town: we bumped into Hansel and Gretel and the Babes in the Wood were just under the big clock. It must be a haven for all lost things, painted on itself that way. Germanic legends slide over those red, peeling roofs like a fantastic shower and the ends of all stories probably lie in the crevasses. We climbed the cathedral tower in whispers, and there it was hidden in the valley, paved with sugar blocks, the home of good witches, and I asked of all the painted statues three wishes

That you should love me

That you love me

You love me!"

Zelda Fitzgerald

From a letter to F. Scott Fitzgerald, written in spring or summer 1931 from a clinic in Nyon, Switzerland, in *Correspondence of F. Scott Fitzgerald,* edited by Matthew J. Bruccoli and Margaret M. Duggan (New York: Random House, 1980), p. 265.

THE CRASH, *TENDER IS THE NIGHT,* "THE CRACK-UP"

In October 1929 the American stock market crashed, precipitating the worldwide Great Depression of the 1930s. The Fitzgeralds owned no stocks, but the trajectory of 1920s boom to 1930s bust was reflected in their lives, a connection drawn by Fitzgerald's *Ledger* heading for September 1929: "The Crash! Zelda + America."[39] Always eccentric, Zelda became increasingly unstable under the strain of her ballet work and her writing. In April 1930 she suffered a mental breakdown, and by June she was placed in a Swiss clinic, where she was diagnosed as schizophrenic. Fitzgerald later wrote in his *Notebooks:* "I left my capacity for hoping on the little roads that led to Zelda's sanitarium."[40] During the sixteen months of her first hospitalization, Fitzgerald lived with Scottie in Paris and in Swiss hotels. To pay for his wife's expensive medical treatment, he wrote seventeen *The Saturday Evening Post* stories, including two masterpieces—"One Trip Abroad" and "Babylon Revisited"—examining the deterioration of Americans in Europe. The Fitzgeralds exchanged sometimes vituperative, sometimes tender letters in which they tried to account for their loss of happiness and the decline of his career. In a letter written in summer 1930, which may never have been sent to his wife, Fitzgerald wrote: "You were going crazy and calling it genius—I was going to ruin and calling it anything that came to hand. And I think everyone far enough away to see us outside of our glib presentation of ourselves guessed at your almost meglomaniacal selfishness and my insane indulgence in drink. . . . I wish the Beautiful and Damned had been a maturely written book because it was all true. We ruined ourselves—I have never honestly thought that we ruined each other."[41]

In September 1931 Zelda was released from the Swiss clinic, and the Fitzgeralds returned permanently to America. They stopped first in Montgomery, where she stayed while Scott spent two months in Hollywood, and then moved to Baltimore, where Zelda was hospitalized in February 1932 following her second breakdown. Shortly thereafter Fitzgerald rented "La Paix," a house near Baltimore. There he returned to work on his novel, which no longer dealt with matricide but instead with the gradual decline of a psychiatrist married to a wealthy mental patient. While in the Baltimore clinic, Zelda wrote an autobiographical novel, *Save Me the Waltz,* that infuriated Fitzgerald because he felt it preempted material from his work-in-progress. At his insistence, she revised the book. Since the drafts of *Save Me the Waltz* do not survive, the extent of Fitzgerald's involvement in the revision process cannot be determined. (He often helped his wife polish her stories and articles, but there is no evidence that she assisted him in revising his work.) Her novel was published to disappointing reviews and sales in October 1932.

Between June 1932 and February 1934 Zelda was well enough to live part of the time with Fitzgerald and Scottie at "La Paix" and then Baltimore. During this period she wrote a play, *Scandalabra,* which was produced by a Baltimore little-theater group, and she worked on paintings, which were exhibited in New York City for one month in early 1934. In February of that year she suffered her third breakdown and for the next six years was confined to hospitals in Maryland, New York, and North Carolina. Fitzgerald mourned her loss, which he now recognized as permanent: "The voices fainter and fainter—How is Zelda, how is Zelda—tell us—how is Zelda."[42] In a July 1938 letter to Scottie, he found in Zelda's tragedy a warning for both their daughter and himself: "She realized too late that work was dignity and the only dignity and tried to atone for it by working herself but it was too late and she broke and is broken forever."[43]

Fitzgerald's conviction that "work was dignity and the only dignity" found its fullest expression in *Tender Is the Night.* On its simplest level the novel can be read as an examination of the corrupting power of riches: psychiatrist Richard Diver is ruined by his marriage to a wealthy mental patient, Nicole Warren, whose illness requires Dick's undivided attention and his acceptance of her luxurious style of living. On a more profound level, the novel reveals that Diver's collapse is caused by weaknesses in himself: he has such a strong need for the love and admiration of others that he pursues these goals rather than dedicating himself to his potentially brilliant career. In her charm, her demands for attention, and her psychotic episodes, Nicole Diver suggests Zelda. More important, in his betrayal of his career for the sake of transitory things, Dick Diver represents Fitzgerald's judgment on himself. Through much of his life, Fitzgerald feared that he was squandering his time and his talent. In a 12 June 1940 letter to Scottie, he wrote: "What little I've accomplished has been by the most laborious and uphill work, and I wish now I'd <u>never</u> relaxed or looked back—but said at the end of <u>The Great Gatsby</u>: 'I've found my line—from now on this comes first. This is my immediate duty—without this I am nothing.'"[44]

Tender Is the Night was serialized in *Scribner's Magazine* between January and April 1934 before it was published in book form on 12 April. The novel enjoyed moderate sales, placing tenth on the *Publishers' Weekly* best-seller lists in April and May and requiring three small printings during the same period. Nonetheless, royalties from the book were not sufficient to pay off Fitzgerald's debts. The majority of the reviews were favorable, though several critics complained that the causes of Dick Diver's collapse were not entirely clear. Most of the contemporary commentators, even the favorable ones, felt that he had failed yet again to fulfill his promise as a novelist.

Fitzgerald's fourth and final collection of short fiction—*Taps at Reveille,* which was published in early 1935 and which included eighteen stories—did not sell well. The disappointing sales of this collection, combined with the apparent failure of *Tender Is the Night,* precipitated Fitzgerald's "Crack-Up" period, named for a series of self-analytical essays—"The Crack-Up," "Pasting It Together," and "Handle with Care"—that he wrote for *Esquire* magazine in 1935 and 1936. In "The Crack-Up" he explained that he no longer believed "Life was something you dominated if you were any good"[45] but instead found himself helpless and emotionally bankrupt, both as a human being and as a writer. In "Pasting It Together" Fitzgerald identified sources of his collapse—intellectual, artistic, political, social, philosophical—and concluded, "So there was not an 'I' any more—not a basis on which I could organize my self-respect—save my limitless capacity for toil that it seemed I possessed no more."[46] Finally, in "Handle with Care," he bitterly concluded that he must "at last become a writer only" and "cease any attempts to be a person—to be kind, just or generous. . . . There was to be no more giving of myself."[47] The "Crack-Up" essays were brilliantly written, but they seemed to some of Fitzgerald's readers self-indulgent and self-pitying. Moreover, they suggested that he might be finished as an author, thereby alarming the magazine editors who were providing most of his income. In truth, at this point in his career, Fitzgerald was finding it increasingly difficult to produce successful commercial stories; in his *Notebooks* he confessed: "It grows harder to write because there is much less weather than when I was a boy and practically no men and women at all."[48] As his stories began to be rejected by *The Saturday Evening*

Post and other mass-market magazines, Fitzgerald's income declined precipitously. His final *Post* story, "'Trouble,'" appeared in March 1937, and thereafter his only reliable short-fiction market was Arnold Gingrich's new magazine, *Esquire,* which paid him $250 per contribution.

During the mid 1930s, Fitzgerald's health deteriorated as his alcoholism intensified, and he was repeatedly hospitalized. He was convinced that he had tuberculosis, although his medical records are unclear on this point. From February 1935 through June 1937 Fitzgerald lived mostly in or near Asheville, North Carolina, where the mountain air was regarded as beneficial to lung patients. In April 1936 he had Zelda transferred from Sheppard-Pratt Hospital in Towson, Maryland, to Highland Hospital at Asheville. He was able to see her occasionally at Highland, and she seemed to respond well to the hospital's regimen of controlled diet and exercise. Scottie lived with her father when he was in Baltimore, or with family friends when he was away. In the fall of 1936 she became a boarding student at the Ethel Walker School in Simsbury, Connecticut, and Harold and Anne Ober, who lived in Scarsdale, New York, functioned as foster parents to her.

In the fall of 1936 Fitzgerald suffered a pair of public humiliations. Hemingway included a contemptuous reference to him in "The Snows of Kilimanjaro," published in the August issue of *Esquire,* and journalist Michel Mok portrayed him as a drunken, pitiful failure in a *New York Post* interview that appeared the day after his fortieth birthday.[49] Shaken by these attacks, Fitzgerald tried to rededicate himself to writing. He worked intermittently on an historical novel set in ninth-century France. Begun in 1934, the novel was never completed, though *Redbook Magazine* bought four installments, now known as the "Count of Darkness" or "Philippe" stories. They are among the worst works of fiction Fitzgerald ever published. Although he was a history buff, he could not make researched material come alive, and he ultimately abandoned the project. He had more success with "Author's House" and "Afternoon of an Author," autobiographical essays or stories that appeared in *Esquire* in 1936. The following year he wrote "Financing Finnegan," a story about an editor and agent who have to support a brilliant but unreliable author; the story, published by *Esquire* in 1938, amusingly reflects Fitzgerald's relationship with Perkins

"Her [Zelda Fitzgerald's] letters are tragically brilliant on all matters except those of central importance. How strange to have failed as a social creature—even criminals do not fail that way—they are the laws 'Loyal Opposition', so to speak. But the insane are always mere guests on earth, eternal strangers carrying around broken dialogues that they cannot read."

F. Scott Fitzgerald

From *The Notebooks of F. Scott Fitzgerald,* edited, with an introduction, by Matthew J. Bruccoli (New York: Harcourt Brace Jovanovich/Bruccoli Clark, 1978), # 2062.

and Ober. Fitzgerald also produced the splendid essay "Early Success," which appeared in the October 1937 *American Cavalcade*. Written at the lowest point of his career, the essay touchingly evokes that period in the early 1920s "when the fulfilled future and the wistful past were mingled in a single gorgeous moment—when life was literally a dream."[50]

HOLLYWOOD, *THE LOVE OF THE LAST TYCOON*, ENDINGS

By the summer of 1937 Fitzgerald was as much as $40,000 in debt. He owed money to Scribners, Perkins, and Ober for loans and advances; he was behind in payments for Zelda Fitzgerald's treatment at Highland Hospital; and he struggled to pay Scottie's private-school tuition. In June 1937 the Hollywood movie studio Metro-Goldwyn-Mayer offered him a six-month contract as a screenwriter at $1,000 per week, which in December was extended for an additional year at $1,250 per week. During his eighteen months at M-G-M, Fitzgerald worked on six movies, including *Three Comrades* (1938), for which he received his only screen credit. Just before he was released from his M-G-M contract, he was loaned to Selznick International, where he worked for one week on *Gone With the Wind* (1939). Thereafter he freelanced as a screenwriter on half a dozen other movies during 1939 and 1940. Fitzgerald was not a successful screenwriter. In a winter 1939 letter to Scottie, he joked that he no longer expected to be made "Czar of the Industry" and then explained: "Seriously, I expect to dip in and out of the pictures for the rest of my natural life, but it is not very soul-satisfying because it is a business of telling stories fit for children and this is only interesting up to a point."[51]

In Hollywood, Fitzgerald paid off most of his debts and stayed on the wagon, except for occasional binges. The most notable of these episodes, a disastrous February 1939 trip to Dartmouth College with the young screenwriter Budd Schulberg to work on the movie *Winter Carnival,* got both writers fired from the project and ended in Fitzgerald's hospitalization. That Fitzgerald remained sober during most of his time in Hollywood was largely the result of his relationship with Sheilah Graham, a young English-born movie columnist whom he met shortly after his arrival in California. Graham, who became his companion for the rest of his life, tried to control his drinking, accompanied him to social events, cared for him when he was ill, and became his student in a two-year course of study, the "College of One," that he designed for her. Graham, who physically resembled Zelda, was the model for Kathleen Moore, who resembles Monroe

Stahr's dead wife, Minna Davis, in Fitzgerald's uncompleted last novel, *The Last Tycoon* (1941). After his death, Graham wrote three books about their relationship.

During his last three and a half years, Fitzgerald rarely saw Zelda and Scottie, though he spent brief resort vacations with his wife and entertained his daughter in Hollywood. He carried on an extensive correspondence with both, however. His letters to Zelda were sometimes admonitory but more often poignantly regretful: "Oh, Zelda, this was to have been such a cold letter, but I dont feel that way about you. Once we were one person and always it will be a little that way."[52] His correspondence with Scottie, who entered Vassar College in September 1938, was filled with stern advice about her classes, her friends, and her behavior; it also recorded some of Fitzgerald's most important reflections on writing and on his own career as an author. In a letter dated 31 October 1939, for example, he wrote: "I am not a great man, but sometimes I think the impersonal and objective quality of my talent and the sacrifices of it, in pieces, to preserve its essential value has some sort of epic grandeur. Anyhow after hours I nurse myself with delusions of that sort."

In the same letter to Scottie, Fitzgerald revealed that he had a new project under way: "Look! I have begun to write something that is maybe great, and I'm going to be absorbed in it four or six months. It may not make us a cent but it will pay expenses and it is the first labor of love I've undertaken since the first part of 'Infidelity' (—do you remember that half finished script the censor stopped . . . ?)."[53] The project, a novel about the movie industry, would be Fitzgerald's final treatment of themes central to his work, particularly the pursuit of the American dream of success and the fulfillment of heroic aspirations. The protagonist of the novel is Monroe Stahr, a brilliant young movie producer who is working himself to death to make quality movies and maintain his standards against hostile studio forces. Based on Irving Thalberg, the "boy wonder" of M-G-M who had died in 1936, Stahr embodies Fitzgerald's vision of the tycoon, the pioneer, who through his quest had dominated American history and had provided a model for Fitzgerald himself: "It is the history of me and of my people. And if I came here yesterday like Sheilah I should still think so. It is the history of all aspiration—not just the American dream but the human dream and if I came at the end of it that too is a place in the line of the pioneers."[54]

Fitzgerald interrupted his work on the novel to write stories for *Esquire* about Hollywood hack-writer Pat Hobby and to adapt "Babylon Revisited" as a screenplay called "Cosmopolitan"; the screenplay was never produced. Despite his heavy workload and his declining health, he was able to complete drafts of seventeen of thirty planned episodes of the novel. In 1941 the unfinished work was posthumously published with *The Great Gatsby* and five Fitzgerald stories in a volume edited by his old friend Edmund Wilson, who combined episodes into chapters and provided the title, *The Last Tycoon,* from a list of rejected working titles in Fitzgerald's notes for the novel. (The same list was the source for *The Love of the Last Tycoon: A Western,* which was Fitzgerald's choice and which was selected as the title for the 1993 Cambridge University Press critical edition.) The reception for *The Last Tycoon* was respectful, with most critics praising the maturity of the book and lamenting the brevity of Fitzgerald's career. Even in its unfinished state, *The Last Tycoon* is regarded as the best American novel about the movies.

F. Scott Fitzgerald died of a heart attack on 21 December 1940 while reading a *Princeton Alumni Weekly* football article in the Hollywood apartment of Sheilah Graham. He was forty-four years old. The newspaper and magazine obituaries were condescending, describing him as a failed writer and ruined man: a "Symbol of 'Jazz Era'" who "Epitomized 'Sad Young Men,'" as *The New York Times* headline put it.[55] Not even Fitzgerald himself would have dared predict that by the mid 1940s a "Fitzgerald revival" would be under way or that by the 1960s he would be elevated to a permanent position as one of the greatest writers who ever lived.

Beginning in April 1940 Zelda Fitzgerald lived as an invalid with her mother in Montgomery. She returned to Highland Hospital in November 1947, and on 10 March 1948 she died with eight other patients in a hospital fire. She was buried beside her husband at Rockville Union Cemetery in Rockville, Maryland; in November 1975 the couple were reinterred at St. Mary's church, Rockville, in the Fitzgerald family plot. Scottie Fitzgerald finished Vassar College with the help of loans from Maxwell Perkins, Harold Ober, and Gerald Murphy. In 1950, having resisted pressure to sell her father's papers piece by piece, she gave Princeton University the magnificent archive that Fitzgerald had preserved. Always a saver of his manuscripts, typescripts, and proofs, Fitzgerald insured that the physical evidence of his genius would be preserved; Scottie's gift guaranteed that it would be readily available to the readers and scholars who fueled the Fitzgerald revival. Scottie, who died on 18 June 1986, is buried with her parents.

NOTES

1. F. Scott Fitzgerald, *F. Scott Fitzgerald: A Life in Letters,* edited by Matthew J. Bruccoli with Judith S. Baughman (New York: Scribners, 1994), p. 233.

2. Fitzgerald, *F. Scott Fitzgerald's Ledger: A Facsimile,* introduction by Bruccoli (Washington, D.C.: NCR Microcard Editions/Bruccoli Clark, 1973), p. 160.

3. Fitzgerald, *Afternoon of an Author,* edited, with an introduction, by Arthur Mizener (New York: Scribners, 1958), p. 185.

4. Ibid., p. 184.

5. Fitzgerald, *A Life in Letters,* p. 5.

6. Michel Mok, "The Other Side of Paradise," *New York Post,* 25 September 1936, pp. 1, 15; reprinted in *F. Scott Fitzgerald In His Own Time,* edited by Bruccoli and Jackson R. Bryer (New York: Popular Library, 1971), p. 296.

7. The story is most readily available in *The Apprentice Fiction of F. Scott Fitzgerald, 1909–1917,* edited by John Kuehl (New Brunswick, N.J.: Rutgers University Press, 1965).

8. Fitzgerald, *Ledger,* p. 165.

9. Fitzgerald, "Homage to the Victorians," in *In His Own Time,* p. 134.

10. Fitzgerald, *This Side of Paradise* (New York: Scribners, 1998), p. 43.

11. Fitzgerald, "Princeton," in *Afternoon of an Author,* p. 79.

12. Fitzgerald, *A Life in Letters,* p. 460.

13. Fitzgerald, *This Side of Paradise,* p. 58.

14. Edmund Wilson, "Thoughts on Being Bibliographed," *Princeton University Library Chronicle,* 5 (February 1944): 54.

15. Fitzgerald, *Ledger,* p. 170.

16. Fitzgerald, "The Crack-Up," in *The Crack-Up,* edited, with an introduction, by Wilson (New York: New Directions, 1945), p. 76.

17. Fitzgerald, *Ledger,* p. 170.

18. Fitzgerald, *Correspondence of F. Scott Fitzgerald,* edited by Bruccoli and Margaret M. Duggan (New York: Random House, 1980), p. 53.

19. Fitzgerald, "My Lost City," in *The Crack-Up,* p. 25.

20. Fitzgerald, *Correspondence,* p. 43.

21. Fitzgerald, "Early Success," in *The Crack-Up,* p. 86.

22. Jackson R. Bryer, ed., *F. Scott Fitzgerald: The Critical Reception* (New York: Burt Franklin, 1978), p. 1.

23. John O'Hara, introduction to *The Portable F. Scott Fitzgerald,* selected by Dorothy Parker (New York: Viking, 1945), p. vii.

24. Fitzgerald, *As Ever, Scott Fitz—,* edited by Bruccoli and Jennifer M. Atkinson, with a foreword by Scottie Fitzgerald Smith (Philadelphia & New York: J. B. Lippincott, 1972), p. 221.

25. Wilson to Arthur Mizener, 3 March 1950, in *Letters on Literature and Politics 1912–1972,* edited by Elena Wilson (New York: Farrar, Straus & Giroux, 1977), p. 478.

26. Fitzgerald, "How to Live on $36,000 a Year," *Saturday Evening Post,* 196 (5 April 1924): 22, 94, 97.

27. Fitzgerald, *Ledger,* p. 176.

28. Scottie Fitzgerald Smith, foreword, in *Bits of Paradise: 22 Uncollected Stories by F. Scott and Zelda Fitzgerald,* selected by Bruccoli with the assistance of Smith (New York: Pocket Books, 1976), p. xii.

29. *The Romantic Egoists: A Pictorial Autobiography from the Scrapbooks and Albums of F. Scott and Zelda Fitzgerald,* edited by Scottie Fitzgerald Smith, Bruccoli, and Joan P. Kerr (New York: Scribners, 1974), p. ix.

30. Fitzgerald, *Correspondence,* p. 600.

31. Fitzgerald, *The Notebooks of F. Scott Fitzgerald,* edited, with introduction, by Bruccoli (New York & London: Harcourt Brace Jovanovich/Bruccoli Clark, 1978), # 1029.

32. Ibid., # 839.

33. Fitzgerald, *Correspondence,* p. 145.

34. Ibid., p. 178.

35. Fitzgerald, "Pasting It Together," in *The Crack-Up,* p. 79.

36. Fitzgerald, *A Life in Letters,* p. 126.

37. Fitzgerald, *Ledger,* p. 180.

38. Ibid., p. 183.

39. Ibid., p. 184.

40. Fitzgerald, *Notebooks,* # 1362.

41. Fitzgerald, *Correspondence,* p. 241.

42. Fitzgerald, *Notebooks,* # 462.

43. Fitzgerald, *A Life in Letters,* p. 363.

44. Ibid., p. 451.

45. Fitzgerald, "The Crack-Up," in *The Crack-Up,* p. 69.

46. Ibid., p. 79.

47. Ibid., pp. 83, 82.

48. Fitzgerald, *Notebooks,* # 447.

49. Mok, "The Other Side of Paradise," pp. 1, 15; reprinted in *In His Own Time,* pp. 294–299.

50. Fitzgerald, "Early Success," in *The Crack-Up,* p. 90.

51. Fitzgerald, *A Life in Letters,* p. 384.

52. Fitzgerald, *Correspondence,* p. 500.

53. Fitzgerald, *A Life in Letters,* p. 419.

54. Fitzgerald, *Notebooks,* # 2037.

55. *New York Times,* 23 December 1940, p. 19.

FITZGERALD AT WORK

GETTING ESTABLISHED

EARLY SUCCESS: Reflecting upon his career in his 1937 essay "Early Success," Fitzgerald declared, "Premature success gives one an almost mystical conception of destiny as opposed to will power—at its worst the Napoleonic delusion. The man who arrives young believes that he exercises his will because his star is shining. The man who only asserts himself at thirty has a balanced idea of what will power and fate have each contributed, the one who gets there at forty is liable to put the emphasis on will alone."[1] In many ways Fitzgerald's early career seemed the product of destiny, of fate. He had served his literary apprenticeship at the St. Paul Academy, the Newman School, and Princeton. During a three-month period in 1917–1918, he had diligently used weekends and leave time from military service to write "The Romantic Egotist," the 120,000-word novel that he later rewrote as *This Side of Paradise*. Nonetheless, Fitzgerald's early success had a fairy-tale quality. He was twenty-three years old when, in the spring of 1920, his first novel was published and his short stories began appearing regularly in *The Saturday Evening Post* and other mass-circulation magazines. *This Side of Paradise* brought him instant critical and popular recognition, and his stories provided him with both a substantial income and a large audience. So much success at such an early age confirmed Fitzgerald's sense that his star was shining, that destiny was guiding him. He might have found his strongest proof of this conviction in his fortunate involvement with two men who would have a significant impact on his career, the editor Maxwell E. Perkins, of Charles Scribner's Sons, and the agent Harold Ober, of the Paul Revere Reynolds literary agency and, later, of Harold Ober Associates.

MAXWELL PERKINS: Maxwell E. Perkins, a Harvard graduate with New England roots, was twelve years older than Fitzgerald. Reserved and conservative in every way but his literary tastes, Perkins seemed an unlikely sponsor for the exuberant young writer and his iconoclastic first novel. Yet when Fitzgerald, with the help and recommendation of Anglo-Irish

Fitzgerald was the first great literary discovery of the now-legendary editor Maxwell Perkins.

writer Shane Leslie, submitted "The Romantic Egotist" to Scribners in 1918, Perkins saw its promise and argued for its publication. Overruled by senior editors, Perkins almost certainly wrote the 19 August 1918 letter of rejection, which praised the novel's originality, provided suggestions for rewriting, and encouraged submission of a revised version. Fitzgerald hastily reworked some of the material, but Perkins again declined the novel in October 1918.

During the spring and early summer of 1919, Fitzgerald suspended work on the novel while he worked for an ad agency in New York City and tried unsuccessfully to have his short fiction published in magazines. In July he returned home to St. Paul and rewrote "The Romantic Egotist." The typescript of the novel, now titled "This Side of Paradise," was delivered in late summer to Perkins, who was again its only supporter when it came up for consideration during a Scribners editorial meeting. Perkins in effect threatened to resign if the novel were not accepted for publication: "My feeling is that a publisher's first allegiance is to talent. And if we aren't going to publish a talent like this, it is a very serious thing. . . . If we're going to turn down the likes of Fitzgerald, I will lose all interest in publishing books."[2] The other editors relented, and in a 16 September 1919 letter Perkins told Fitzgerald: "I am very glad, personally, to be able to write you that we are all for publishing your book, 'This Side of Paradise.'"[3] In Perkins, Fitzgerald had discovered a perceptive editor and steadfast friend; in Fitzgerald, Perkins had found the first of his stable of geniuses—including Ernest Hemingway, Thomas Wolfe, and Ring Lardner—which made him America's most famous literary editor.

As an editor Perkins was not concerned with line-editing—restructuring writers' sentences, correcting or questioning possible factual errors, pointing out problems in grammar or usage—nor was he a good proofreader. His great strength was in structure and character development, but his editorial role with Fitzgerald—as with all of his authors—was advisory, not collaborative. His contributions to *This Side of Paradise* cannot be determined with certainty since the setting-copy typescript and proofs of the novel are lost, but correspondence between author and editor in late 1919 and early 1920 suggests that Perkins did not require significant changes by Fitzgerald. Moreover, when in December 1921 Perkins advised Fitzgerald to soften character Maury Noble's cynical discussion of the Bible in *The Beautiful and Damned,* and the novelist responded with a strong defense of the passage, Perkins replied, "Don't ever *defer* to my judgment. You won't on any vital point, I know, and I should be ashamed, if it were possible to have made you; for a writer of any account must speak solely for himself."[4] Perkins then explained the reasons for his objections to the passage—that flippant language undercut the effectiveness of the scene—and Fitzgerald, admitting the soundness of his editor's advice, made revisions.

When Perkins received the typescript for *The Great Gatsby,* he recognized its brilliance, as his 20 November 1924 letter to Fitzgerald reveals:

> . . . The amount of meaning you get into a sentence, the dimensions and intensity of the impression you make a paragraph carry, are most extraordinary. The manuscript is full of phrases which make a scene blaze with life. If one enjoyed a rapid railroad journey I would compare the number and vividness of pictures your living words suggest, to the living scenes disclosed in that way. It seems in reading a much shorter book than it is, but it carries the mind through a series of experiences that one would think would require a book of three times its length.
>
> The presentation of Tom, his place, Daisy and Jordan, and the unfolding of their characters is unequalled so far as I know. The description of the valley of ashes adjacent to the lovely country, the conversation and the action in Myrtle's apartment, the marvelous catalogue of those who came to Gatsby's house,— these are such things as make a man famous. And all these things, the whole pathetic episode, you have given a place in time and space, for with the help of T. J. Eckleberg and by an occasional glance at the sky, or the sea, or the city, you have imparted a sort of sense of eternity. You once told me you were not a <u>natural</u> writer—my God! You have plainly mastered the craft, of course; but you needed far more than craftsmanship for this.[5]

Yet, Perkins also suggested that the novel would be strengthened if Gatsby's character and the source of his wealth were made clearer and if his biography were presented "bit by bit" in the "regular flow" of the narrative rather than in longer sections. Fitzgerald revised and rewrote the book in galley proofs and thereby created a masterpiece.

For Fitzgerald, Perkins's encouragement and expressions of confidence were extremely important, particularly during the 1930s, when the writer fell upon hard times. In a 14 May 1930 letter Perkins wrote: "I have never found any flaw in your judgment about your work, yet. . . . The only thing that has ever worried me about you was the question of health. . . . But don't blame me for being impatient once in a while. It is only the impatience to see something one expects greatly to enjoy and admire, and wishes to see triumph. That's the truth."[6] Fitzgerald in a January 1932 letter expressed his recognition of Perkins's unfailing support: ". . . you're the only one whose ever consistently felt faith in me. . . ."[7] On 4 August 1933, Perkins told Fitzgerald, "Whenever any of these new writers come up who are brilliant, I always realize that you have more talent and more skill than any of them;—but circumstances have prevented you from realizing upon the fact for a long time,"[8] and on 9 March 1938 he wrote of *The Great Gatsby*: "What a pleasure it was to publish that! It was as perfect a thing as I ever had any share in publishing.—One does not seem to get such satisfactions as that any more."[9] During the mid 1930s, when Scribners no longer granted Fitzgerald cash advances on future books, his editor provided personal loans, and after Fitzgerald's death Perkins not only helped manage his literary properties but also, with Harold Ober and Gerald Murphy, lent Scottie Fitzgerald money so that she could complete her education at Vassar.

Many commentators have suggested that Perkins, who had five daughters, functioned as a surrogate father to the younger men who became his three greatest authors. In a 2 April 1934 letter to Wolfe, Fitzgerald referred to "our common parent, Max."[10] In a 23 April 1938 letter to Perkins—written when Hemingway seemed obsessed by the Spanish Civil War, Wolfe had bitterly broken with Perkins and Scribners, and Fitzgerald himself appeared finished as a novelist—Fitzgerald again drew the father-sons connection between the editor and his authors: "What a time you've had with your sons, Max—Ernest gone to Spain, me gone to Hollywood, Tom Wolfe reverting to an artistic hill-billy."[11]

HAROLD OBER: Harold Ober, like Perkins a New Englander and a Harvard graduate, became Fitzgerald's literary agent in November 1919. In October of that year Fitzgerald had sent the typescript of a story to the Paul Revere Reynolds literary agency, where Ober was a partner. The Reynolds Agency sold Fitzgerald's story, "Head and Shoulders," to *The Saturday Evening Post* for $400; published in the 21 February 1920 issue, the story was Fitzgerald's first appearance in the magazine. In a January 1925 letter to Ober, Fitzgerald recalled his jubilation at breaking into the mass-circulation or slick-magazine market: "I was twenty-two when I came to New York and found that you'd sold <u>Head and Shoulders</u> to the Post. I'd like to get a thrill like that again but I suppose its only once in a lifetime."[12]

Harold Ober, Fitzgerald's literary agent

Fitzgerald's connection with Ober, first at the Reynolds agency and beginning in 1929 at Ober's own agency, helped shape the writer's career. Earning a 10 percent commission, Ober handled magazine and movie sales for Fitzgerald but did not represent him in book deals with Scribners, with whom the novelist made his own contractual arrangements. Ober was extremely successful in selling Fitzgerald's stories, particularly to *The Saturday Evening Post*. Between 1920 and 1937 *The Post* was his major short-story market, at least in part because in 1924 Ober gave the magazine first refusal rights on his author's short fiction. Sixty-five of Fitzgerald's 160 stories appeared in the magazine, which during the 1920s cost five cents per issue and had a circulation of 2.75 million. Some twenty-five more of Fitzgerald's stories were published in such other high-paying mass-market magazines as *Red Book, Liberty, Collier's,* and *McCall's.* The author became better known in his own time as a short-story writer than as a novelist.

Until he went to Hollywood in 1937, an arrangement also brokered by Ober, Fitzgerald made most of his money through sales of stories. His *Ledger* shows that during 1920 he cleared some $18,850, all but $6,775 from story and movie sales handled by his agent.[13] According to his *Ledger* for 1925, the year that *The Great Gatsby* was published, Fitzgerald earned, after commissions to Ober, $11,025 on five stories, plus $2,402 on "Misselaeneous" items, including an advance on a stage version of *The Great Gatsby,* second serial rights on the novel, and English sales of two stories. His income that same year from three novels and three collections of stories was $4,906.61. Thus, $13,427 of his $18,333.61 in earnings that year came from projects handled by Ober.[14] By 1929 Fitzgerald's *Saturday Evening Post* rate peaked at $4,000 per story, and even between 1932 and 1937, when his talent for sustained short fiction had abandoned him and his pay rate had fallen, he earned $1,000 to $3,000 per story from *The Saturday Evening Post* and other slicks, though fewer of his stories were being accepted.

At the beginning of his career Fitzgerald enjoyed writing for the magazines. Three stories published in May 1920 issues of *The Saturday Evening Post*—"Bernice Bobs Her Hair" (1 May), "The Ice Palace" (22 May), and "The Offshore Pirate" (29 May)—reveal the charm, wit, and power of observation that he could command in the commercial short-story form. All three of these early *Post* stories entertainingly treat young American women trying to define themselves in the contemporary world, and Fitzgerald inscribed a copy of *Flappers and Philosophers,* in which they were collected, "For Harold Ober who chaperoned these debutantes."[15] Yet, the writer soon became disillusioned with *The Post* and the other slicks because, he felt, they discouraged serious material. As early as September 1922 Fitzgerald complained "that the magazines want only flapper stories from me,"[16] and in April 1926 he reminded his agent that editors at *The Post* were "hostile, as you know, to the general cast of thought that permeates my serious work."[17] He was unfair to *The Post.* Although it and the other mass-circulation magazines had declined two of his brilliant novelettes—the naturalistic "May Day" (1920) and the satiric "The Diamond as Big as the Ritz" (1922), which were ultimately published by H. L. Mencken's journal *The Smart Set*—*The Post* did print several of his most enduring serious stories, including "The Last of the Belles" (2 March 1929), "One Trip Abroad" (11 October 1930), and "Babylon Revisited" (21 February 1931). Fitzgerald's real complaint arose from his growing conviction that the necessity to produce income-generating stories stole time he needed to work on novels. He therefore began to denigrate his work for the magazines. In a 9 September 1929 letter to Hemingway he described himself as an "old whore" turning $4,000 tricks for *The Post.*[18]

In the course of their nearly twenty years together as author and agent, Fitzgerald and Ober built a strong professional relationship. Ober was a skilled marketer of Fitzgerald's stories, and, even when the author's reputation was at its lowest, in 1937, Ober was able to engineer the $1,000-per-week M-G-M screenwriting contract—with an option to renew at $1,250 per week—that took Fitzgerald to Hollywood and, for a year and a half, eased his financial worries. When he first became an Ober client in 1919, Fitzgerald received payment (less commission) only when stories were sold. By the early 1920s he was requesting payment when stories were delivered to but not yet sold by Ober, and shortly thereafter he began depending upon his agent's advances against unwritten stories.

In a spring 1926 letter to Ober, Fitzgerald mused, "I must owe you thousands—three at least—maybe more. I am forever under obligations to you for your kindness. . . . I honestly think I cause you more trouble and bring you less business than any of your clients. How you tolerate it I don't know—but thank God you do."[19] Ober, in fact, earned a good income from commissions on sales of Fitzgerald's work, but he had to endure substantial risks to do so. By the time Fitzgerald went to Hollywood in July 1937, he owed Ober $12,511.69, which he was able to repay by the end of 1938 from his M-G-M salary.

In July 1939, after Fitzgerald's contract with M-G-M had expired and he was yet again short of money, he pressed Ober to resume their old system of advances against promised work. Ober made one small loan but then advised Fitzgerald that he could do no more because the Depression had eaten into the profit margin of his agency and he needed to save money for his two sons' college educations. In a letter dated 19 July Fitzgerald expressed shock and dismay at his agent's "sudden change in policy."[20] Although Ober continued to handle Fitzgerald's previously published work, the writer henceforth acted as his own agent for his new work, a practice he had already begun in 1934 with his low-paying essays and stories for *Esquire*.

Despite his break with Fitzgerald, Ober and his wife, Anne, continued to act as surrogate parents to Scottie Fitzgerald, a role they had filled since 1936 when she had enrolled at the Ethel Walker School in Simsbury, Connecticut. When Fitzgerald died, Ober was a major contributor to the loan that allowed Scottie to complete her Vassar education. (She later provided a moving tribute to Ober in the foreword to *As Ever, Scott Fitz—*, a collection of Fitzgerald's correspondence with Ober.) Both Perkins and Ober helped Judge John Biggs Jr., the executor of Fitzgerald's estate, manage his literary properties, and Harold Ober Associates, the agency Ober founded, still handles these properties.

SUBJECTS AND THEMES

MATERIAL: Throughout his twenty-year career as a professional writer, Fitzgerald was often regarded as a not-quite-serious literary figure. This assessment was fueled by his image as a free-spending, heavy-drinking playboy and by the material he often exploited: the interests—usually romantic—of young people; the pursuit of wealth, success, and happiness by ambitious poor boys; the concerns of affluent, upper-middle-class men and women. Fitzgerald's material seemed, in short, the stuff of popular, escapist fiction rather than of enduring literature. In his introduction to the 1934 Modern Library reprint of *The Great Gatsby,* Fitzgerald stated that certain reviewers had attacked the novel in 1925 because "the pages weren't loaded with big names of big things and the subject not concerned with farmers (who were the heroes of the moment). . . . I had recently been kidded half haywire by critics who felt that my material was such as to preclude all dealing with mature persons in a mature world. But, my God! it was my material, and it was all I had to deal with."[21]

Writers' material—the subjects, experiences, ideas that they examine and re-examine—is what makes them the kinds of authors they are. Writers and material are inseparable, as Fitzgerald explained in his 1933 essay "One Hundred False Starts":

> Mostly, we authors must repeat ourselves—that's the truth. We have two or three great and moving experiences in our lives—experiences so great and moving that it doesn't seem at the time that anyone else has been so caught up and pounded and dazzled and astonished and beaten and broken and rescued and illuminated and rewarded and humbled in just that way ever before.
>
> Then we learn our trade, well or less well, and we tell our two or three stories—each time in a new disguise—maybe ten times, maybe a hundred, as long as people will listen.[22]

Fitzgerald's statement emphasizes the intensely personal nature of a writer's material, which is drawn from the most important and most emotionally involving experiences in his or her life. For Fitzgerald these experiences included his growing up with a sense of being a poor boy in a rich man's world but also with a sense of his own special destiny: both perceptions led him to believe in and pursue the American dream of success, personal fulfillment, and wealth. Another of his formative experiences was his dramatic early success as a writer and celebrity, which was followed by his later collapse into emotional bankruptcy and anonymity: his greatest work from the late 1920s through the mid 1930s examines the decline of potential heroes, a decline colored by their own and their creator's sense of regret. In his *Notebooks* Fitzgerald wrote, "Show me a hero and I will write you a tragedy."[23] Still another of his life- and work-shaping experiences was the intense romance and devastating misfortune of his relationship with Zelda Sayre Fitzgerald: virtually all of his important female characters reflect some facet of Zelda and his involvement with her.

CHARACTERIZATION: Theme is most dramatically expressed through character, and Fitzgerald used the people he created to convey his personal vision of the world. In his five novels and 160 stories, he portrayed a wide range of characters. Though he may be most closely identified with his debutantes, college boys, and ambitious young men seeking the fulfillments promised by wealth, social standing, and personal happiness, he also provided memorable portraits of other kinds of people: the deranged priest, Father Adolphus Schwartz, with his vision of a place where "'things go glimmering all the time'"[24] in "Absolution" (1924); the vulgar, vital, lower-class Myrtle Wilson with her own meretricious dreams in *The Great Gatsby*; the sinister Meyer Wolfshiem with his human-molar cuff buttons and his "gonnegtions"[25] with the underworld in *Gatsby*; and the wealthy Anson Hunter with his sense of superiority in "The Rich Boy" (1926). The best of these characters emerge as recognizable, credible individuals rather than stock figures. Fitzgerald's novella "The Rich Boy" opens with the line "Begin with an individual, and before you know it you find that you have created a type; begin with a type, and you find that you have created—nothing."[26] It is only through portraying individuals, Fitzgerald writes, that an author is able to convey their social identities. In a 20 November 1924 letter about the unrevised draft version of *The Great Gatsby*, Perkins commented on Fitzgerald's ability both to draw individuals and to invest them with the symbolic importance of the "type," or representative figure. Praising the novel's "set of characters marvelously palpable and vital," Perkins remarked, "I would know Tom Buchanan if I met him on the street and would avoid him. . . ."[27]

Because they are drawn from his own experience, many of Fitzgerald's characters manifest recognizably Fitzgeraldian qualities. His men often combine ambition for early success with the desire for romantic love and the achievement of an ideal life. Amory Blaine, the protagonist of *This Side of Paradise*, pursues romantic attachments but, more important, engages in a quest to fulfill his promise, intelligence, idealism, and sense of "aristocratic egotism."[28] Jay Gatsby, the title figure of *The Great Gatsby*, is inspired by his "heightened sensitivity to the promises of life"[29] to amass the fortune that he believes will enable him to recover Daisy Fay Buchanan, his lost love. Dexter Green, the central male character in the short story "Winter Dreams," becomes a prosperous businessman partly in response to the splendid world represented by selfish, beautiful, rich Judy Jones, whom he loves. Fitzgerald's men often lack the hardness to fulfill their dreams: Amory is thwarted by love and life, though he remains determined to continue his quest; Gatsby is defeated and destroyed by the Buchanans, who "smashed up things and creatures and then retreated back into their money or their vast carelessness or whatever it was that kept them together . . .";[30] Dexter not only fails to

"A personality is what you thought you were, what this Kerry and Sloane you tell me of evidently are. Personality is a physical matter almost entirely; it lowers the people it acts on—I've seen it vanish in a long sickness. But while a personality is active, it overrides 'the next thing.' Now a personage, on the other hand, gathers. He is never thought of apart from what he's done. He's a bar on which a thousand things have been hung—glittering things sometimes, as ours are, but he uses those things with a cold mentality back of them."

Monsignor Darcy to Amory Blaine

From F. Scott Fitzgerald, *This Side of Paradise* (New York: Scribners, 1920).

win Judy but is devastated by news of her lost beauty, which symbolizes for him the loss of "the country of illusion, of youth, of the richness of life, where his winter dreams had flourished."[31] Certain of Fitzgerald's male characters are actually weak—notably Anthony Patch in *The Beautiful and Damned* and Gordon Sterrett in "May Day"—but the majority of the men portrayed by Fitzgerald fail because the objects of their pursuit do not and cannot measure up to the men's conceptions of them. Because the quests of Fitzgerald's best male characters usually are played out in the real world, their objects, their dreams, are assailed by mutability—by inevitable change and loss—so that youthful beauty fades; innocence hardens into cynicism; and aspirations fade when tested against harsh experience. "'Can't repeat the past?' [Gatsby] cried incredulously. 'Why of course you can!'"[32] Gatsby is wrong, but his faith makes him unforgettable.

Women like Fitzgerald's female characters scarcely existed in American fiction before 1920. Part of the appeal of *This Side of Paradise* and much of Fitzgerald's early short fiction resulted from their portrayals of the new American girl in revolt against conventional standards for women. Ardita Farnam in "The Offshore Pirate" is imaginative, independent, and outspoken; in an authorial intrusion into the narrative, Fitzgerald connects her most compelling quality with her membership in the postwar generation of women: "To me the interesting thing about Ardita is the courage that will tarnish with her beauty and youth."[33] Fitzgerald recognizes that Ardita's courage will fail her as she grows older, less attractive, and more similar in interests and values to the middle-aged, prewar generation of women, but he also celebrates her present-day youthful power. Rosalind Connage, one of the major female characters in *This Side of Paradise,* is described as willful and self-centered, but, says the omniscient narrator, "in the true sense she is not spoiled. Her fresh enthusiasm, her will to grow and learn, her endless faith in the inexhaustibility of romance, her courage and fundamental honesty—these things are not spoiled."[34] The best of Fitzgerald's heroines are brave, determined, beautiful (or at least attractive), intelligent (but not educated), and chaste (though willing to exchange pre-engagement kisses with their love interests). These young women, many of them still in their teens, also understand that their lives depend upon the marital choices they make. Rosalind eventually breaks with Amory Blaine because she knows that the "little flat,"[35] which is all that he can presently provide, would ruin their relationship and their future. The Fitzgerald woman's marital concerns are further explicated in a 1931 story, "A New Leaf," in which Julia Ross tells her fiancé, Dick Ragland, that she will not marry him until he proves that he can stop drinking: "'Remember, I'm also deciding for my children.'"[36]

Fitzgerald clearly admired attractive, independent, unconventional women like the characters Ardita, Rosalind, and Julia, and his wife, Zelda, but he also tended to treat his most fully developed women characters rather critically. Both Nicole Warren Diver and Daisy Fay Buchanan are undeniably charming figures—beautiful, desirable, intelligent—but they have flaws. Nicole's history as a mental patient causes her to drain her husband's energies and thus prevent him from fulfilling his promise as a brilliant young psychiatrist; her possession of a fortune has accustomed her to a luxurious lifestyle, and its comforts and requirements further weaken Dick Diver's resolve. Daisy lacks the courage to commit herself to Gatsby, either when they first meet in 1917 or when they are reunited in 1922. She is romantically drawn to him in both periods of her life but, because of fear, twice rejects the uncertain promises offered by Gatsby and instead chooses the old wealth and secure upper-class social position provided by Tom Buchanan, a hard and unfaithful man. Nicole and Daisy, like many of Fitzgerald's most complex female characters, are incapable of sharing the lofty dreams and aspirations of the men who love them.

MORAL STANCE/DOUBLE VISION: Fitzgerald was not a purely objective reporter or chronicler of the Jazz Age and the 1930s but instead brought a strong moral perspective to his work. His central characters undergo processes of self-assessment (Amory Blaine, for example), or they judge others (Nick Carraway), or they are judged by Fitzgerald himself, who constantly measured the behavior of characters against implicit standards of responsibility, honor, and courage. "Action is character,"[37] Fitzgerald wrote in his *Notebooks,* and by *character* he meant the moral qualities of the fictional being that are defined by his or her actions. In a 4 November 1939 letter to his daughter, Fitzgerald commented on musical-comedy writers Cole Porter, Richard Rodgers, and Lorenz Hart: "Sometimes I wish I had gone along with that gang, but I guess I am too much a moralist at heart and really want to preach at people in some acceptable form rather than to entertain them."[38]

One of Fitzgerald's major methods for achieving this acceptable form of preaching was his adoption of a perspective that the critic Malcolm Cowley labeled "double vision"—the perception of events both as an insider and as an outsider: "It was as if all his novels described a big dance to which he had taken . . . the prettiest girl . . . and as if at the same time he stood outside the ballroom, a little Midwestern boy with his nose to the glass, wondering how much the tickets cost and who paid for the music."[39] One of the best and most familiar embodiments of double vision in Fitzgerald's work is the narrator of *The Great Gatsby,* Nick Carraway, who both participates in and comments on the action of the novel. In the second chapter Nick describes himself as "entangled in" as well as a "watcher" over the events that unfold in Myrtle Wilson's apartment: "I was within and without, simultaneously enchanted and repelled by the inexhaustible variety of life."[40] His position as both insider and outsider remains intact throughout the novel, though at its end he rejects the carelessness of the Buchanans for a firmer moral stance. Of his final meeting with Tom, Nick says: "I couldn't forgive him or like him but I saw that what he had done was, to him, entirely justified. . . . I shook hands with him; it seemed silly not to, for I felt suddenly as though I were talking to a child. Then he went into the jewelry store to buy a pearl necklace—or perhaps only a pair of cuff buttons—rid of my provincial squeamishness forever."[41] Nick fully understands Tom's behavior, but he ultimately rejects it for his own more mature and responsible moral position; he continues to observe objectively but also to draw his own moral judgments. Nick thus fulfills Fitzgerald's declaration in his 1936 essay "The Crack-Up" that "the test of a first-rate intelligence is the ability to hold two opposed ideas in the mind at the same time, and still retain the ability to function."[42]

In "The Diamond as Big as the Ritz" Fitzgerald employs a mixture of literary modes to develop his doubleness of vision and unmistakable moral stance. In the annotated table of contents for *Tales of the Jazz Age,* in which "Diamond" was collected, Fitzgerald explained that the novelette "was designed utterly for my own amusement. I was in a mood characterized by a perfect craving for luxury, and the story began as an attempt to feed that craving on imaginary food."[43] "Diamond" seems at first an elaborate joke. The protagonist, John T. Unger, who comes from a small town named Hades, enrolls at St. Midas', the most expensive prep school in the world, and then accompanies his classmate Percy Washington through the arid Montana town of Fish to the hidden Washington family estate built on "'a diamond bigger than the Ritz-Carlton Hotel.'"[44] Much of the charm of the story results from its elements of fantasy:

Fitzgerald's descriptions at the end of section II and throughout section III of the opulence of the Washingtons' "exquisite château"[45] and of their lifestyle, in which a bath, for example, becomes a measure of their voluptuous "standards of living."[46] The fantasy continues in Fitzgerald's descriptions of John's romantic involvement with Percy's beautiful younger sister, Kismine, who in a parody of romance conventions utters such lines as "'We can't let such an inevitable thing as death stand in the way of enjoying life while we have it'"[47] (this in response to John's realization that he will be murdered to prevent him from disclosing the source of the Washingtons' wealth) and "'We'll be poor, won't we? Like people in books. And I'll be an orphan and utterly free. Free and poor! What fun!'"[48] (this as the couple begin their flight from the mountain as the aerial attack is launched in section IX).

The novelette also develops into a religious allegory: John escapes Hades (in section I Fitzgerald indulges in elaborate jokes on the heat of the place) for St. Midas' (but Midas, the legendary king with the gift for turning everything he touches to gold, also turns his food to gold). John then passes the wasteland presided over by the twelve men of Fish (the fish, of course, is a Christian symbol, but the twelve men are weary, dispirited apostles) before he enters the apparent paradise of the Washingtons' estate. The allegory may not be entirely successful, particularly in its rather inconsistent treatment of Hades at the beginning and end, but the story provides a convincing condemnation of misused wealth even as it seems to celebrate its luxurious manifestations. Braddock Tarleton Washington—the richest man in the world and father to Percy, Kismine, and another daughter, Jasmine—is revealed as an amoral autocrat who keeps African American slaves, imprisons or murders all intruders, shields his children from reality, and even offers a bribe to God. In his scene of crisis, Washington intrudes his perspective upon the omniscient-narrator voice: "God had His price, of course. God was made in man's image, so it had been said: He must have His price."[49] John watches as Washington offers the bribe, and God and all the natural world seem momentarily to pause in their activities. Then "The dawn and the day resumed their place in a time, and the risen sun sent hot waves of yellow mist that made its path bright before it. The leaves laughed in the sun, and their laughter shook the trees until each bough was like a girl's school in fairyland. God had refused to accept the bribe."[50] God and nature triumph over the soulless man's immense wealth and lead Washington to destroy himself, his wife and son, and all his material possessions, including the diamond as big as the Ritz. Through his merging of fantasy and allegory—a brilliant demonstration of his double vision and moral stance—Fitzgerald portrays both the apparent attractions of wealth and its terrible corruptions.

In one of his greatest stories, "Babylon Revisited," Fitzgerald develops a protagonist, Charlie Wales, who has lived a life of dissipation in 1920s Paris. He has been at least partially responsible for the death of his wife, Helen, by locking her out in the snowy Parisian streets after a night of drunkenness and marital discord, and he has surrendered the guardianship of his young daughter, Honoria, to his wife's sister and brother-in-law, Marion and Lincoln Peters. As the story begins, Charlie has returned to Depression-era Paris, where Honoria lives with the Peterses and their children. Wales is an apparently changed man. He runs a successful business in Prague; he limits himself to one drink a day "'so that the idea of alcohol won't get too big in my imagination'"[51]; and he now wishes to take Honoria with him to Prague and thus restore their family life. He clearly understands the consequences of his earlier irresponsible life in Boom-era Paris:

> . . . All the catering to vice and waste was on an utterly childish scale, and he suddenly realized the meaning of the word "dissipate"—to dissipate into thin air; to make nothing out of something. . . .

> He remembered thousand-franc notes given to an orchestra for playing a single number, hundred-franc notes tossed to a doorman for calling a cab.

> But it hadn't been given for nothing.

> It had been given, even the most wildly squandered sum, as an offering to destiny that he might not remember the things most worth remembering, the things that now he would always remember—his child taken from his control, his wife escaped to a grave in Vermont.[52]

Charlie's failure in the course of the story to win custody of his daughter at first seems unfair, the result of others' inability to recognize the very real changes he has made in his life. His neurotic sister-in-law, Marion, continues to dislike and distrust him, and the drunken Duncan Schaeffer and Lorraine Quarrles, who show up at the Peterses' apartment just as Marion is about surrender Honoria's guardianship to Charlie, assume that he is still the reveler they have known in the past. He is not. Yet, as Fitzgerald reveals through his skillful handling of characterization and action, Charlie has not entirely reformed. He is still drawn to the Babylon of 1920s Paris. The beginning and ending of the story find him in the Ritz bar, a symbol of 1920s extravagance. He returns to the cabarets and nightclubs of Montmartre, which recall for him both the exhilaration and "utter irresponsibility"[53] of those days; he refuses to give up alcohol altogether and leaves the Peterses' address with the Ritz barman for Duncan Schaeffer, both acts revealing his partial attraction to the past; and he constantly engages in self-pity and rationalization, imagining that his dead wife would want Honoria to be with him again: "He was absolutely sure Helen wouldn't have wanted him to be so alone."[54] Charlie clearly recognizes the extent of his earlier culpability when in section V of the story he tells Paul, the Ritz bartender, that he had lost everything he wanted in the boom—wife, child, sense of purpose—by "selling short."[55] But Charlie also suggests that his behavior in the 1920s was perhaps not really so blameworthy because the rules of that time were different from those of present time, the 1930s: "—The men who locked their wives out in the snow, because the snow of twenty-nine wasn't real snow. If you didn't want it to be snow, you just paid some money."[56] Charlie wants to have it both ways: his pride of reform in the present, and his nostalgia for the good and bad old days of the 1920s. He therefore does not deserve to regain Honoria (his lost honor) because he cannot finally surrender his remaining allegiances to the past. Through the characterization of Charlie Wales, "Babylon Revisited" exploits the double vision that conveys the moral stance in the best of Fitzgerald's work.

THE AMERICAN DREAM: Gertrude Stein said of the younger American writers who gathered in Paris in the 1920s, "You are all a lost generation,"[57] a line that Hemingway used as an epigraph for *The Sun Also Rises* (1926). Stein's statement described many of the American expatriates who had witnessed the battlefield carnage of World War I and thus had become disillusioned with the political and philosophical tenets that brought about the war. These writers and intellectuals were also dismayed by what they regarded as clear signs of provincialism in the United States during the 1920s: Prohibition, religious and political conservatism, rampant consumerism, and the conformist behavior that found its label in the title character of Sinclair Lewis's 1922 novel, *Babbitt*. For many of the young expatriate writers, the American dream—the belief that aspirations could be fulfilled through imagination and hard work—seemed dead or at least terribly corrupted. They thus moved to Europe, which appeared to offer a freer, more stimulating, and perhaps less hypocritical environment.

Although Fitzgerald lived abroad for nearly six years and was one of the major American writers to emerge during the 1920s, he did not share the disillusionment with or contempt for their country of certain expatriate Americans. Instead, he was unabashedly patriotic, believing that America remained the land of opportunity, of idealism, of great potentialities and possibilities. For Fitzgerald, the American dream was bound up inextricably with the country's history, which he called in a note accompanying material for *The Love of the Last Tycoon* "the most beautiful history in the world."[58] Yet he also recognized that however beautiful this history, its real meaning was elusive. In the coda to his 1929 story "The Swimmers" Fitzgerald wrote: "France was a land, England was a people, but America, having about it still that quality of the idea, was harder to utter—it was the graves at Shiloh and the tired, drawn, nervous faces of its great men, and the country boys dying in the Argonne for a phrase that was empty before their bodies withered. It was a willingness of the heart."[59]

In his novels and stories Fitzgerald revealed not only the fulfillment of the American dream but also the many ways it could be debased and distorted. His most evocative protagonists—among them Jay Gatsby, Dick Diver, and Monroe Stahr—share "that quality of the idea" and "willingness of the heart" defined by Fitzgerald as quintessentially American. Although they are frequently disappointed in their quests, it is not finally the dream that fails them but instead something else: some weakness or corruption in themselves or others. In *The Great Gatsby*, for example, Gatsby's dreams are noble, even incorruptible; but as Nick Carraway says, it is "what preyed on Gatsby, what foul dust floated in the wake of his dreams"[60] that destroys him: his own innocence about the differences between new and old wealth, and the hardness and carelessness of the Buchanans. At the end of the novel Nick, Fitzgerald's spokesman, reasserts the validity and pervasiveness of the American dream by tying Gatsby's vision to that of the historical Dutch sailors catching their first sight of the "fresh, green breast of the new world" with all of its rich if elusive promises to the brave and adventurous: "something commensurate to [their] capacity for wonder."[61]

In *Tender Is the Night* Dick Diver's pursuit of the American dream of success and fulfillment is defeated by weakness in himself. His promise as a young American psychiatrist—before his self-indulgent and self-sacrificing marriage to the wealthy mental patient Nicole Warren—is revealed early in Book II of the novel, which begins with a flashback to Zürich. At the end of the first chapter of Book II, the omniscient narrator declares, "The foregoing has the ring of a biography, without the satisfaction of knowing that the hero, like Grant, lolling in his general store in Galena, is ready to be called to an intricate destiny."[62] The connection of Dick with Ulysses S. Grant, who worked in a Galena, Illinois, general store before rising to commander of the Union army during the Civil War and president of the United States later, suggests Diver's splendid potential, just as the repetition of the image in the novel's final sentence[63] emphasizes the enormity of his fall.

Almost from the beginning of his story in Book II, Diver is torn between his desire to devote himself to his work while enduring material privations and his equally strong desire to enjoy the "grace and adventure"[64] associated with affluence:

"God, am I like the rest after all?"— So he used to think starting awake at night—"Am I like the rest?"

This was poor material for a socialist but good material for those who do much of the world's rarest work. . . . In the dead white hours in Zürich staring into a stranger's pantry across the upshine of a street-lamp, he used to think that he wanted to be good, he wanted to be kind, he wanted to be brave and wise, but it was all pretty difficult. He wanted to be loved, too, if he could fit it in.[65]

Both his eloquent oration at the World War I battlefield Beaumont Hamel in Book I, chapter 13, and his meditation on his father's death in Book II, chapters 18 and 19, reveal that after his marriage to Nicole, Dick retains his capacity to respond to dedication and sacrifice— two principles implicit in the fulfillment of the American dream. In his Beaumont Hamel speech he declares, "'All my beautiful lovely safe world blew itself up here with a great gust of high-explosive love,'" but he then confesses his own helplessness in combating his sense of loss: "'. . . an old romantic like me can't do anything about it.'"[66] Hearing of his father's death, he praises the Reverend Mr. Diver's "'good instincts,' honor, courtesy, and courage," but as

"'See that little stream—we could walk to it in two minutes. It took the British a month to walk to it—a whole empire walking very slowly, dying in front and pushing forward behind. And another empire walked very slowly backward a few inches a day, leaving the dead like a million bloody rugs. No Europeans will ever do that again in this generation.'

'Why, they've only just quit over in Turkey,' said Abe. 'And in Morocco—'

'That's different. This Western Front business couldn't be done again, not for a long time. The young men think they could do it but they couldn't. They could fight the First Marne again but not this. This took religion and years of plenty and tremendous sureties and the exact relation that existed between the classes. The Russians and Italians weren't any good on this front. You had to have a whole-souled sentimental equipment going back further than you could remember. You had to remember Christmas, and postcards of the Crown Prince and his fiancée, and little cafés in Valence and beer gardens in Unter den Linden and weddings at the mairie, and going to the Derby, and your grandfather's whiskers.

.   .   .

'. . . Why, this was a love battle—there was a century of middle-class love spent here. This was the last love battle.'"

Dick Diver

From F. Scott Fitzgerald, *Tender Is the Night*, text established by Matthew J. Bruccoli (London: Everyman, 1996), Book I, chapter 13, pp. 61–62.

he lays his father to rest in his ancestral Virginia churchyard, Dick symbolically acknowledges his own inability to live up to the elder Diver's standards: "'Good-by, my father—good-by, all my fathers.'"[67] This scene represents Dick Diver's final surrender of his sense of duty and purpose. Thereafter his decline is both precipitous and inevitable.

In his final, unfinished novel, *The Love of the Last Tycoon*, Fitzgerald develops a protagonist who has achieved the American dream of success and fulfillment. Monroe Stahr, a young Jew from a lower-middle-class background, has made himself through genius and hard work the most respected producer in the Hollywood movie industry, which by the mid 1930s had become the world's most popular and powerful medium for conveying images of the American dream. Fitzgerald's plan for the novel included Stahr's death in a plane crash near the end. Yet, in the sections of the book that were written, the protagonist maintains his standards and his work ethic despite formidable obstacles: efforts by rival movie executives and labor organizers to wrest control of his studio from him; complications arising from his involvement with Kathleen Moore, who resembles his dead actress wife, Minna Davis; and concerns caused by his failing health. By refusing to compromise his vision and his work, Stahr fulfills the implicit requirements of the American dream and thereby becomes the only major Fitzgerald protagonist who both achieves and maintains his success.

Fitzgerald, who was an avid student of history, provided his final hero with historical associations. Stahr is connected by the narrator, Cecelia Brady, with royalty—"he had looked out on all the kingdoms,"[68] he was "a little like the Emperor and the Old Guard. . . . the last of the princes"[69]—and with legendary figures of the movie industry, "Edison and Lumière and Griffith and Chaplin."[70] He is identified by cameraman Pete Zavras with great figures from ancient Greece—"'You are the Aeschylus and the Diogenes of the moving picture. . . . Also the Asclepius and the Menander.'"[71] More significantly, Stahr is connected with tycoons from American history—Jay Gould, Cornelius Vanderbilt, Andrew Carnegie, and John Jacob Astor—and when writer Wylie White objects to Stahr's calling himself a "merchant" by citing historian Charles Francis Adams's negative assessment of the early American tycoons, the producer responds, "'Adams was probably a sour belly. . . . He wanted to be headman himself but he didn't have the judgement or else the character.'"[72] Most significantly of all, Stahr is associated with Abraham Lincoln, who was martyred for his successful efforts to preserve the country's union. (*The Oxford English Dictionary* notes that the word *tycoon* was applied to Lincoln.) In a scene in episode 10, the Danish prince Agge, who accom-

It was as if they could say, "Neither of us has anything; we shall be poor together"—just as delightful that they should be rich instead.

An hour later Anson awoke in a fog of nervous agony through which he perceived after a moment the figure of his uncle standing by the door.

". . . . I said, are you better?"

"Do you feel better, old man?"

"Terrible," murmured Anson.

"I'm going to try you with another bromo. It'll do you good to sleep another hour."

With an effort Anson slid his legs from the bed and stood up.

"I'm all right," he said dully.

"Take it easy."

"I think if you gave me a glass of brandy, I could go down!"

"Oh, no—"

"Yes, that's the only thing. I'm all right now—I suppose I'm in Dutch down there."

"They know you're a little under the weather," said his uncle deprecatingly. "But what's the difference? Jack Schuler didn't even get here. He died in the locker-room over at the links."

31

Illustration by F. R. Gruger of Anson Hunter and Paula Legendre; "The Rich Boy" appeared in the January and February 1926 issues of *Red Book Magazine*. (Matthew J. and Arlyn Bruccoli Collection of F. Scott Fitzgerald, Thomas Cooper Library, University of South Carolina)

panies Stahr on a studio tour, is moved by the sight of an actor dressed as Lincoln: "—This then, he thought, was what they all meant to be."[73] Agge refers in general to Americans, but in particular to Stahr, who at the end of his meeting with the prince reinforces his identification with the presidential preserver of the union by declaring that in the world of the studio, "'I'm the unity.'"[74] Later in the novel, the English screenwriter Boxley, who has begun to master his trade through Stahr's instruction, even more clearly connects the producer with the president, thereby emphasizing the magnitude of Stahr's efforts: "Stahr like Lincoln was a leader carrying on a long war on many fronts."[75] In his final novel, then, Fitzgerald makes explicit both the imaginative and historical validity of his twenty-year investigation of the American dream.

FITZGERALD AND MONEY: More than any other writer of his time, with the possible exception of Theodore Dreiser, Fitzgerald was aware of the influence of money on American life and character. Because he wrote seriously about money, aspiration, and love, which were usually inseparable in his fiction, Fitzgerald has been labeled a materialist by his detractors. He also has been regarded as an uncritical worshipper of the rich, a view promulgated by Ernest Hemingway's crack in his 1936 story "The Snows of Kilimanjaro" that "poor Scott Fitzgerald" was ruined by his "romantic awe" of the rich.[76]

Fitzgerald wrote about the rich, but his understanding of the effects of money on character was complex. His most-quoted statement on the subject appears in his 1926 story "The Rich Boy": "Let me tell you about the very rich. They are different from you and me. They possess and enjoy early, and it does something to them, makes them soft where we are hard, and cynical where we are trustful, in a way that, unless you were born rich, it is very difficult to understand. They think, deep in their hearts, that they are better than we are because we had to discover the compensations and refuges of life for ourselves. Even when they enter deep into our world or sink below us, they still think that they are better than we are. They are different."[77] This passage reflects the ambivalence of Fitzgerald's attitude: his attraction to and his distrust of the rich.

For Fitzgerald, money was an important part of the American dream because it provided not just luxuries but also opportunities unavailable to less affluent people. Money therefore had its obligations. As Fitzgerald told Hemingway in his 16 July 1936 letter of reply to "The Snows of Kilimanjaro": "Riches have <u>never</u> facinated me, unless combined with the greatest charm or distinction."[78] Wealthy people who wasted or perverted the opportunities that their money gave them were objects of Fitzgerald's disappointment or disapproval. In "The Rich Boy," for example, Anson Hunter's sense of superiority prevents him from committing himself to meaningful human relationships, and he thus becomes increasingly isolated as he grows older. In *The Beautiful and Damned* Anthony Patch's expectations of an inheritance cause him to waste his talents and life. In *The Great Gatsby* the Buchanans' money makes them careless, hard, and directionless: "They had spent a year in France, for no particular reason, and then drifted here and there unrestfully wherever people played polo and were rich together."[79] In "The Diamond as Big as the Ritz" the Washingtons' vast wealth enslaves them, making them emotionally and spiritually arid. In *Tender Is the Night* Dick Diver has "been swallowed up like a gigolo, and somehow permitted his arsenal to be locked up in the Warren safety-deposit vaults."[80] Fitzgerald clearly understood that money had the power to corrupt its possessors, just as it had the potential to increase their fulfillment.

Fitzgerald's responses to money were formed by his family's ambiguous social position in St. Paul and by his exposure to the sons and daughters of the affluent at prep school and Princeton. In a 4 March 1938 letter to Anne Ober about Scottie Fitzgerald's upcoming private-school graduation ceremony, Fitzgerald wrote: ". . . we will watch all the other little girls get diamond bracelets and Cord roadsters. I am going to a costumer's in New York and buy Scotty some phoney jewelry so she can pretend they are graduation presents. Otherwise, she will have to suffer the shame of being a poor girl in a rich girl's school. That was always my experience—a poor boy in a rich town; a poor boy in a rich boy's school; a poor boy in a rich man's club at Princeton. So I guess she can stand it. However, I have never been able to forgive the rich for being rich, and it has colored my entire life and works."[81]

Fitzgerald's sense of being excluded from the freedom and opportunities provided by money had been further intensified by his inability to marry Zelda right away because of his failures in New York following his army discharge. As he declared in "Pasting It Together":

The man with the jingle of money in his pocket who married the girl a year later would always cherish an abiding distrust, an animosity, toward the leisure class—not the conviction of a revolutionist but the smouldering hatred of a peasant. In the years since then I have never been able to stop wondering where my friends' money came from, nor to stop thinking that at one time a sort of *droit de seigneur* might have been exercised to give one of them my girl.

> For sixteen years I lived pretty much as this latter person, distrusting the rich, yet working for money with which to share their mobility and the grace that some of them brought into their lives.[82]

Because Fitzgerald's response to wealth was complex, mixing resentment and strong attraction, his fictional treatment of this material is both profound and extensive.

EMOTIONAL BANKRUPTCY: Fitzgerald employed a financial metaphor, "emotional bankruptcy," to label a theme that pervades his work. He believed that people—in and out of fiction—have a fixed amount of emotional capital and that when this capital is depleted by reckless expenditure, it cannot be replaced. Fitzgerald developed this idea from his own struggles with money, personal relationships, and internal and external impediments to his work. In "The Crack-Up" he charged himself with being "only a mediocre caretaker of most of the things left in my hands, even of my talent."[83] From the early 1920s on, he often lamented the dissipations of his life: his *Ledger* headings include "a bad year. No work" (1921–1922), "dangerous and deteriorating year" (1922–1923), "The most miserable year since I was nineteen" (1923–1924), "Total loss" (1926–1927), "Increasingly unhappy. . . . Ominous" (1932–1933).[84] When he was working, it was usually on the short stories that he increasingly resented. During the 1930s he confided in his *Notebooks,* "I have asked a lot of my emotions—one hundred and twenty stories, The price was high, right up with Kipling, because there was one little drop of something not blood, not a tear, not my seed, but me more intimately than these, in every story, it was the extra I had. Now it is gone and I am just like you now."[85] In "Pasting It Together" Fitzgerald again described his sense of emotional bankruptcy through financial metaphors, declaring that "like a man over-drawing at his bank," he felt "a vast irresponsibility toward every obligation, a deflation of all my values."[86]

"There are no second acts in American lives," Fitzgerald wrote in both the *Notebooks*[87] and his 1932 essay "My Lost City."[88] In this statement he suggested that both he and his countrymen, engaged in quests for the quintessential American dream of success, wealth, and happiness, must almost inevitably exhaust their energies and resources. "I began to realize," he admitted in "The Crack-Up," "that I had been mortgaging myself physically and spiritually up to the hilt,"[89] a phenomenon that he saw repeated in certain of his associates during the 1930s and that he treated in important fictional works of that decade. Charlie Wales in "Babylon Revisited" employs financial imagery—"selling short" and "you just paid some money"[90]—to describe his surrender to the affluence and dissipations of the expatriate life that had undermined his commitment to responsible behavior. Josephine Perry, the teenaged protagonist of the short story "Emotional Bankruptcy" (1931), discovers that she is unable to love the man she wants to love because she has squandered her emotional capital on frivolous earlier romances: "She was very tired and lay face downward on the couch with that awful, awful realization that all the old things are true. One cannot both spend and have."[91] Similarly, in the 1930 story "One Trip Abroad" Nelson and Nicole Kelly, who have come to Europe to study painting and singing, respectively, expend their energies on restless travel and meaningless social connections until, their health and spirits broken, they are forced to enter a Swiss sanatorium. There they discover in horror that the young couple they have observed from time to time during their years in Europe—she now marked by "ill health" and "unwholesomeness" and he appearing "weak and self-indulgent"[92]—are, in fact, themselves. In "Afternoon of an Author," a highly autobiographical 1936 story or essay (it has been variously labeled), Fitzgerald's ill, weary writer-protagonist grasps for inspiration that he hopes will refresh his exhausted material, as he glimpses a pair of young lovers from the upper deck of a bus: "Their isolation moved him and he knew he would get something out of it professionally, if only in contrast to the growing seclusion of his life and the increasing necessity of picking over an already well-picked past. He needed reforestation and he was well aware of it, and he hoped the soil would stand one more growth. It had never been the very best soil for he had had an early weakness for showing off instead of listening and observing."[93] Most significantly, Dick Diver, having given too much to too many people, fades from once-brilliant psychiatrist to failed small-town doctor in *Tender Is the Night*. The final sentence of the novel is a much-admired example of Fitzgerald's perfectly controlled tone and rhythm as he conveys Diver's emotional bankruptcy and obscurity: "Perhaps, so she [Nicole Diver] liked to think, his career was biding its time, again like Grant's in Galena; his latest note was post-marked from Hornell, New York, which is some distance from Geneva and a very small town; in any case he is almost certainly in that section of the country, in one town or another."[94]

TECHNIQUES AND STYLE

TRADITIONALIST: With the publication of *This Side of Paradise* in 1920, Fitzgerald became known as a daring writer primarily because of his material and themes rather than because of his technical innovations. His questing young men and courageous young women, who challenged conventional standards of behavior, seemed emblematic of the new decade of

"He tried to find the visible act that revealed a moral quality inherent in a certain moment of time. He was haunted by time, as if he wrote in a room full of clocks and calendars. He made lists by the hundred, including lists of the popular songs, the football players, the top debutantes (with the types of beauty they cultivated), the hobbies and the slang expressions of a given year; he felt that all these names and phrases belonged to the year and helped to reveal its momentary color. 'After all,' he said in an otherwise undistinguished magazine story, 'any given moment has its value; it can be questioned in the light of after-events, but the moment remains. The young prince in velvet gathered in lovely domesticity around the queen amid the hush of rich draperies may presently grow up to be Pedro the Cruel or Charles the Mad, but the moment of beauty was there.'"

Malcolm Cowley

From the introduction to *The Stories of F. Scott Fitzgerald*, edited by Cowley (New York: Scribners, 1951), pp. xiii–xiv.

the 1920s, thereby attracting youthful readers and unsettling many older ones. Fitzgerald, however, was not essentially a modernist or an experimental writer, as were many of his contemporaries. Except for a brief passage in Book II, chapter 5, of *This Side of Paradise* and for Book II, chapter 10, of *Tender Is the Night*— Nicole Diver's account of the development of her relationship with her husband—he avoided the stream-of-consciousness technique perfected by British writers James Joyce and Virginia Woolf. Fitzgerald also rejected what he called the "infectious style,"[95] with its short declarative sentences and simple diction, of Ernest Hemingway, as well as the collage-like "Newsreel" and "Camera Eye" techniques used by John Dos Passos in his *U.S.A.* trilogy.

Fitzgerald's techniques and writing style were traditional because his vision of the world was at least in part drawn from pre–World War I assumptions. Lionel Trilling correctly observed that "Fitzgerald was perhaps the last notable writer to affirm the Romantic fantasy, descended from the Renaissance, of personal ambition and heroism, of life committed to, or thrown away for, some ideal of self."[96] Whereas Hemingway's and Dos Passos's male protagonists often express their disillusionment with "all faiths,"[97] Fitzgerald's best male figures adhere to these faiths, though they may question them and may be— indeed, usually are—defeated in their quests. In his *Notebooks* Fitzgerald wrote, "The two basic stories of all times are Cinderella and Jack the Giant Killer—the charm of women and the courage of men. The 19th century glorified the merchant's cowardly son. Now a reaction."[98] Observing this "reaction" in the often nihilistic themes and experimental techniques of his most distinguished contemporaries, Fitzgerald asserted his allegiance to the older, nineteenth-century tradition: "I am the last of the novelists for a long time now."[99]

Fitzgerald was, above all, a storyteller who achieved a close relationship with the reader through the voice of his fiction, which was intimate, warm, and witty. Trilling defined this quality as "his power of love": "Even in Fitzgerald's early, cruder books, or even in his commercial stories, and even when the style is careless, there is a tone and pitch to the sentences which suggest his warmth and tenderness, and, what is rare nowadays and not likely to be admired, his gentleness without softness. . . . [H]e was gifted with the satiric eye; yet we feel that in his morality he was more drawn to celebrate the good than to denounce the bad. . . . [W]e know this the more surely because we perceive that he loved the good not only with his mind but also with his quick senses and his youthful pride and desire."[100] Hard-boiled novelist Raymond Chandler made a similar point about Fitzgerald's distinctive voice: "He had one of the rarest qualities in all literature, and it's a great shame that the word for it has been thoroughly debased by the cosmetic racketeers, so that one is almost ashamed to use it to describe a real distinction. Nevertheless, the word is charm— charm as Keats would have used it. Who has it today? It's not a matter of pretty writing or clear style. It's a kind of subdued magic, controlled and exquisite, the sort of thing you get from good string quartettes. Yes, where would you find it today?"[101]

NOVELIST OF SELECTION: Most practitioners of American social fiction tend to saturate their texts with details of character and place—Sinclair Lewis, John O'Hara, or Thomas Wolfe, for example—but Fitzgerald in his mature work employed a different method. He recognized the genius of his Scribners stablemate Wolfe, but in a July 1937 letter to him, Fitzgerald suggested that the younger writer's saturation method blunted his artistic effects: "The novel of selected incidents has this to be said that the great writer like Flaubert has consciously left out the stuff that Bill or Joe, (in his case Zola) will come along and say presently. . . . So Mme Bovary becomes eternal while Zola already rocks with age."[102]

Critics have observed that in *This Side of Paradise* Fitzgerald employed the saturation method, mixing a variety of styles and forms— verse and short plays, for example, are included within his narrative—as well as at least two sometimes inconsistent points of view: Amory Blaine's and the author's own omniscient voice. The reviewer for *The New Republic* described the novel as "the collected works of F. Scott Fitzgerald."[103] *The Beautiful and Damned* is more tightly constructed than *This Side of Paradise,* though it still suffers from inconsistent style and tone, authorial intrusions, and awkwardly interpolated material from other genres. With *The Great Gatsby,* however, Fitzgerald truly became the novelist of selection, disciplining his wealth of literary sources and his fertile imagination.

Great fiction is great social history. Although Fitzgerald is one of the best practitioners of American social fiction and *The Great Gatsby* is regarded as a bible of the 1920s, the novel includes surprisingly little anthropological data. Only six songs—most of them romantic ballads, not jazz—are mentioned. Though many cars figure in the narrative and careless driving becomes a motif of the novel, only a few—including Nick Carraway's "old Dodge"[104] and George Wilson's "dust-covered wreck of a Ford which crouched in a dim corner"[105] of his gas-station/garage—are identified by make. The most famous automobile in American literature, Gatsby's yellow car, is not defined as a Rolls-Royce or a Duesenberg but is instead labeled by Tom Buchanan as a "'circus wagon'"[106] and described by Nick Carraway as "a rich cream color, bright with nickel, swollen here and there in its monstrous length with triumphant hatboxes and supper-boxes and tool-boxes, and terraced with a labyrinth of wind-shields that mirrored a dozen suns."[107] Fitzgerald uses carefully selected details of description to convey through each automobile the character and vision of its owner: Nick's unostentatious pragmatism; Wilson's trapped, poverty-stricken, crouching desperation; and Gatsby's "gorgeous,"[108] grandiose "Platonic conception of himself" in "service of a vast, vulgar and meretricious beauty."[109]

Similarly, Fitzgerald's celebrated catalogue at the beginning of chapter 4 of Gatsby's party guests does not list actual people but instead, through suggestive naming, provides a cross-section of members of 1920s society who have either succeeded in the world's terms or aspire to do so. Several critics have commented on Fitzgerald's use of imagery drawn from unappealing animal or aquatic life—the "Leeches," "Doctor Webster Civet," "A whole clan named Blackbuck," "the Fishguards," "James B. ('Rot-gut') Ferret," "S. B. Whitebait," for example—and his fondness for incongruous combinations: "the Willie Voltaires," "the Stonewall Jackson Abrams of Georgia," "Mrs. Ulysses Swett." Others have celebrated his pure comic or satiric invention in naming: "the Cheadles," "S. W. Belcher and the Smirkes," "the Chromes and the Backhyssons," and the interchangeable young women whose "last names were either the melodious names of flowers and months or the sterner ones of the great American capitalists whose cousins, if pressed, they would confess themselves to be."[110] In his treatment both of automobiles and the guest list, Fitzgerald proved himself a master of the selective, evocative detail.

STYLIST: Throughout his best work Fitzgerald's writing style is impressionistic: his details evoke sensory responses in the reader and, in the description of Nicole Diver's shopping trip in Book I, chapter 12, of *Tender Is the Night,* permit omniscient-narrator response:

> . . . She bought colored beads, folding beach cushions, artificial flowers, honey, a guest bed, bags, scarfs, love birds, miniatures for a doll's house and three yards of some new cloth the color of prawns. She bought a dozen bathing suits, a rubber alli-

gator, a travelling chess set of gold and ivory, big linen handker-
chiefs for Abe, two chamois leather jackets of kingfisher blue and
burning bush from Hermès—bought all these things not a bit like
a high-class courtesan buying underwear and jewels, which were
after all professional equipment and insurance—but with an
entirely different point of view. Nicole was the product of much
ingenuity and toil. For her sake trains began their run at Chicago
and traversed the round belly of the continent to California; chi-
cle factories fumed and link belts grew link by link in factories;
men mixed toothpaste in vats and drew mouthwash out of cop-
per hogsheads; girls canned tomatoes quickly in August or
worked rudely at the Five-and-Tens on Christmas Eve; half-breed
Indians toiled on Brazilian coffee plantations and dreamers were
muscled out of patent rights in new tractors—these were some of
the people who gave a tithe to Nicole, and as the whole system
swayed and thundered onward it lent a feverish bloom to such
processes of hers as wholesale buying, like the flush of a fireman's
face holding his post before a spreading blaze. She illustrated
very simple principles, containing in herself her own doom, but
illustrated them so accurately that there was grace in the proce-
dure, and presently Rosemary [Hoyt] would try to imitate it.[111]

Here Fitzgerald astonishes the reader with the variety and luxury of
Nicole's purchases, then suggests the price that her extravagant needs
exact both upon poorer people everywhere and upon herself—she "con-
tain[s] in herself her own doom"—and, in a final brilliant imaginative
leap, concedes her exciting "feverish bloom" and "grace" as she fulfills
her privileges as a wealthy woman.

In other places Fitzgerald's style evokes mood. At the beginning
of chapter 3 of *The Great Gatsby,* for example, Nick Carraway begins his
first description of a Gatsby party with these lines: "There was music from
my neighbor's house through the summer nights. In his blue gardens men
and girls came and went like moths among the whisperings and the
champagne and the stars."[112] The language and the rhythm of the first sentence—especially in the phrase "through the summer nights"—establish
a romantic scene that is reinforced by the apparently magical "blue gardens" filled with "men and girls" in the second sentence. As this sentence
develops, however, Nick suggests that these couples are in constant and
meaningless flux—they "came and went like moths"—and that they are
absorbed equally by "the whisperings" (romantic murmurings or rumors
about Gatsby) and "the champagne" (beverage associated with celebration or drunkenness) and "the stars" (normally a symbol of lofty aspira-

tions or destiny, but here perhaps no more than a prop for the make-believe world Gatsby has created). Fitzgerald, through his narrator Nick, employs language that subtly suggests both the magic and corruption that fill the world of the novel. When Nick remarks, as the scene draws to a close, that "the orchestra is playing yellow cocktail music,"[113] he strikingly combines color and sound through a rhetorical device known as synesthesia.

Many literary critics have attempted to identify distinctive elements of Fitzgerald's style.[114] They have focused on his dramatic use of verbs—Wilson's car that "crouched in a dim corner"—or his pattern of linking adjectives that seem contradictory: Jordan Baker's "charming, discontented face"[115] and Nicole Diver's "hard and lovely and pitiful" face.[116] Critics have also cited his linkage of apparently incompatible nouns and adjectives to produce startling but thematically evocative effects: the "triumphant hatboxes" of Gatsby's car and the "blue gardens" of his parties, both suggesting the grandeur but unreality of his vision of self. Similarly, *Tender Is the Night* begins with a description of Gausse's Hôtel des Étrangers, which is fronted by "Deferential palms"; here the oddly paired adjective and noun evoke the artificial splendor of this hotel for strangers—wealthy expatriates—and its equally artificial "bright tan prayer rug of a beach,"[117] where these expatriates worship the leisure their wealth provides. Moreover, in Cecelia Brady's meditation on Monroe Stahr at the end of the first chapter of *The Love of the Last Tycoon,* she envisions him in flight, gazing down on and measuring the "jerky hopes and graceful rogueries and awkward sorrows" of the less heroic people surrounding him; here, through her linkage of apparently disparate adjectives and nouns, she emphasizes Stahr's penetrating but compassionate response as "he came here from choice to be with us to the end."[118]

SYMBOLIST: Commentators have given much attention to symbolism in Fitzgerald's novels and short fiction, particularly to his expansion of color imagery into larger symbolic patterns, his persistent drawing upon figures and episodes from American history, and, above all, his pervasive concern with time and mutability, or inevitable change.[119] (In *The Great Gatsby* there are at least 450 words that have to do with time, and in *Tender Is the Night,* 840 words.) In "May Day" Fitzgerald examines the failure of virtually all social classes in the United States to fulfill the promises of the American dream, and, as a scene near the end of the story reveals, he uses symbolism to convey his message. In this scene several major characters—weak, unsuccessful artist Gordon Sterrett; Sterrett's lower-class, blackmailing lover, Jewel Hudson; discharged soldier and ignorant rioter Gus Rose; and drunken Yalemen Philip Dean and Peter Himmel—are brought together in Childs', a New York restaurant, at four o'clock in the morning. At the end of the scene the sun rises, turning the plate-glass front of the restaurant "a blue that seemed to press close upon the pane as if to crowd its way into the restaurant. Dawn had come up in Columbus Circle, magical, breathless dawn, silhouetting the great statue of the immortal Christopher, and mingling in a curious and uncanny manner with the fading yellow electric light inside."[120] Here Fitzgerald uses the blue light of dawn and the yellow electric light of the restaurant to link the statue of Christopher Columbus, the heroic discoverer of the New World, and the degraded Americans assembled in Childs'. Through his symbolism Fitzgerald subtly but profoundly suggests how far the modern Americans of the story have fallen from the New World dreams embodied in Columbus.

"MAY DAY"

"This somewhat unpleasant tale, published as a novelette in the Smart Set in June, 1920, relates a series of events which took place in the spring of the previous year. Each of the three events made a great impression upon me. In life they were unrelated, except by the general hysteria of that spring which inaugurated the Age of Jazz, but in my story I have tried, unsuccessfully I'm afraid, to weave them into a pattern—a pattern which would give the effect of those months as they appeared to at least one member of what was then the younger generation."

F. Scott Fitzgerald

From the annotated table of contents for *Tales of the Jazz Age* (New York: Scribners, 1922).

A single example from *The Great Gatsby*—a novel filled with evocative symbols—illustrates Fitzgerald's skill in handling this device. The green light at the end of Daisy's dock becomes an emblem of Gatsby's devotion to her and to the dream that she personifies for him. The light appears at three important positions in the novel and evolves on each appearance. At the end of chapter 1, Nick has his first glimpse of Gatsby standing in the darkness of his lawn and trembling as he stretches his arms out toward the green light across the bay;[121] his posture suggests the enormous importance he attaches to the object, though its meaning remains a mystery to both Nick and the reader at this point in the book. In chapter 5, the fulcrum of the novel, Gatsby and Daisy are reunited, and near the end of the scene he mentions the green light. Noticing Gatsby's apparent absorption in what he has said, Nick speculates, "Possibly it had occurred to him that the colossal significance of that light had now vanished forever. Compared to the great distance that had separated him from Daisy it had seemed very near to her, almost touching her. It had seemed as close as a star to the moon. Now it was again a green light on a dock. His count of enchanted objects had diminished by one."[122] Daisy, the actual woman, may already have fallen a bit short of his vision of her. In chapter 9, as the novel concludes, Nick again evokes the light, which with Daisy's betrayal and Gatsby's destruction has resumed magical properties; now, however, it represents the magnitude and essential incorruptibility of Gatsby's dream that also lives on, despite impossible odds, in all who aspire greatly. "Gatsby believed in the green light, the orgastic future that year by year recedes before us," Nick declares. In the final lines of the novel, he makes Gatsby's experience the reader's experience by changing the third-person pronouns to first-person: "It eluded us then, but that's no matter—tomorrow we will run faster, stretch out our arms farther [recalling Gatsby's gesture in the first chapter]. . . . So we beat on" but are, like Gatsby, "borne back ceaselessly into the past."[123] Thus, the green light becomes symbolic not only of Gatsby's dreams but also of the elusive "American dream" that all readers presumably share.

MASTER OF POINT OF VIEW AND STRUCTURE: Fitzgerald has been particularly praised for his handling of point of view and structure, especially in *The Great Gatsby*. His adoption of a partially involved narrator for the novel—a technique that he probably learned from reading British fiction writer Joseph Conrad—allowed Fitzgerald both to bring structural complexity to the novel and to increase readers' belief in and sympathy for his title character. Nick, who tells Gatsby's story, declares at the beginning of the novel that he is "inclined to reserve all judgements,"[124] but as he is drawn into relationships with Tom, Daisy, Gatsby, and Jordan Baker, this intelligent, observant, and essentially moral man is forced to judge the conduct of the other characters. As he says in the preface to his story: "Conduct may be founded on the hard rock or the wet marshes but after a certain point I don't care what it's founded on. When I came back from the East last autumn I felt that I wanted the world to be in uniform and at a sort of moral attention forever;. . . ."[125]

Fitzgerald rewrote and restructured *The Great Gatsby* in galley proofs, primarily by breaking up and moving forward in the novel sections of Nick's account of Gatsby's history. This structural decision on Fitzgerald's part complicates the time scheme of the novel, but it also increases reader interest as author, narrator, and reader become collaborators in discovering the truths of Gatsby's story. Nick functions as a filter for and commentator on the history, which appears in chapters 4, 6, 8, and 9 of the published novel, and in each case he documents his sources.

In chapter 4, during their automobile ride to New York, Nick reports Gatsby's false, highly romantic autobiography, which Nick says is "like skimming hastily through a dozen magazines"[126] and to which he responds with incredulity—until Gatsby produces both a photo of himself at Oxford and his war medal from Montenegro. At the end of the chapter Nick reports Jordan Baker's account of Gatsby's courtship of Daisy in 1917 Louisville (an account that focuses on Daisy); her restlessness when the young military officer leaves for the war; her wedding to Tom Buchanan following a drunken episode provoked by a mysterious letter; and her early happiness with Tom, which is destroyed by his infidelity. Jordan then relays Gatsby's request that Nick manage a reunion between the former lovers, which takes place in chapter 5.

In chapter 6 Nick tells the story of Gatsby's youth, when he was named James Gatz, and his early years with Dan Cody, a self-made millionaire; the narrator clearly stipulates both the source of his information and his reason for divulging it at this point: "He told me all this very much later, but I've put it down here with the idea of exploding those first wild rumors about his antecedents, which weren't even faintly true. Moreover he told it to me at a time of confusion, when I had reached the point of believing everything and nothing about him."[127] This piece of Gatsby's story is followed by scenes in which Tom and two of his friends stop by Gatsby's house for a drink and the Buchanans attend a Gatsby party, which in turn is followed by Nick's post-party meeting with Gatsby, during which Gatsby makes his startlingly romantic statement about the possibility of repeating the past.[128] Nick provides an eloquent account of the moment Gatsby had "forever wed his unutterable visions to [Daisy's] perishable breath"[129] but then resumes his usual, more pragmatic voice by commenting on Gatsby's "appalling sentimentality."[130]

At the beginning of chapter 8, following the confrontation between Tom and Gatsby at the Plaza Hotel; the death of Tom's lover, Myrtle Wilson; and Gatsby's vigil outside the Buchanan home in chapter 7, Nick and Gatsby meet before dawn at Gatsby's house. Nick, revealing that this was the night Gatsby told him of his early years with Dan Cody,[131] retells the story of Gatsby's courtship of Daisy (an account that focuses on Gatsby), his heroism during the war, and his forlorn return to Louisville, where he begins his efforts to recapture the past. Nick's narrative is interrupted by Gatsby's extraordinary remark about Daisy's relationship with Tom—"'In any case . . . it was just personal'"—which Nick interprets as reflecting "some intensity in his conception of the affair that couldn't be measured."[132] By this point in the novel, because of Nick's skillful telling of Gatsby's story, the reader is prepared to shout with him to Gatsby, "'They're a rotten crowd. . . . You're worth the whole damn bunch put together.'"[133]

In chapter 9, following Gatsby's murder by George Wilson at the end of chapter 8, Nick provides after-biographies balancing Mr. Gatz's account of his son's early preparation for transforming himself into

Gatsby against Wolfshiem's brief testimonial about his own role in helping Gatsby to acquire the wealth that allowed him to pursue his dream. Both narratives miss the point about the magnitude of Gatsby's effort, but they ironically reinforce Nick's conclusions about the title character in his prefatory meditation: "No—Gatsby turned out all right at the end; it is what preyed on Gatsby, what foul dust floated in the wake of his dreams that temporarily closed out my interest in the abortive sorrows and short-winded elations of men."[134] Nick may "temporarily" have lost his interest, but he and his creator then retell Gatsby's story, increasing its effectiveness through brilliant handling of point of view and structure.

Fitzgerald intended to employ a similar partially involved narrator, Cecelia Brady, in *The Love of the Last Tycoon,* but because the unfinished novel is fragmentary and Fitzgerald's notes and outlines for the complete work are unclear about Cecelia's role, it is impossible to say whether she would have been the only narrator of *Tycoon.* In *Tender Is the Night,* however, Fitzgerald abandoned the first-person narrator and developed instead another complex structural plan. The novel is divided into three books employing an omniscient narrator, but Book I (twenty-five chapters)—which describes events that occur on the Riviera and Paris during a two-week period in the summer of 1925—is seen primarily through the eyes of Rosemary Hoyt, a young American actress. Because Rosemary is naive and becomes infatuated with the central character of the novel, Dr. Dick Diver, her perspective makes him and his wife, Nicole, seem elegant, glamorous, and in control of their world, until Nicole's breakdown at the end of this section. Book II (twenty-three chapters) abandons Rosemary's perspective in favor of the omniscient narrator and begins with a flashback to 1917, when Dick, then a brilliant young psychiatrist, comes to Zürich, meets and marries the wealthy mental patient Nicole Warren, and begins to become dependent on her money. In Book II, chapter 10, Nicole provides a stream-of-consciousness account of her life with Dick, an account that concludes with her apprehensive notice of Rosemary's arrival on the Riviera beach in summer 1925, thereby bringing the novel back to its starting point in Book I. The remainder of Book II employs the omniscient narrator to trace Dick's gradual decline through 1928 into purposelessness, alcoholism, and infidelity. Book III (thirteen chapters), again related by the omniscient narrator, rapidly chronicles Dick's complete deterioration in 1928 and 1929: his increasing alcoholism, his final abandonment of his career as a psychiatrist, and his desertion by both Rosemary and Nicole. This third book produces a cataclysmic effect; in its final postscript chapter the narrator matter-of-factly reveals Diver as a total failure living in obscurity in upstate

New York. The point of view and structure of the novel brilliantly convey the tragedy of Diver's collapse, moving as they do from Rosemary's romanticized vision of him in Book I, through the richly detailed omniscient-narrator account of his rise and fall in Book II, to the understated but devastating omniscient-narrator report of his final degradation in Book III. Fitzgerald, who regarded his ambitious 1934 novel as "a confession of faith,"[135] was so disappointed by its contemporary critical reception that he restructured his own copy in straight chronological order. This so-called "Author's Final Version," published in 1951, demonstrated the effectiveness of the original plan.

CODA: Fitzgerald was clearly a master of stylistic and technical devices that are often identified with great writing. Author James Thurber recognized an effect of this mastery when he wrote in 1942, "Fitzgerald's perfection of style and form, as in 'The Great Gatsby,' has a way of making something that lies between your stomach and your heart quiver a little."[136] Modernist writer Gertrude Stein declared in 1933 that Fitzgerald was "the only one of the younger writers who wrote naturally in sentences,"[137] and she could have added that he combined his sentences into fully developed, integrated paragraphs. But Fitzgerald was more than a brilliant technician and stylist. In an October 1936 letter to his daughter, who was trying to write short stories, Fitzgerald offered advice drawn from his own experience: "If you have anything to say, anything you feel nobody has ever said before, you have got to feel it so desperately that you will find some way to say it that nobody has ever found before, so that the thing you have to say and the way of saying it blend as one matter—as indissolubly as if they were conceived together."[138] Fitzgerald's accomplishments as a fiction writer were, finally, the product of his remarkable fusion of technique and style with material, theme, and a distinctive personal voice.

SUBJECT TO REVISION

WRITING HABITS: Fitzgerald is an authentic instance of an author who wrote by ear, the way a composer writes music. His prose is rhythmical, and he punctuated for sound, not for sight or in accordance with mechanical rules. He has been unnecessarily ridiculed for his bad spelling, which does not diminish the brilliance and control of his prose: literature is not a spelling bee. Fitzgerald felt that it was his publisher's responsibility to correct misspellings and other mechanical and usage errors, but because the Scribners proofreading standards were low, his books—particularly *This Side of Paradise* and *Tender Is the Night*—were published with errors for which he was blamed. In addition to spelling and usage problems, factual errors occur. In *The Great Gatsby,* for example, the description of the eyes on Dr. T. J. Eckleburg's billboard includes the line "their retinas are one yard high";[139] since retinas cannot be seen, Fitzgerald probably meant *irises.* The blunder was Fitzgerald's, but a good copyeditor should have caught it. Though Fitzgerald committed factual and mechanical errors, he evoked emotions, moods, and sensory responses through delicate self-editing. Every word mattered to him. As he wrote in a 13 August 1936 letter to publisher Bennett Cerf, "[S]ometimes by a single word one can throw a new emphasis or give a new value to the exact same scene or setting."[140] Thus, in the description of Monroe Stahr's unfinished house in section 14 of *The Love of the Last Tycoon,* Fitzgerald wrote "the skeleton of Stahr's house" and then substituted *fuselage* for *skeleton* to emphasize the connections between Stahr and flight.[141]

Fitzgerald was a painstaking writer and rewriter. His first drafts were done in pencil on legal-size paper and then were turned over to a typist, who prepared a triple-spaced text with one or two carbon copies. Fitzgerald then revised the ribbon copy and sometimes the carbons in pencil. One of these revised typescripts, which incorporated all corrections, went back to the typist, who prepared a new typescript. After another round of pencil corrections, this typescript was usually submitted for publication, but it might be retyped if the corrections were extensive. Fitzgerald then polished the galley proofs, not hesitating to revise or rewrite so heavily that the proofs had to be reset.

ACHIEVING MASTERPIECES: The composition process for Fitzgerald's novels was more elaborate than for his short fiction, involving layers of rewriting and revisions in both typescript and proofs. Authors are normally expected to read their proofs for typographical errors only; the writing process is supposed to be finished before the work is set in type. Fitzgerald, however, regarded proofs as just another typescript; he refused to leave his work alone while there was an opportunity to improve it. He revised, rewrote, and restructured *The Great Gatsby* in galley proofs, and he revised *Tender Is the Night* in magazine serial proofs, book galleys, and book page proofs. He did not engage in nervous tinkering: examination of his revised typescripts and proofs reveals that the work got better in each layer of revision. The alterations ranged from single-word substitutions to rewrites of complete scenes as Fitzgerald endeavored to achieve the work that existed in his mind.

Because Fitzgerald was a saver and preserved his manuscripts, typescripts, and proofs, it is possible to reconstruct the writing of *The*

Great Gatsby and *Tender Is the Night*—and to see how they became masterpieces. The process is clearer for *Gatsby*, for which the extant documents are the pencil manuscript, the untouched first galley proofs, and the revised/rewritten galleys; the typescript has not survived. This intricately structured short novel achieved its narrative control in the galley stage. Fitzgerald's changes were so extensive that the proofs had to be entirely reset.

When Perkins read the typescript for the unrevised text of *The Great Gatsby*, he wrote Fitzgerald, who was in Europe, a long letter that most significantly focused on the structure of the novel:

> There is one other point: in giving deliberately Gatsby's biography when he gives it to the narrator you do depart from the method of the narrative in some degree, for otherwise almost everything is told, and beautifully told, in the regular flow of it,—in the succession of events or in accompaniment with them. But you can't avoid the biography altogether. I thought you might find ways to let the truth of some of his claims like "Oxford" and his army career come out bit by bit in the course of actual narrative. I mention the point anyway for consideration in this interval before I send the proofs.[142]

Fitzgerald responded in a December 1924 letter:

> (b) Chapters VI + VII I know how to fix
>
> (c) Gatsby's business affairs I can fix. I get your point about them.
>
> (d) His vagueness I can repair by <u>making more pointed</u>—this doesn't sound good but wait and see. It'll make him clear
>
> (e) But his long narrative in Chap VIII will be difficult to split up. Zelda also thought I was a little out of key but it is good writing and I don't think I could bear to sacrifice any of it
>
> (f) I have 1000 minor corrections which I will make on the proof + several more large ones which you didn't mention.[143]

After publication of *The Great Gatsby* Fitzgerald gave his editor credit for improving the novel: "Max, it amuses me when praise comes in on the structure of the book—because it was you who fixed up the structure, not me."[144] Fitzgerald was extravagant in his expression of gratitude: he did all of his own work in restructuring *Gatsby* by transposing, cutting, and replacing episodes in the galley proofs. The novel became a masterpiece in the process.

As he told Perkins, Fitzgerald recognized that Gatsby's long biography in proof chapter 8 withheld necessary information from the reader. His solution was to transpose the facts about Gatsby's past from proof chapters 7 and 8 to the beginning and end of book chapter 6.

The Restructuring of *The Great Gatsby*

Unrevised Galleys	Revised Galleys & Book
Chapter 6	**Chapter 6**
Tom & friends visit Gatsby	Biography of Gatsby (Cody)
Buchanans attend party	Tom & friends visit Gatsby
	Buchanas attend party
	Gatsby tells Nick about love for Daisy
Chapter 7	**Chapter 7**
Gatsby tells Nick about love for Daisy	Lunch at Buchanan home
Lunch at Buchanan home	Tom stops for gas
Tom stops for gas	Plaza & confrontation
Plaza & confrontation	Death of Myrtle
Death of Myrtle	Nick & Gatsby outside Buchanan home
Nick & Gatsby outside Buchanan	
Chapter 8	**Chapter 8**
Biography of Gatsby (Cody)	Gatsby's courtship & Daisy's marriage
Gatsby's courtship & Daisy's marriage	Flashback to garage
Flashback to garage	Murder of Gatsby
Murder of Gatsby	

The large proof revisions were accompanied by thousands of minute changes: single-word substitutions and alterations of sentence rhythms. Comparison of the manuscript and revised proof texts for the eloquent closing of the novel reveals Fitzgerald's painstaking concern with every word.

And as I sat there, brooding on the old unknown world I thought of gatsby, ~~wonder~~ when he picked out the green light at the end of Daisy's dock. He had come a long way to this blue lawn but now his dream must have seemed so close that he could hardly fail to grasp it. He did not know that ~~he had left it behind him before, it lay somew~~ it was all behind him, ~~somewhere~~ back in that vast obscurity on the other side of the city, where the dark fields of the republic rolled on under the night.

He believed in the green glimmer, in the orgastic future that year by year recedes before us. It eluded us then but never mind — tomorrow we will run faster, stretch out our arms farther. And one fine morning—

So we beat on, a boat against the current, borne back ceaselessly into the past

Manuscript final page of *The Great Gatsby*, which Fitzgerald substantially revised before publication (Princeton University Library)

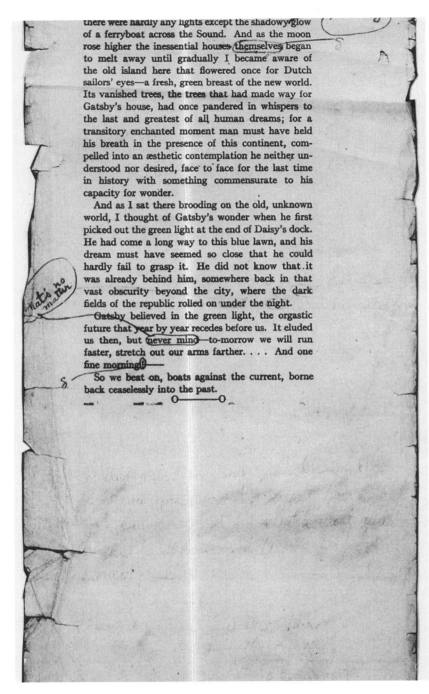

there were hardly any lights except the shadowy glow of a ferryboat across the Sound. And as the moon rose higher the inessential houses *themselves* began to melt away until gradually I became aware of the old island here that flowered once for Dutch sailors' eyes—a fresh, green breast of the new world. Its vanished trees, the trees that had made way for Gatsby's house, had once pandered in whispers to the last and greatest of all human dreams; for a transitory enchanted moment man must have held his breath in the presence of this continent, compelled into an æsthetic contemplation he neither understood nor desired, face to face for the last time in history with something commensurate to his capacity for wonder.

And as I sat there brooding on the old, unknown world, I thought of Gatsby's wonder when he first picked out the green light at the end of Daisy's dock. He had come a long way to this blue lawn, and his dream must have seemed so close that he could hardly fail to grasp it. He did not know that it was already behind him, somewhere back in that vast obscurity beyond the city, where the dark fields of the republic rolled on under the night. *That's no matter—* Gatsby believed in the green light, the orgastic future that *year* by year recedes before us. It eluded us then, but *never mind*—to-morrow we will run faster, stretch out our arms farther. . . . And one fine *morning*——

So we beat on, boats against the current, borne back ceaselessly into the past.

Revised galley proof for the final page of *The Great Gatsby*, which shows Fitzgerald improving the rhythm of a sentence (Princeton University Library)

Fitzgerald worked on the novel that became *Tender Is the Night* between 1925 and 1933, but his writing was frequently interrupted, and the novel evolved through three different plotlines and seventeen stages before its publication in 1934. His original story centered on Francis Melarky, a young American movie technician who meets charming American expatriates Seth and Dinah Piper (also called Roreback) and alcoholic Abe Grant (Herkimer) on the Riviera while traveling with his mother. In this version Melarky was to murder the domineering Mrs. Melarky, and the work-in-progress was variously titled "The Boy Who Killed His Mother," "Our Type," "The World's Fair," and "The Melarky Case." Fitzgerald worked intermittently on the Melarky matricide plot between 1925 and 1930, producing five drafts, no one of which was longer than four chapters. Three of the drafts used a third-person narrator and two employed an unidentified first-person narrator. In 1929 Fitzgerald briefly shifted his focus to a new plotline involving movie director Lew Kelly and his wife, Nicole, who meet a young actress named Rosemary while traveling to Europe on an ocean liner. Only two manuscript chapters of this version survive, and in early 1930 Fitzgerald returned to the Melarky story.

Zelda's first psychological breakdown in April 1930 and Fitzgerald's growing sense of his own failures during the late 1920s and early 1930s provided him with new, deeply felt material, which in turn generated a new plotline. He abandoned the Melarky-Kelly versions, though clearly the Pipers and Nicole Kelly contributed to the Divers, Abe Grant evolved into Abe North, and Francis Melarky and the actress Rosemary were combined and transformed into Rosemary Hoyt in *Tender Is the Night*. Between 1931 and 1933 the final version of the novel went through eleven stages: notes, manuscript, four sets of typescripts and carbons, revised galleys and revised pages proofs for its serial appearance in *Scribner's Magazine*,[145] the serial itself, and revised book galley proofs and book page proofs. Fitzgerald used several different working titles for the novel, including "The Drunkard's Holiday," "Dr. Diver's Holiday," and "Richard Diver," before settling on *Tender Is the Night*, drawn from "Ode to a Nightingale" by his favorite poet, the nineteenth-century British Romantic John Keats. His drafts for the Diver version reveal that he settled on the flashback structure from the beginning of his work on this plotline. Though his posthumously published "Author's Final Version" placed chapters in chronological order, there is no evidence that

Fitzgerald experimented with a straight chronological narrative while he was working on the novel published in 1934.[146]

STORIES AND NOVELS: The working relationship between Fitzgerald's short stories and novels is not generally understood. The stories have been disparaged as hackwork that took time away from his serious fiction. Although this view was endorsed by Fitzgerald, who resented the necessity to produce commercial work, careful reading of the stories reveals close connections with the novels. Fitzgerald's stories can be regarded as trial drafts for elements in his novels; in certain of these "cluster stories" he tested themes, scenes, and characters that were developed in his next novel. The most instructive of the cluster stories are associated with *The Great Gatsby* and *Tender Is the Night*. Fitzgerald described "Winter Dreams" (1922) as "A sort of 1st draft of the Gatsby idea,"[147] for it tells the story of a poor boy inspired to succeed by a desirable rich girl who betrays him. "Absolution," "'The Sensible Thing,'" and "The Diamond as Big as the Ritz" also have meaningful connections with *Gatsby*. Because *Tender Is the Night* was nine years in gestation and composition, at least thirty-seven magazine stories relate to it, notably "Babylon Revisited" and "One Trip Abroad." Both analyze the deterioration of Americans in Europe during the boom years. Fitzgerald did not include "One Trip Abroad" in his final volume of stories, *Taps at Reveille*, perhaps because he regarded it as too close to *Tender Is the Night*.

The reciprocity between his stories and novels resulted in problems for Fitzgerald because he had a firm rule against repeating pieces of his writing in his novels and story collections. When he was working on *The Great Gatsby*, he transferred short passages from magazine stories to the novel but then removed and replaced those passages before reprinting the stories in one of his collections. If a story had been too heavily mined to be salvaged for book republication, Fitzgerald designated it in his *Ledger* as "Permanently Buried."

This system worked well for *The Great Gatsby*, but it resulted in difficulties for *Tender Is the Night*. During the long period while Fitzgerald wrote and rewrote *Tender Is the Night*, he borrowed material from the novel-in-progress for the short stories he was producing for ready money, and he stripped material from stories for use in the novel.[148] The completed novel therefore included material originally written for stories as well as story material borrowed from the novel and then re-borrowed back into the novel. This process was not a literary crime: many authors have recycled their own writings. Never-

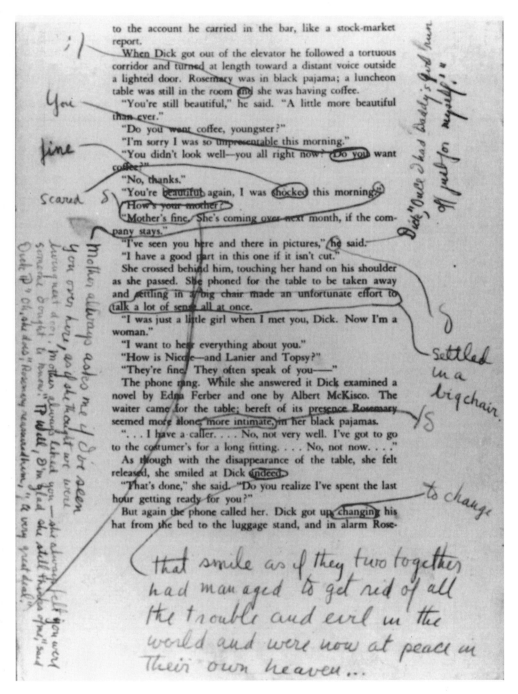

Revised galley proof for Book II, chapter 20, of *Tender Is the Night,* the 1928 reunion of Dick Diver and Rosemary Hoyt (Princeton University Library)

"The taxi driver regarded me indulgently while I stumbled here and there in the knee-deep underbrush, looking for my youth in a clapboard or a strip of roofing or a rusty tomato can. I tried to sight on a vaguely familiar clump of trees, but it was growing darker now and I couldn't be quite sure they were the right trees.

'They're going to fix up the old race course,' Ailie called from the car. 'Tarleton's getting quite doggy in its old age.'

No. Upon consideration they didn't look like the right trees. All I could be sure of was this place that had once been so full of life and effort was gone, as if it had never existed, and that in another month Ailie would be gone, and the South would be empty for me forever."

F. Scott Fitzgerald

From "The Last of the Belles" (1929), in *The Short Stories of F. Scott Fitzgerald,* edited, with a preface, by Matthew J. Bruccoli (New York: Scribners, 1989), pp. 462–463.

theless, Fitzgerald did regard the repetition of passages in his story volumes and novels as improper. When Perkins suggested that Fitzgerald was overly conscientious in this regard, he replied: "The fact that Ernest [Hemingway] has let himself repeat here and there a phrase would be no possible justification for me doing the same. Each of us has his virtues and one of mine happens to be a great sense of exactitude about my work. He might be able to afford a lapse in that line where I wouldn't be and after all I have got to be the final judge of what is appropriate in these cases."[149]

The symbiotic relationship between Fitzgerald's commercial short-story work and his novels must be understood in terms of his own standards: he did not write down for magazines, nor did he write carelessly for them. The plots of the stories are sometimes gimmicky, and the happy endings may be contrived, but his writing maintains Fitzgerald's standards. He always wrote the only way he knew how to write. Moreover, the recycling and polishing of material is characteristic of Fitzgerald's practice of refining his prose through layers of revision. Even the disparaged *Saturday Evening Post* stories underwent this process, which is one of the reasons they were so successful.

NOTES:

1. F. Scott Fitzgerald, *The Crack-Up,* edited, with an introduction, by Edmund Wilson (New York: New Directions, 1945), p. 89.

2. A. Scott Berg, *Max Perkins: Editor of Genius* (New York: Congdon/Dutton, 1978), p. 16.

3. *Dear Scott/Dear Max: The Fitzgerald-Perkins Correspondence,* edited, with an introduction, by John Kuehl and Jackson R. Bryer (New York: Scribners, 1971), p. 21.

4. Ibid., p. 47.

5. Maxwell Perkins to Fitzgerald, in *F. Scott Fitzgerald: A Life in Letters,* edited by Matthew J. Bruccoli (New York: Scribners, 1994), p. 88.

6. Fitzgerald, *Correspondence of F. Scott Fitzgerald,* edited by Bruccoli and Margaret M. Duggan (New York: Random House, 1980), p. 236.

7. Fitzgerald, *A Life in Letters,* p. 208.

8. Fitzgerald, *Dear Scott/Dear Max,* p. 180.

9. Ibid., p. 242.

10. Fitzgerald, *A Life in Letters,* p. 253.

11. Ibid., pp. 360.

12. Fitzgerald, *As Ever, Scott Fitz—: Letters Between F. Scott Fitzgerald and His Literary Agent Harold Ober, 1919–1940,* edited by Bruccoli and Jennifer M. Atkinson (Philadelphia & New York: Lippincott, 1972), p. 73.

13. Fitzgerald, *F. Scott Fitzgerald's Ledger: A Facsimile,* introduction by Bruccoli (Washington, D.C.: NCR Microcard Editions/Bruccoli Clark, 1973) , p. 52.

14. Ibid., pp. 58–59.

15. Fitzgerald, *As Ever, Scott Fitz—,* p. 19.

16. Ibid., p. 48.

17. Ibid., p. 90.

18. Fitzgerald, *A Life in Letters,* p. 169.

19. Fitzgerald, *As Ever, Scott Fitz—,* p. 85.

20. Ibid., p. 402.

21. Bruccoli and Bryer, eds., *F. Scott Fitzgerald in His Own Time* (New York: Popular Library, 1971), p. 156.

22. Fitzgerald, *Afternoon of an Author,* edited by Arthur Mizener (New York: Scribners, 1958), p. 132.

23. Fitzgerald, *The Notebooks of F. Scott Fitzgerald,* edited, with an introduction, by Bruccoli (New York & London: Harcourt Brace Jovanovich/Bruccoli Clark, 1978), # 316.

24. Fitzgerald, *The Short Stories of F. Scott Fitzgerald,* edited, with a preface, by Bruccoli (New York: Scribners, 1989), p. 270.

25. Fitzgerald, *The Great Gatsby,* preface and notes by Bruccoli (New York: Collier Books/Scribner Classic, 1992), p. 75.

26. Fitzgerald, *The Short Stories,* p. 317.

27. Fitzgerald, *A Life in Letters,* p. 87.

28. Fitzgerald, *This Side of Paradise* (New York: Scribners, 1998), p. 26.

29. Fitzgerald, *The Great Gatsby,* p. 6.

30. Ibid., pp. 187–188.

31. Fitzgerald, *The Short Stories,* p. 236.

32. Fitzgerald, *The Great Gatsby*, p. 116.

33. Fitzgerald, *The Short Stories*, p. 89.

34. Fitzgerald, *This Side of Paradise*, p. 175.

35. Ibid., p. 198.

36. Fitzgerald, *The Short Stories*, p. 643.

37. Fitzgerald, *Notebooks*, # 2070.

38. *The Letters of F. Scott Fitzgerald*, edited, with an introduction, by Andrew Turn-bull (New York: Scribners, 1963), p. 63.

39. Malcolm Cowley, "Third Act and Epilogue," *New Yorker*, 21 (30 June 1945): 54.

40. Fitzgerald, *The Great Gatsby*, p. 40.

41. Ibid., pp. 187–188.

42. Fitzgerald, *The Crack-Up*, p. 69.

43. Fitzgerald, *The Short Stories*, p. 182.

44. Ibid., p. 185.

45. Ibid., p. 188.

46. Ibid., p. 191.

47. Ibid., p. 205.

48. Ibid., p. 209.

49. Ibid., p. 212.

50. Ibid., p. 213.

51. Ibid., p. 624.

52. Ibid., p. 620.

53. Ibid., p. 629.

54. Ibid., p. 633.

55. Ibid.

56. Ibid.

57. James R. Mellow, *Charmed Circle: Gertrude Stein & Company* (New York: Praeger, 1974), p. 273.

58. Fitzgerald, *Notebooks*, # 2037.

59. Fitzgerald, *The Short Stories*, p. 512.

60. Fitzgerald, *The Great Gatsby*, p. 6.

61. Ibid., p. 189.

62. Fitzgerald, *Tender Is the Night: A Romance,* text established by Bruccoli (London: Everyman, 1996), p. 123.

63. Ibid., p. 321.

64. Ibid., p. 139.

65. Ibid., p. 140.

66. Ibid., p. 62.

67. Ibid., pp. 212–213.

68. Fitzgerald, *The Love of the Last Tycoon: A Western,* edited, with a preface and notes, by Bruccoli (New York: Scribner Paperback Fiction, 1994), p. 20.

69. Ibid., p. 27.

70. Ibid., p. 28.

71. Ibid., p. 61.

72. Ibid., p. 17.

73. Ibid., p. 49.

74. Ibid., p. 58.

75. Ibid., p. 107.

76. Ernest Hemingway, "The Snows of Kilimanjaro," *Esquire,* 6 (August 1936): 200.

77. Fitzgerald, *The Short Stories,* p. 318.

78. Fitzgerald, *A Life in Letters,* p. 302.

79. Fitzgerald, *The Great Gatsby,* p. 10.

80. Fitzgerald, *Tender Is the Night,* p. 209.

81. Fitzgerald, *As Ever, Scott Fitz—,* p. 357.

82. Fitzgerald, *The Crack-Up,* p. 77.

83. Ibid., p. 71.

84. Fitzgerald, *Ledger,* pp. 176–178, 181.

85. Fitzgerald, *Notebooks,* # 885.

86. Fitzgerald, *The Crack-Up,* pp. 77–78.

87. Fitzgerald, *Notebooks,* # 428.

88. Fitzgerald, *The Crack-Up,* p. 72.

89. Ibid.

90. Fitzgerald, *The Short Stories,* p. 633.

91. Ibid., p. 560.

92. Ibid., pp. 595–596.

93. Ibid., p. 738.

94. Fitzgerald, *Tender Is the Night,* p. 321.

95. Fitzgerald, "Pasting It Together," in *The Crack-Up,* p. 79.

96. Lionel Trilling, *The Liberal Imagination* (New York: Viking, 1950), p. 249.

97. Fitzgerald, *This Side of Paradise,* p. 284.

98. Fitzgerald, *Notebooks,* # 1071.

99. Ibid., # 2001.

100. Trilling, *The Liberal Imagination,* pp. 244–245.

101. Raymond Chandler to David Warren, 13 November 1950, in *Selected Letters of Raymond Chandler,* edited by Frank MacShane (New York: Columbia University Press, 1981), p. 239.

102. Fitzgerald, *A Life in Letters,* p. 332.

103. Quoted in *F. Scott Fitzgerald: The Critical Reception,* edited by Bryer (New York: Burt Franklin, 1978), p. 22.

104. Fitzgerald, *The Great Gatsby,* p. 7.

105. Ibid., p. 29.

106. Ibid., p. 128.

107. Ibid., p. 68.

108. Ibid., p. 6.

109. Ibid., p. 104.

110. Ibid., pp. 65–67. For useful analyses of Fitzgerald's catalogue of guests, see Ruth Prigozy, "Gatsby's Guest List and Fitzgerald's Technique of Naming," in *Fitzgerald/Hemingway Annual 1972,* edited by Bruccoli and C. E. Frazer Clark Jr. (Washington, D. C.: NCR Microcard Editions, 1972), pp. 99–112; and Lottie R. Crim and Neal B. Houston, "The Catalogue of Names in *The Great Gatsby,*" *Research Studies,* 36 (June 1968): 113–130.

111. Fitzgerald, *Tender Is the Night,* p. 59.

112. Fitzgerald, *The Great Gatsby,* p. 43.

113. Ibid., p. 44.

114. See particularly Daniel J. Schneider, "Color-Symbolism in *The Great Gatsby,*" *University Review,* 31 (October 1964): 13–17; F. H. Langman, "Style and Shape in *The Great Gatsby,*" *Southern Review* [Adelaide, Australia], 6 (March 1973): 48–67; W. J. Harvey, "Theme and Texture in *The Great Gatsby,*" *English Studies,* 38 (February 1957): 12–20; Bryer, "Style as Meaning in *The Great Gatsby:* Notes Toward a New Approach," in *Critical Essays on F. Scott Fitzgerald's The Great Gatsby,* edited by Scott Donaldson (Boston: G. K. Hall, 1984), pp. 117–129; John Stark, "The Style of *Tender Is the Night,*" in *Fitzgerald/Hemingway Annual 1972,* pp. 89–95; and George Garrett, "Fire and Freshness: A Matter of Style in *The Great Gatsby,*" in *New Essays on The Great Gatsby,* edited by Bruccoli (Cambridge: Cambridge University Press, 1985), pp. 101–116.

115. Fitzgerald, *The Great Gatsby,* p. 15.

116. Fitzgerald, *Tender Is the Night,* p. 10.

117. Ibid., p. 7.

118. Ibid., p. 21.

119. See particularly Anne R. Gere, "Color in Fitzgerald's Novels," in *Fitzgerald/Hemingway Annual 1971,* edited by Bruccoli and Clark (Washington, D.C.: NCR Microcard Editions, 1971), pp. 333–339; Kermit W. Moyer, "*The Great Gatsby:* Fitzgerald's Meditation on American History," in *Fitzgerald/Hemingway Annual 1972,* pp. 43–57; Marius Bewley, "Scott Fitzgerald and the Collapse of the American Dream," in his *The Eccentric Design* (New York: Columbia University Press, 1953), pp. 259–287; Robert Ornstein, "Scott Fitzgerald's Fable of East and West," *College English,* 18 (December 1956): 139–143; Jeffrey Steinbrink, "'Boats Against the Current': Mortality and the Myth of Renewal in *The Great Gatsby,*" *Twentieth Century Literature,* 26 (Summer 1980): 157–170; and Robert Sklar, *F. Scott Fitzgerald: The Last Laocoön* (New York: Oxford University Press, 1967).

120. Fitzgerald, *The Short Stories,* p. 135.

121. Fitzgerald, *The Great Gatsby,* pp. 25–26.

122. Ibid., p. 98.

123. Ibid., p. 189.

124. Ibid., p. 5.

125. Ibid., p. 6.

126. Ibid., p. 71.

127. Ibid., p. 107.

128. Ibid., p. 116.

129. Ibid., p. 117.

130. Ibid., p. 118.

131. Ibid., p. 155.

132. Ibid., p. 160.

133. Ibid., p. 162.

134. Ibid., pp. 6–7.

135. Fitzgerald, 1934 inscription to Philip Lenhart, in *A Life in Letters,* p. 252.

136. James Thurber, "Taps at Assembly," *New Republic,* 106 (9 February 1942): 211–212; reprinted in *F. Scott Fitzgerald: The Critical Reception,* pp. 380–382.

137. Gertrude Stein, *The Autobiography of Alice B. Toklas* (New York: Harcourt, Brace, 1933), p. 268.

138. Fitzgerald, *A Life in Letters,* p. 313.

139. Fitzgerald, *The Great Gatsby,* p. 27.

140. Fitzgerald, *A Life in Letters*, pp. 306–307.

141. Fitzgerald, *The Love of the Last Tycoon*, p. 81.

142. Perkins to Fitzgerald, 20 November 1924, in *A Life in Letters*, p. 88.

143. Ibid., p. 89.

144. Ibid., p. 125.

145. The novel appeared in four issues of *Scribner's Magazine* from January through April 1934.

146. For an extended discussion of the evolution of the novel, see Bruccoli, *The Composition of Tender Is the Night: A Study of the Manuscripts* (Pittsburgh: University of Pittsburgh Press, 1963).

147. Fitzgerald, ca. 1 June 1995, in *A Life in Letters*, p. 121.

148. See George Anderson, "F. Scott Fitzgerald's Use of Story Strippings in *Tender Is the Night*," in Bruccoli and Judith S. Baughman, *Reader's Companion to F. Scott Fitzgerald's Tender Is the Night* (Columbia: University of South Carolina Press, 1996), pp. 213–261.

149. *Dear Scott/Dear Max*, p. 207.

FITZGERALD'S ERAS

SOCIAL AND POLITICAL BACKGROUNDS
OF THE 1920s AND 1930s

An era is not just a time span; it is a period characterized by major events and the responses to them—political, social, and cultural. An era is defined by the way people felt about what was happening to them and around them.

F. Scott Fitzgerald is now automatically identified with the 1920s. He is regarded as an exemplary figure for that decade, embodying and expressing its charm, ebullience, waste, genius, dissipation, and confidence. Yet Fitzgerald was a professional writer from 1920 through 1940; connecting him exclusively with the 1920s distorts the shape and significance of his life and career. The dominant American historical influences during his lifetime were World War I (The Great War, 1914–1918 in Europe) and the Great Depression of the 1930s. In between there was the Boom, the Roaring Twenties, and the Jazz Age—named by Fitzgerald. His own history reflected the history of his time: his success and fame in the 1920s, his crack-up and relative obscurity in the 1930s.

PREWAR TO 1920: Born in 1896, Fitzgerald grew up with the manners, values, standards, and culture of the late nineteenth century. The world of his boyhood was a time of great American fortunes and enormous inequalities. Workers were wage slaves; there were no social security benefits, and pensions were rare. Women were denied career opportunities, as well as the vote until 1920. Low taxes and the availability of servants enabled the upper-middle and upper classes to live very well. After Fitzgerald's father lost his job as a Procter & Gamble salesman in 1908, the family of four lived comfortably on Mollie Fitzgerald's income of $5,000 or $6,000 a year from her inheritance.

The class system was rigid, but Americans still believed that their country was the land of opportunity. The self-made man was a model. Successful businessmen and moguls were heroes. The prewar years were also a period of social reform and the Progressive Era. Republican Theodore Roosevelt, president from 1901 to 1909, was known as the Trust Buster for his opposition to unregulated corporations; he sponsored pure food and drug legislation and was regarded as a conservationist. This period also witnessed the establishment of the International Workers of the World (known as the Wobblies) and the beginnings of American socialism. Fitzgerald was never politically active, but like other privileged collegians he regarded himself as a socialist. His first novel, *This Side of Paradise,* ends with a denunciation of capitalist inequality.

Democrat President Woodrow Wilson (1913–1921) promulgated the New Freedom, which involved reforms such as tariff reduction and antitrust measures. The idealism of the Progressive Movement facilitated America's involvement in World War I with such slogans as "The War to End all Wars" and "The War to Make the World Safe for Democracy." Socialist labor leader Eugene V. Debs was imprisoned for his opposition to America's involvement in the war. Fitzgerald's reasons for joining the army had little to do with patriotism: it was a way out of his academic difficulties at Princeton, and it was the gentlemanly thing to volunteer.

The war, in which he did not see battle, changed Fitzgerald's world, erasing the old certainties and faiths. In 1920 he was both the product of the great change in American society and its herald-prophet. In "My Generation" (1939) he wrote that "We were born to power and intense nationalism":

That America passed away somewhere between 1910 and 1920; and the fact gives my generation its uniqueness—we are at once prewar and postwar. We were well-grown in the tense Spring of 1917, but for the most part not married and settled. The peace found us almost intact—less than five percent of my college class were killed in the war, and the colleges had a high average compared to the country as a whole. Men of our age in Europe simply did not exist. I have looked for them often, but they are twenty-five years dead.

So we inherited two worlds—the one of hope to which we had been bred; the one of disillusion which we had discovered early for ourselves. And that first world was growing as remote as another country, however close in time.[1]

The prolonged slaughter of trench warfare (more than one million casualties in the 1916 Battle of the Somme) and the victors' quarreling over the spoils resulted in the disillusionment and political cynicism that characterized the American 1920s. There were 117,000 American casualties and an estimated ten million British, French, Germans, and Russians killed in battle; many Americans concluded that the Great War had been a misdirected massacre. During the 1920s America was isolationist, refusing to join the League of Nations. Americans distrusted politicians and noble causes. Ernest Hemingway spoke for his generation in *A Farewell to Arms* (1929):

> . . . I was always embarrassed by the words sacred, glorious, and sacrifice and the expression in vain. We had heard them, sometimes standing in the rain almost out of earshot, so that only the shouted words came through, and had read them, on proclamations that were slapped up by billposters over other proclamations, now for a long time, and I had seen nothing sacred, and the things that were glorious had no glory and the sacrifices were like the stockyards at Chicago if nothing was done with the meat except to bury it. There were many words that you could not stand to hear and finally only the names of places had dignity. Certain numbers were the same way and certain dates and these with the names of the places were all you could say and have them mean anything. Abstract words such as glory, honor, courage, or hallow were obscene beside the concrete names of villages, the numbers of roads, the names of rivers, the numbers of regiments and the dates.[2]

"The identification of Fitzgerald with the Twenties—which represented half his professional life—has contributed to the distorted popular impression of him as the totemic figure who embodied or was even somehow responsible for the excesses of the boom and the punitive Depression. The ways in which his career duplicated the national moods are almost too neat—like something inept novelists invent. After achieving sudden success with *This Side of Paradise* in the spring of 1920, for the next decade he was rewarded for retelling people their favorite fables about youth and love and ambition and success and happiness. It wasn't that simple, of course, for amidst the echolalia of his parties there was a quest for values operating in his work. As the Twenties lurched or sprinted forward, Fitzgerald's warning notes became clearer. Yet the preacher was unable to heed his own sermons. He could only send out messages from within the hysteria. The moralist had to be a participant. By 1929 Fitzgerald knew he had lost something. Not his genius, not his capacity to feel intensely, not even his capacity for work. He had lost his belief that 'life was something you dominated if you were any good.'"

Matthew J. Bruccoli

From *Some Sort of Epic Grandeur: The Life of F. Scott Fitzgerald,* revised edition (New York: Carroll & Graf, 1993), p. 340.

Warren G. Harding won the Presidency in 1920 on a platform of "not nostrums but normalcy"[3] and presided over a crooked administration. His successor, Calvin Coolidge, announced that "The business of America is business."

The Russian Revolution during World War I resulted in the spread of world communism. Before—and even after—the horrors of

Stalinism were manifest in the Moscow show trials of 1935, 1936, and 1937, many American intellectuals and liberals—the terms became interchangeable in the 1930s—embraced the ideals of communism. During the 1920s most Americans regarded communism as a foreign threat to the American way of life. Immigrants suspected of radical activities were deported during the "Red Scare." The Sacco and Vanzetti case became the most passionately argued political cause of the decade when two immigrant Italian anarchists were executed by the state of Massachusetts in 1927 for their participation in a payroll robbery-murder. Their trial was conducted in an atmosphere of prejudice, and many writers believed that shoemaker Niccolo Sacco and fish-peddler Bartelomeo Vanzetti were electrocuted for their political beliefs. In his *U.S.A.* trilogy John Dos Passos denounced this injustice, declaring that "we are two nations."[4] Although Fitzgerald's friends were passionately engaged in the defense of Sacco and Vanzetti, he made no statement on the case.

THE 1920s: The decade of the 1920s was known as the Boom because of general prosperity and ebullience—despite the 1921 recession—and the seemingly easy money to be made in stock-market speculation. So-called paper profits were made by playing the market on margin: that is, paying as little as 10 percent of the purchase price for stocks and borrowing the rest with the stocks as collateral. This method worked while the price of the stocks rose; but when stocks fell, the speculator was required to put up more cash (a margin call) or lose the stocks. (The Dow-Jones average fell from 381 to 198 after 29 October 1929).[5] Most Americans were not "in the market"; nonetheless, stories abounded about barbers and bootblacks who retired on stock tips. There was a get-rich-quick, gold-rush mentality at the end of the decade. Fitzgerald's characters were in the market, but he never owned a share of stock. His investment portfolio consisted of two $500 bonds that he sold at a loss.

Two major achievements of the reform impulse were the Eighteenth and Nineteenth Amendments to the U.S. Constitution—Prohibition and voting rights for women—both of which were ratified by 1920. The impact of the Nineteenth Amendment is difficult to assess. Women did not become a political force during the 1920s, although both political parties tried to appeal to "the women's vote" by building "family values" into their platforms; the child-labor laws were credited to the influence of women voters. Yet, there were few women in important elected positions. The Volstead Act, which implemented the Eighteenth Amendment by prohibiting the manufacture and sale of alcoholic beverages in the United States, had powerful social and economic consequences—not because it was enforced, but because it was unenforceable. Prohibition changed American drinking habits and manners. Debate continues about whether Prohibition increased alcohol consumption. Speakeasies (illegal establishments, so named because patrons were required to speak to the doorman through a peephole in order to get inside) became centers of social and literary life. Men who had not patronized saloons before Prohibition frequented speakeasies. For the first time women who were not prostitutes drank and smoked in public. The speakeasies provided venues for jazz music. It really was the Jazz Age: the term *jazz,* which originally had sexual connotations, referred to the music as well as the "revolt of youth" associated with jazz.

Prohibition fostered the rise of organized crime as bootlegging (dealing in alcohol) became a major industry. The most famous gangster, Al Capone, controlled the liquor trade in Chicago as well as the city. The Mafia was restricted to Italians—mostly Sicilians—but other racketeers included Jews (Murder, Inc., and the Detroit Purple Gang) and Irishmen (the O'Banion Gang). The Chicago St. Valentine's Day massacre in 1929 was Capone's response to competition from Bugs Moran. With the help of the movies such as *Public Enemy* (1931), *Little Caesar* (1931), and *Scarface* (1932), the gangster joined the cowboy as an American character type.

Prohibition was the most fervently debated domestic issue of the 1920s. In general, the Republicans defended Prohibition as "a noble experiment," and the Democrats advocated repeal—except in the South. Protestants were dry, and Catholics were wet; the small towns were dry, and the big cities were wet. There were no class boundaries with regard to alcohol: rich and poor drank. In 1928 pro-repeal Democrat Al Smith ran against Republican Herbert Hoover for the presidency and was badly defeated. Smith's Roman Catholicism resulted in the first defection of the Solid South from the Democratic Party to a Republican candidate.

After Smith's defeat it was generally held that a Catholic could never be elected president. The 1920s and 1930s were characterized by racial and religious prejudice—both unthinking bias and active intolerance. Segregation of blacks was the law of the South and the practice in the rest of the country. Southern blacks endured de facto slavery and the danger of lynching. Catholics, Jews, and foreigners were included with African Americans on the hate list of the Ku Klux Klan, whose power reached beyond the South into the border states and the Midwest. The KKK claimed five million members in 1923. Anti-Semitism was in force. Jews were excluded from hotels and restaurants that displayed the sign "Restricted"; good neighborhoods were restricted. There were quotas

COLLEGE TUITIONS (EXCLUSIVE OF ROOM AND BOARD), 1925

University of Iowa . . . . $45 per semester (liberal arts)

University of Illinois . . . . $32.50 per semester

University of Wisconsin . . . . . . $62 per academic year

University of South Carolina . . . $40 per academic year

Princeton University . . . . $350 per academic year

Harvard University . . . . $300 per academic year

restricting the number of Jews in private schools and colleges. To a lesser extent there were similar Catholic quotas.

The 1920s were also the collegiate decade. University enrollments increased, especially at the state schools, as uneducated parents sent their children to college. Between 1915 and 1930 the student bodies doubled at larger universities: University of Illinois, from 5,439 to 12,709; University of Iowa, from 2,680 to 4,860; and University of Wisconsin, from 5,128 to 9,401. These figures do not represent government support of veterans: there was no G.I. bill after World War I. However, tuition was low ($90 per year at the University of Iowa), and many students were able to work their way through college.

The growth in college and university population was accompanied by a collegiate culture: college styles, college slang, and college manners were widely imitated. Fitzgerald's *This Side of Paradise* was the first of many popular 1920s college novels. College football became big business. In 1927 thirty million football tickets were bought for $50 million.

THE 1930S: Fitzgerald's reputation or image functioned as a barometer of his times. He was the darling of the 1920s and the sacrificial victim of the 1930s. The Great Depression began with the October 1929 stock-market crash. The crash was not the only or even the main cause for the Depression, but millions of Americans who were not speculators or investors suffered. Factories closed; workers were dismissed; wages were cut; banks failed; farms were foreclosed; Hoovervilles—shack clusters sarcastically named for the president—appeared in cities; and the dispossessed and unemployed took to the roads. Between 1930 and 1939 unemployment went from 4,340,000 to 9,480,000—having reached 12,830,000 in 1932, when 25 percent of the labor force was out of work. In May 1932 twenty thousand veterans marched on Washington to demand early payment of the World War I bonus. The Bonus Army was dispersed by the regular army. Social security and unemployment benefits were unknown before Franklin D. Roosevelt's New Deal sponsored pro-labor legislation. The 1930s brought the expansion of American labor unions and major—often bloody—strikes in the coal, auto, and steel industries. Labor leaders emerged as national figures: John L. Lewis

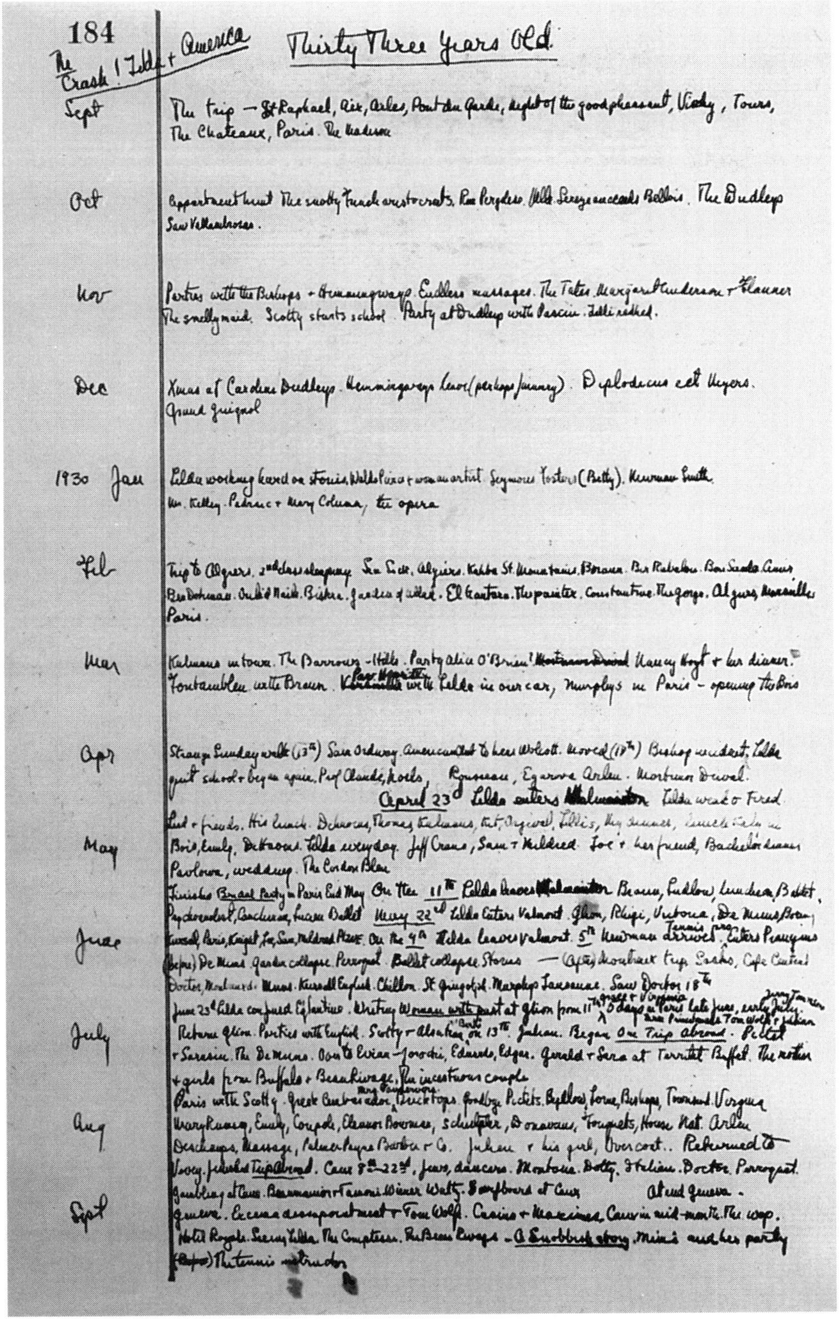

184

The Crash / Zelda + America

Thirty Three Years Old

Sept

Oct

Nov

Dec

1930 Jan

Feb

Mar

Apr

May

June

July

Aug

Sept

This page from Fitzgerald's *Ledger* for September 1929 through September 1930 notes in the upper left the American stock-market crash and Zelda Fitzgerald's first breakdown (Washington, D.C.: Microcard/Bruccoli Clark, 1973).

of the United Mine Workers and the C.I.O. (Congress of Industrial Organizations) and Walter Reuther of the United Auto Workers.

There were fears of communist revolution from the Left and, after Adolf Hitler became chancellor of Germany in 1933, of fascist revolution from the Right. Radical political groups were visible, but their actual strength was limited. The most votes a communist candidate for president polled was William Z. Foster's 102,000 in 1932, when socialist Norman Thomas received 881,000 votes. There was no American fascist party, although the pro-Nazi German-American Bund and profascist Silver Shirts were active.

The broad economic, political, and social programs of the Roosevelt New Deal, commencing in 1933, bandaged some of the worst wounds of the Depression and permanently changed what Americans expected from government. Roosevelt became the most adored and hated president since Lincoln. His supporters asserted that he had saved the country from revolution; his detractors asserted that he had eroded American liberty and self-reliance by means of a massive bureaucracy and punitive taxation. Inheritance taxes were instituted to break up large fortunes, but the big rich remained rich. Roosevelt's political genius and personality enabled him to maintain a working relationship between the conservative Southern Democrats and the liberal Northern Democrats. Opposition to Roosevelt for having gone too far or not far enough was constant during the 1930s. His opponents included Dr. Francis E. Townsend, whose Old Age Revolving Pension Program proposed that all retirees over sixty receive $200 per month on the condition that they spend it. Roosevelt's Social Security Act of 1935 was regarded as the result of the Townsend plan. U.S. Senator Huey P. Long of Louisiana, murdered in 1935, propounded a Share-the-Wealth program and called for a guaranteed $2,500 income for everyone, along with a $5,000 homestead allowance. Father Charles E. Coughlin, the "Radio Priest," began as a Roosevelt adherent but turned against him as too radical. Hard-line radical writers believed that Roosevelt had failed to do enough to equalize American life, particularly with regard to what was called "The Negro Question." Fitzgerald was a Democrat and voted for Roosevelt, but he did not engage in political activity.

During the 1930s American liberals were concerned by Hitler's Nazi Germany and his anti-Semitic actions and, to a lesser extent, by Benito Mussolini's Fascist Italy. European intellectuals, including many Jews, fled to America, where they exerted a strong influence on the arts and science. Among these figures were Thomas Mann, Albert Einstein, Billy Wilder, Bertolt Brecht, Kurt Weill, Vladimir Horowitz, Arthur

Rubinstein, Enrico Fermi, and Vladimir Nabokov (whose wife was a Jew). American writers turned to the political Left out of conviction or conformity.

Liberal orthodoxy became a test of literary merit. The "fellow travelers"—those who did not join the Communist Party but accepted the doctrines of marxism and supported the party—hailed Russia as "the workers' paradise"; the country's famines, purges, and executions were ignored, denied, or alibied. There were also anti-Stalinist American Marxists, usually followers of Leon Trotsky. The Hitler-Stalin pact of 1939, which parceled eastern Europe into German and Soviet spheres of influence, disillusioned many American communists and fellow travelers, but the hard-liners defended Stalin. From 1937 to his death in 1940 Fitzgerald worked as a Hollywood screenwriter among $1,000-a-week communists. He remained apart from radical causes, although his friends engaged in procommunist or antifascist activities. Fitzgerald did not lend his name to leftist causes, did not join political groups, and did not even sign petitions.

Another European war was anticipated after Germany and Italy armed and commenced their territorial demands. Most Americans were still isolationists who remembered the slaughter of World War I and wanted to keep out of another foreign war. The Spanish Civil War (1936–1939) was regarded as a rehearsal for World War II by both the Left and Right. Many American writers and intellectuals sided with the elected socialist government of Spain (the Loyalists or Republicans), supported by Russia, against the Nationalist forces of General Francisco Franco, aided by Germany and Italy. The American government maintained a strict neutrality, but Americans volunteered for the Loyalist Abraham Lincoln Brigade and other international units. Hemingway was a pro-Republican war correspondent. John Dos Passos supported the Republicans until he learned that the communist-controlled Loyalists were suppressing disagreement among their own ranks by means of executions—as were the Nationalists. Franco's victory was seen by liberals as the defeat of democracy and as an omen of Nazi conquest.

Fitzgerald was an ardent student of history and had been influenced by the German writer Oswald Spengler's *The Decline of the West* (translated into English in 1926), which predicted twentieth-century wars and dictatorships. Nevertheless, he was too deeply concerned about his own financial, professional, family, and health problems to become involved with the Spanish Civil War or other causes of the 1930s. In 1936 he wrote essays for *Esquire*—a men's fashion magazine expensively priced for that time at fifty cents—analyzing his collapse. Known as the

"Crack-Up" series (after the title of one of the essays), these confessional articles damaged his reputation by causing him to be regarded as a symbolic 1920s figure who had been condignly punished for his frivolity, dissipation, and irresponsibility. Hemingway was writing for *Esquire* at the same time as Fitzgerald, but Hemingway's contributions—mostly about hunting and fishing—were not condemned.

After the outbreak of World War II in September 1939, America was officially neutral but in fact pro-British, providing lend-lease support to England. A peacetime draft was imposed, and it became manifest that America would become involved in the war.

CULTURE AND SOCIETY IN THE 1920s

The popular impression of the 1920s as a time of hedonism, alcoholic orgies, and high jinks is in some part based on misreadings of Fitzgerald's fiction. Jay Gatsby's party in *The Great Gatsby* has become the quintessential 1920s party. Fitzgerald's characters have become confused with the cartoons of sheiks in raccoon coats and flappers in short skirts drawn by John Held Jr. Fitzgerald's play *The Vegetable* and his story collection *Tales of the Jazz Age* had Held dust jackets, and he titled his first story volume *Flappers and Philosophers*. The term *flapper,* which had frivolous connotations in America, originated in England to describe young women in a society where there was a shortage of men during and after the war.

Fitzgerald's view of the 1920s was serious and complex, for he recognized the glamour as well as the waste, the charm as well as the self-destruction. In "Early Success" (1937) he wrote: "All the stories that came into my head had a touch of disaster in them—the lovely young creatures in my novels went to ruin, the diamond mountains of my short stories blew up, my millionaires were as beautiful and damned as Thomas Hardy's peasants."[6] He wrote in "Echoes of the Jazz Age" (1931), his postmortem for the decade he named, that "It was an age of miracles, it was an age of art, it was an age of excess, and it was an age of satire."[7] After the party ended, Fitzgerald declined to cry mea culpa:

> It is the custom now to look back ourselves of the boom days with a disapproval that approaches horror. But it had its virtues, that old boom: Life was a great deal larger and gayer for most people, and the stampede to the spartan virtues in time of war and famine shouldn't make us too dizzy to remember its hilarious glory. There were so many good things. These eyes have been hallowed by watching a man order champagne for his two thou-

sand guests, by listening while a woman ordered a whole staircase from the greatest sculptor in the world, by seeing a man tear up a good check for eight hundred thousand dollars.[8]

More than any other American decade the 1920s were a period of heroes and hero-worship, resulting from the defining American belief in individuality and the possibility of greatness. Charles A. Lindbergh's 1927 solo flight from New York to Paris made him the most admired and celebrated figure of the decade. (His popularity was diminished by his isolationism and admiration for Germany in the 1930s.) Never before had there been so many sports idols: tennis players Helen Wills and Bill Tilden; boxers Jack Dempsey and Benny Leonard; golfer Bobby Jones; football players Red Grange and The Four Horsemen; thoroughbred racing champion Man o' War; and baseball players Babe Ruth, Lou Gehrig, Ty Cobb, and Walter Johnson. Ruth, the highest salaried athlete of the 1920s, signed a three-year contract in 1927 calling for $70,000 a year. Dempsey's cut of the first million-dollar gate in his bout with Georges Carpentier in July 1921 was $300,000 plus 25 percent of the movie rights. Professional sports were segregated—except for boxing, in which blacks were often required to lose to whites. In baseball the Negro Leagues produced pitcher Satchel Paige, catcher Josh Gibson ("The Black Babe Ruth"), and other stars who earned little money.

The 1920s were the golden decade of American popular music. The songs of the decade were by Irving Berlin; George and Ira Gershwin; Cole Porter; Richard Rodgers and Lorenz Hart; Jerome Kern; Vincent Youmans; DaSylva, Henderson, and Brown; and Harry Ruby and Bert Kalmar. These composers and lyricists continued their work in the 1930s, but they were identified with the 1920s. Lavish musical revues of the Ziegfeld Follies genre typified Broadway productions. The black jazz giants emerged: King Oliver, Louis Armstrong, Jelly Roll Morton, Duke Ellington, and Bessie Smith. Paul Whiteman's orchestra performed white jazz with the legendary Bix Beiderbecke on cornet.

The 1920s generated the second—and greater—American literary renaissance after the nineteenth-century New England Renaissance. These are the writers—some of whom began earlier—who were published during that miraculous decade: fiction writers Fitzgerald, Hemingway, William Faulkner, Thomas Wolfe, Ring Lardner, Dashiell Hammett, Gertrude Stein, Theodore Dreiser, Sinclair Lewis, Sherwood Anderson, John Dos Passos, John Steinbeck, Willa Cather, Edith Wharton, and James Gould Cozzens; poets T. S. Eliot, Ezra Pound, Robert Frost, E. E. Cummings, and Wallace Stevens; and critic H. L. Mencken. It was a time of wit and satire before the laughter ended in 1930. Robert Benchley, Dorothy Parker, Donald Ogden Stewart, George S. Kaufman, Alexander Woollcott, Franklin P. Adams, Don Marquis, James Thurber, S. J. Perelman, and a flock of newspaper columnists provided the laughs. Eugene O'Neill established himself as the greatest American dramatist with a run of innovative plays: *Beyond the Horizon, The Emperor Jones, Diff'rent* (1920); *Gold, The Straw, Anna Christie* (1921); *The First Man, The Hairy Ape* (1922); *Welded, Desire Under the Elms* (1924); *The Fountain* (1925); *The Great God Brown* (1926); *Marco Millions, Strange Interlude, Lazarus Laughed* (1928); and *The Dynamo* (1929). All was not high culture in the 1920s. *Abie's Irish Rose,* a corny comedy about love between a Jewish boy and an Irish girl, ran for 2,327 performances on Broadway.

The writers were not the products of college creative-writing courses because there were none. Some of the best writers served their apprenticeships on newspapers. The 1920s were a time of great newspapermen, columnists, and editors: reporter and short-story writer Damon Runyon; columnist Heywood Broun; and editors Harold Ross (*The New Yorker*), Herbert Bayard Swope (*The New York World*), Henry Luce and Britten Hadden (*Time*), George Horace Lorimer (*The Saturday Evening Post*), and H. L. Mencken and George Jean Nathan (*The Smart Set* and *The American Mercury*). The historically Protestant American book-publishing industry was stimulated by the founding of new houses by energetic Jews: Bennett Cerf and Donald S. Klopfer (Random House); Richard Simon and M. Lincoln Schuster (Simon and Schuster, which published the first crossword-puzzle books); Alfred A. Knopf; the Boni brothers and Horace Liveright (Boni and Liveright); and Harold Guinzberg and George Oppenheimer (Viking Press). Though not experimental or avant-garde publishers, these commercial houses were receptive to the books of younger writers.

The innovations in literature and the other arts were connected with the expatriation tropism that made Paris seem an American creative colony during the 1920s. American writers and artists went to France because they could live affordably there, drink there, satisfy sexual proclivities there, and get published there by the little magazines and small presses—or start their own journals and imprints. The rate of exchange was crucial to this migration. The franc fluctuated from fifteen to thirty-five to the dollar; a meal with wine cost four or five francs. Prohibition has been exaggerated as an impetus for expatriation. Bootleg booze was readily available in the United States, but some Americans who could afford to leave home proclaimed that they could not tolerate living in a society that interfered with their freedom to drink.

Under the influence of Sigmund Freud, men and women shed their repressions and inhibitions. Psychoanalysis became fashionable among the affluent. The general loosening of moral and sexual restrictions liberated American women, whose activities had been circumscribed by custom. Corsets were abandoned; skirts rose; and the double standard eroded as birth-control information became available. Women gained more educational opportunities and held some jobs that were previously reserved for men. Nonetheless, the best colleges and universities remained sexually segregated, and women were blocked from executive positions. The freedoms of the 1920s—which began during the war—contended against entrenched puritanism. Censorship of printed matter was usual. Copies of the Paris-published *Ulysses* (1922) by James Joyce could not be brought into America; Hemingway's *A Farewell to Arms* (1929) and an issue of *The American Mercury* were banned in Boston. Mencken attacked American prudery and ignorance, labeling the South "The Sahara of the Bozart" (that is, the desert of the beaux arts) and defining puritanism as the fear that somebody was having a good time.

REPRESENTATIVE AMERICAN SALARIES, 1920–1939

1920–1924	
Stenographer	$25–$30 per week
Maid	$12–$14 per week
Public school teacher	$970–$1,269 per year
1925–1929	
Carpenter	60¢ per hour
Public school teacher	$1,299–$1,445 per year
1930–1934	
Cook	$15 per week
Painter	$2.50 per day
Public school teacher	$1,265–$1,455 per year
1935–1939	
Stenographer	$12 per week
Maid	$485–$544 per year
Dentist	$40 per week
Public school teacher	$1,293–$1,403 per year

From *The Value of a Dollar: Prices and Incomes in the United States, 1860–1989*, edited by Scott Derks (Detroit: Gale/ Manly, 1994).

Americans became mobile, and the automobile was the most powerful agent of social change. During the 1920s there were more cars in the United States than in all of the rest of the world. A new Model-T Ford cost $260 in 1928; most American families could afford a used Tin Lizzie for $50 or less. The proliferation of automobiles influenced sexual conduct. A popular song of 1928 celebrated the Model-A Ford ($545): "You don't have to do it any more / With one foot sticking out the door / Since Henry made a lady out of Lizzie."

The prosperity of the boom years was not very prosperous by present standards: the average annual salary for public-school teachers rose from $970 to $1,445 between 1920 and 1929; stenographers were paid $25 to $30 per week; maids got $12 to $14 dollars per week; carpenters earned sixty cents per hour. Textile mills in the South paid men $18 and women $9 for a seventy-hour work week. Mobs of job seekers came when Ford offered $5 a day to assembly-line workers. Food and rent were commensurately cheaper; nonetheless, $5 a day did not provide luxury. It is almost impossible to convert the buying power of the 1920s dollar to the value of the current dollar, but the usual conversion factor is seven to ten times. Thus $5 would be worth $35 to $50 now.

The 1920s brought a vast expansion in what became known as the media. The mass-circulation slick-paper magazines (*The Saturday Evening Post, Collier's, Liberty, Cosmopolitan*) paid Fitzgerald and other popular writers very well. The pulp-paper genre magazines (detective, adventure, western, romance, sports, and science fiction) paid only a penny or two cents a word, but they provided places for writers to publish and perhaps develop. The magazines were competing with the new forms of mass entertainment: the movies and radio. Silent movies, especially Charlie Chaplin's comedies, had huge audiences. Movies evolved from one-reelers to epics such as director D. W. Griffith's *The Birth of a Nation* (1915) and *Intolerance* (1916). The talkies—commencing in 1927 with *The Jazz Singer,* starring Al Jolson—enlarged the audience and influence of movies on style, morals, and manners. It was the age of the movie palaces, and Americans attended the movies religiously. The stars of the silents included Mary Pickford ("America's Sweetheart"), Douglas Fairbanks, Rudolph Valentino, Buster Keaton, and Harold Lloyd. John Barrymore ("The Great Profile") and Greta Garbo successfully made the transition to talkies; John Gilbert did not. The great directors included Cecil B. DeMille, Erich von Stroheim, and Mack Sennett. The Hollywood studio system flourished; Metro-Goldwyn-Mayer (M-G-M) was organized in 1924. Although Fitzgerald regarded the talkies as a threat to printed fiction, he tried unsuccessfully to master screenwriting for its financial rewards.

The 1920s brought the second industrial revolution as the production of American consumer goods was driven by advertising. Radio was the most effective means of reaching prospective customers. Radio networks emerged in the 1920s. KDKA in Pittsburgh broadcast the presidential-election returns for the first time in 1920 as Harding defeated James M. Cox; by 1925 there were fifty million radio listeners. The first radios for home use were marketed in 1920—bulky, expensive contraptions that operated on large batteries. The National Broadcasting Company (NBC) was organized in 1926, followed by the Columbia Broadcasting System (CBS) in 1927. There was life before television, which was experimentally introduced in 1929 but did not succeed until after World War II. The most popular radio program during the 1920s and 1930s was *Amos 'n' Andy*. The comic treatment of blacks impersonated by two white men did not arouse objections. The humor of the day depended heavily on racial, religious, and national stereotypes and dialects. White (Al Jolson and Eddie Cantor) and black (Bert Williams) blackface performers were staples of show business, as were Yiddish comedians. The sale of fragile seventy-eight-r.p.m. shellac phonograph records that played for three minutes was not impeded by radio; broadcasts provided exposure for songs and performers. Bing Crosby became the most popular crooner of the twentieth century on both radio and records. Phonograph records disseminated black jazz on what were known as "race records." The blues singers, including the incomparable Bessie Smith, were initially available only on black labels, which were white-owned.

Blacks achieved limited literary recognition during the "Harlem Renaissance" as African American writers came to New York during the 1920s. The most prominent figures in this group were Jean Toomer (*Cane*, 1923), Countee Cullen (*Color*, 1925), Langston Hughes (*Fine Clothes to the Jew*, 1927), Claude McKay (*Home to Harlem*, 1928), and Wallace Thurman (*The Blacker the Berry*, 1929). The publication of black writers by white-owned houses was concomitant with the discovery of black culture and folklore by white critics and intellectuals. Literature was still mostly segregated: black characters in fiction by whites were clowns, devoted servants, or criminals; in the movies they were clowns, servants, or dancers.

CULTURE AND SOCIETY IN THE 1930s

In literature and the other arts the 1930s became known as the proletarian decade. Art was expected to deliver the correct—that is, leftist—messages; the acceptable material and characters were from the working class. Critics and other opinion-makers applied the test of social, political, and economic significance to literature. Fitzgerald's *Tender Is the Night* (1934) had been labeled a casualty of the 1930s, but the reviews were mainly respectful. Its disappointing fifteen-thousand-copy sales cannot be attributed to hostile political action: readers had temporarily lost interest in Fitzgerald. The new fashion was for fiction about strikes, migrant workers, and proletarian hero-victims. John Steinbeck's *In Dubious Battle* (1936), *Of Mice and Men* (1937), and especially *The Grapes of Wrath* (1939) satisfied the requirements for meaningful literature. Clifford Odets was the most admired younger playwright, with his strike dramas *Waiting for Lefty* and *Awake and Sing!* (both 1935). New writers of and from the proletariat were welcomed: Michael Gold for *Jews Without Money* (1930) and Henry Roth for his overpraised *Call It Sleep* (1934). James T. Farrell's Studs Lonigan trilogy (1932–1935) and his other works about Irish working-class characters in Chicago were well received. Another Chicago writer, Nelson Algren, wrote his first novel about drifters, *Somebody in Boots* (1935). Proletarian material did not guarantee success: Daniel Fuchs wrote three excellent novels about poor Jews in Brooklyn—*Summer in Williamsburg* (1934), *Homage to Blenholt* (1936), and *Low Company* (1937)—that had poor sales. Richard Wright's *Uncle Tom's Children* (1938) established him as the most highly regarded black fiction writer to emerge in the 1930s. Novelist and folklorist Zora Neale Hurston published her best-known novel, *Their Eyes Were Watching God,* in 1937.

The most innovative and influential radical novels were John Dos Passos's *U.S.A.* trilogy (*The 42nd Parallel,* 1930; *1919,* 1932; and *The Big Money,* 1936). These books combined historical commentary with technical experiments, but before the decade ended, Dos Passos rejected marxism and consequently lost much of his standing. Two major nonpolitical social novelists to emerge in the 1930s were James Gould Cozzens (*The Last Adam,* 1933) and John O'Hara (*Appointment in Samarra,* 1934); both examined the effects of social stratification and community structure.

The critics wanted redeeming social value, but most readers wanted pleasure and escape from the Depression. The biggest sellers of the 1930s were historical romances such as Hervey Allen's *Anthony Adverse* (1933) and Margaret Mitchell's *Gone With the Wind* (1936), which provided the story for the most profitable movie of the decade. Southern fiction perpetuated the legend of an aristocratic antebellum Eden, but novels about the dispossessed and deprived in the contemporary South also achieved recognition. Erskine Caldwell's white-sharecropper novels combined naturalism with grotesqueness. Jack Kirkland's stage adaptation of Caldwell's *Tobacco Road* (1932) opened on Broadway in 1933 and ran for more than three thousand performances. Although Faulkner won critical respect in the 1930s, his books sold poorly, except for *Sanctuary* (1931). General readers preferred Caldwell to Faulkner.

A $2 novel was a luxury during the 1930s. The first American mass-market paperbacks were introduced by Pocket Books in 1939; they were priced at 25¢. Since many public libraries did not provide popular fiction, readers rented books for 5¢ a day from the lending libraries or circulating libraries. There were no authorial royalties on these rented copies. Writers and artists joined the federal WPA (Works Progress

Administration) projects or—if they were lucky—found work in the movies or radio.

Hemingway managed to have it both ways. After writing about bullfighting in *Death in the Afternoon* (1932) and big-game hunting in *Green Hills of Africa* (1935), both of which were criticized for their lack of social conscience, he wrote a novel with a proletarian hero, *To Have and Have Not* (1937), that ridicules proletarian writers. In *Green Hills of Africa* Hemingway declared:

> A country, finally, erodes and the dust blows away, the people all die and none of them were of any importance permanently, except those who practiced the arts, and these now wish to cease their work because it is too lonely, too hard to do, and is not fashionable. A thousand years makes economics silly and a work of art endures forever, but it is very difficult to do and now is not fashionable. People do not want to do it any more because they will be out of fashion and the lice who crawl on literature will not praise them.[9]

Fitzgerald did not climb on the prole bandwagon and was unable to deny the attractions of the 1920s, writing in "Echoes of the Jazz Age" that "it all seems rosy and romantic to us who were young then, because we will never feel quite so intensely about our surroundings any more."[10]

In contrast to the hero-seeking and hero-worshipping impulse of the 1920s, the 1930s had a paucity of heroes apart from New Deal politicians and labor leaders. Among sports figures, Joe Louis, who won the heavyweight championship in 1937, became the first black sports hero widely admired by white fans. The two Louis bouts against German Max Schmeling had strong political overtones, as Schmeling was associated in the public eye with the Nazis. Joe DiMaggio, who succeeded Babe Ruth as the star player for the New York Yankees in 1936, had none of the flamboyance of the Sultan of Swat.

The American automobile industry held its own during the 1930s with no foreign competition. The Ford V-8 was introduced in 1932. Automatic transmissions were made available by Chrysler (Fluid Drive, 1938) and Oldsmobile (Hydramatic, 1939). Duesenberg, Pierce-Arrow, Marmon, and Stutz did not survive the decade.

Americans were more concerned with making a living than with having a good time. The movies maintained their audience because they were cheap: 10¢ for children and 20¢ for adults in the neighborhood theaters, with raffles on bank nights and free dishes. Patrons expected a lot for their money: two features, newsreel, cartoon, travelogues, and other "selected short subjects." Movies were not required to be socially meaningful; the customers knew about poverty—they wanted entertainment. Warner Bros. produced gritty crime movies, but the lavish M-G-M productions filled the theaters. What has been called the greatest year in movie history came at the end of the Depression in 1939: *Gone With the Wind* (Victor Fleming), *Mr. Smith Goes to Washington* (Frank Capra), *Stagecoach* (John Ford), *The Wizard of Oz* (Victor Fleming), *Wuthering Heights* (William Wyler), *Only Angels Have Wings* (Howard Hawks), and *Gunga Din* (George Stevens).

Radio comedy flourished in the 1930s: Fred Allen, Jack Benny, George Burns and Gracie Allen, and a ventriloquist and his dummy, Edgar Bergen and Charlie McCarthy. Al Capp's satiric comic strip, *Li'l Abner*, began in 1934. In music the 1930s were the swing era; the big bands of Benny Goodman, Artie Shaw, Tommy Dorsey, Duke Ellington, and Glenn Miller developed huge followings through radio. They were dance bands, and the jitterbug and lindy replaced the Charleston. Jay Gorney and E. Y. "Yip" Harburg's "Brother, Can You Spare a Dime?" was banned from many radio stations because it was too depressing, as were Rodgers and Hart's "Ten Cents a Dance" and Cole Porter's "Love for Sale," which were both depressing and suggestive.

The peacetime draft began in September 1940. During 1941 there was a national sense of impending vast changes. The next era began on 7 December 1941.

NOTES

1. F. Scott Fitzgerald, "My Generation," *Esquire,* 70 (October 1968): 119, 121.

2. Ernest Hemingway, *A Farewell to Arms* (New York: Scribner Library, 1929), pp. 184–185.

3. Harding's only lasting achievement was to put the neologism "normalcy" into the American language.

4. John Dos Passos, *U.S.A.* (New York: Modern Library, 1937), p. 462.

5. The Dow-Jones hit 11,200 on the day this sentence was written in 1999.

6. Fitzgerald, "Early Success," in *The Crack-Up,* edited, with an introduction, by Edmund Wilson (New York: New Directions, 1945), p. 87.

7. Fitzgerald, "Echoes of the Jazz Age," in *The Crack-Up,* p. 14.

8. Fitzgerald, *The Notebooks of F. Scott Fitzgerald,* edited by Matthew J. Bruccoli (New York: Harcourt Brace Jovanovich/Bruccoli Clark, 1978), # 1769.

9. Hemingway, *Green Hills of Africa,* (New York: Scribner Library, 1935), p. 109.

10. Fitzgerald, "Echoes of the Jazz Age," in *The Crack-Up,* p. 22.

FITZGERALD'S WORKS

WORKS BY F. SCOTT FITZGERALD[1]

BOOKS

Arranged chronologically, this list omits most limited editions and keep-sakes.

Fie! Fie! Fi-Fi! Cincinnati, New York & London: The John Church Co., 1914. Musical comedy; plot and seventeen song lyrics by Fitzgerald.

The Evil Eye. Cincinnati, New York & London: The John Church Co., 1915. Musical comedy; seventeen song lyrics by Fitzgerald.

Safety First. Cincinnati, New York & London: The John Church Co., 1916. Musical comedy; twenty-one song lyrics by Fitzgerald.

This Side of Paradise. New York: Scribners, 1920; London: Collins, 1921. Novel.

Flappers and Philosophers. New York: Scribners, 1920; London: Collins, 1922. Stories.

The Beautiful and Damned. New York: Scribners, 1922; London: Collins, 1922. Serialized in *Metropolitan Magazine,* September 1921 – March 1922. Novel.

Tales of the Jazz Age. New York: Scribners, 1922; London: Collins, 1923. Stories.

The Vegetable. New York: Scribners, 1923. Play.

The Great Gatsby. New York: Scribners, 1925; London: Chatto & Windus, 1926. Novel.

All the Sad Young Men. New York: Scribners, 1926. Stories.

Tender Is the Night. New York: Scribners, 1934; London: Chatto & Windus, 1934. Serialized in *Scribner's Magazine,* January–April 1934. *Tender Is the Night,* "With the Author's Final Revisions," edited, with an introduction, by Malcolm Cowley. New York: Scribners, 1951; London: Grey Walls, 1953. Novel.

Taps at Reveille. New York: Scribners, 1935. Stories.

The Last Tycoon, edited, with an introduction, by Edmund Wilson. New York: Scribners, 1941; London: Grey Walls, 1949. Unfinished novel, with *The Great Gatsby* and five stories.

The Crack-Up, edited, with an introduction, by Wilson. New York: New Directions, 1945; Harmondsworth, U.K.: Penguin, 1965. Essays, selections from the notebooks, and letters.

Afternoon of an Author, edited, with an introduction, by Arthur Mizener. Princeton: Princeton University Library, 1957; New York: Scribners, 1958; London: Bodley Head, 1958. Stories and essays.

The Pat Hobby Stories, edited, with an introduction, by Arnold Gingrich. New York: Scribners, 1962; Harmondsworth, U.K.: Penguin, 1967.

The Apprentice Fiction of F. Scott Fitzgerald, 1909–1917, edited, with an introduction, by John Kuehl. New Brunswick, N.J.: Rutgers University Press, 1965.

F. Scott Fitzgerald In His Own Time: A Miscellany, edited, with an introduction, by Matthew J. Bruccoli and Jackson R. Bryer. Kent, Ohio: Kent State University Press, 1971.

The Basil and Josephine Stories, edited, with an introduction, by Bryer and Kuehl. New York: Scribners, 1973.

Bits of Paradise, selected by Scottie Fitzgerald Smith and Bruccoli, foreword by Smith, preface by Bruccoli. London: Bodley Head, 1973; New York: Scribners, 1974. Stories by Fitzgerald and by Zelda Fitzgerald.

The Cruise of the Rolling Junk, introduction by Bruccoli. Bloomfield Hills, Mich. & Columbia, S.C.: Bruccoli Clark, 1976. Three travel articles.

F. Scott Fitzgerald's Screenplay for Three Comrades by Erich Maria Remarque, edited, with an afterword, by Bruccoli. Carbondale & Edwardsville: Southern Illinois University Press, 1978.

F. Scott Fitzgerald's St. Paul Plays, 1911–1914, edited, with an introduction, by Alan Margolies. Princeton: Princeton University Library, 1978.

The Price Was High: The Last Uncollected Stories of F. Scott Fitzgerald, edited, with an introduction, by Bruccoli. New York & London: Harcourt Brace Jovanovich/Bruccoli Clark, 1979; London: Quartet, 1979.

Poems 1911–1940, edited by Bruccoli, introduction by James Dickey. Bloomfield Hills, Mich. & Columbia, S.C.: Bruccoli Clark, 1981.

Babylon Revisited: The Screenplay, introduction by Budd Schulberg, afterword by Bruccoli. New York: Carroll & Graf, 1993.

LETTERS, DIARIES, NOTEBOOKS

The Letters of F. Scott Fitzgerald, edited, with an introduction, by Andrew Turnbull. New York: Scribners, 1963; London: Bodley Head, 1964.

Thoughtbook of Francis Scott Key Fitzgerald, introduction by John Kuehl. Princeton: Princeton University Library, 1965.

Dear Scott/Dear Max: The Fitzgerald–Perkins Correspondence, edited, with an introduction, by Kuehl and Jackson R. Bryer. New York: Scribners, 1971; London: Cassell, 1973.

As Ever, Scott Fitz—: Letters Between F. Scott Fitzgerald and His Literary Agent Harold Ober, 1919–1940, edited by Matthew J. Bruccoli and Jennifer M. Atkinson, foreword by Scottie Fitzgerald Smith. Philadelphia & New York: Lippincott, 1972; London: Woburn, 1973.

F. Scott Fitzgerald's Ledger: A Facsimile, introduction by Bruccoli. Washington, D.C.: NCR Microcard Editions/Bruccoli Clark, 1973.

The Notebooks of F. Scott Fitzgerald, edited, with an introduction, by Bruccoli. New York & London: Harcourt Brace Jovanovich/Bruccoli Clark, 1978.

Correspondence of F. Scott Fitzgerald, edited, with an introduction, by Bruccoli and Margaret M. Duggan, with Susan Walker. New York: Random House, 1980.

F. Scott Fitzgerald: A Life in Letters, edited, with an introduction, by Bruccoli, with Judith S. Baughman. New York: Scribners, 1994.

EDITIONS AND COLLECTIONS

The Portable F. Scott Fitzgerald, selected by Dorothy Parker, introduction by John O'Hara. New York: Viking, 1945.

The Stories of F. Scott Fitzgerald, edited, with an introduction, by Malcolm Cowley. New York: Scribners, 1951.

The Bodley Head Scott Fitzgerald, 6 volumes. London: Bodley Head, 1958–1963.

The Stories of F. Scott Fitzgerald, 5 volumes. Harmondsworth, U.K.: Penguin, 1962–1968.

F. Scott Fitzgerald on Writing, edited by Larry W. Phillips. New York: Scribners, 1985.

The Short Stories of F. Scott Fitzgerald, edited, with a preface, by Matthew J. Bruccoli. New York: Scribners, 1989; London: Scribners, 1991.

The Cambridge Edition of the Works of F. Scott Fitzgerald. Cambridge: Cambridge University Press, 1991– . Comprises *The Great Gatsby,* edited, with an introduction, by Bruccoli, 1991; *The Love of the Last Tycoon: A Western,* edited, with an introduction, by Bruccoli, 1993; and *This Side of Paradise,* edited, with an introduction, by James L. W. West III, 1995.

Tender Is the Night, edited by Bruccoli. London: Samuel Johnson, 1995. Facsimile of emended copy of the first printing.

Tender Is the Night, Centennial Edition, edited, with an introduction and notes, by Bruccoli. London: Everyman, 1996.

F. Scott Fitzgerald on Authorship, edited, with an introduction, by Bruccoli, with Judith S. Baughman. Columbia: University of South Carolina Press, 1996.

F. Scott Fitzgerald: The Jazz Age, introduction by E. L. Doctorow. New York: New Directions, 1996.

F. Scott Fitzgerald: The Princeton Years, edited, with an introduction, by Chip Deffaa. Fort Bragg, Cal.: Cypress House Press, 1996.

FACSIMILES

The Great Gatsby: A Facsimile of the Manuscript, edited, with an introduction, by Matthew J. Bruccoli. Washington, D.C.: Bruccoli Clark/NCR Microcard Editions, 1973.

F. Scott Fitzgerald: Inscriptions. Columbia, S.C.: Matthew J. Bruccoli, 1988.

F. Scott Fitzgerald Manuscripts, 18 volumes, edited by Bruccoli. New York & London: Garland, 1990–1991. Comprises *This Side of Paradise, The Beautiful and Damned, The Great Gatsby* galleys, *Tender Is the Night, The Last Tycoon, The Vegetable,* stories, and articles.

Fie! Fie! Fi-Fi!, introduction by Bruccoli. Columbia: University of South Carolina Press for the Thomas Cooper Library, 1996. Music score and previously unpublished acting script.

Trimalchio: A Facsimile Edition of the Original Galley Proofs for The Great Gatsby, afterword by Bruccoli. Columbia: University of South Carolina Press in Cooperation with the Thomas Cooper Library, 2000.

WORKS BY ZELDA FITZGERALD[2]

Save Me the Waltz. New York: Scribners, 1932; London: Grey Walls, 1953. Corrected edition, edited by Matthew J. Bruccoli. Carbondale & Edwardsville: Southern Illinois University Press, 1967. Novel.

Bits of Paradise, selected by Scottie Fitzgerald Smith and Bruccoli, foreword by Smith, preface by Bruccoli. London: Bodley Head, 1973; New York: Scribners, 1974. Includes ten stories by Zelda Fitzgerald.

Scandalabra, foreword by Meredith Walker. Bloomfield Hills, Mich. & Columbia, S.C.: Bruccoli Clark, 1980. Play.

Zelda Fitzgerald: The Collected Writings, edited by Bruccoli, introduction by Mary Gordon. New York: Scribners, 1991.

PLOT SUMMARIES

NOVELS

THIS SIDE OF PARADISE, 1920

Book I: The Romantic Egotist. Amory Blaine, who believes himself "a boy marked for glory,"[3] spends most of his early youth traveling with his wealthy, eccentric mother, Beatrice. When he is thirteen, his mother has a nervous breakdown, and he lives for two years with his aunt and uncle in Minneapolis, where he experiences upper-middle-class American adolescent life and indulges favorite daydreams: "the one about becoming a great halfback, or the one about the Japanese invasion, when he was rewarded by being made the youngest general in the world."[4] At fifteen he enrolls in St. Regis' prep school in Connecticut,

"My Very Very Dear Marie:
I got your little note
For reasons very queer Marie
You're mad at me I fear Marie
You made it very clear Marie
    You cared not what you wrote.

"The letter that you sent Marie
    Was niether swift nor fair
I hoped that you'd repent Marie
Before the start of Lent Marie
But Lent could not prevent Marie
    From being debonaire

"So write me what you will Marie
    Altho' I will it not
My love you can not kill Marie
And tho' you treat me ill Marie
Believe me I am still Marie
    Your fond admirer
                Scott"

               F. Scott Fitzgerald

Poem written in 1915 for Marie Hersey, a St. Paul friend with whom Fitzgerald corresponded while they were both away at school; in *F. Scott Fitzgerald: A Life in Letters,* edited by Matthew J. Bruccoli, with Judith S. Baughman (New York: Scribners, 1994), p. 11.

where he is at first unpopular but then enjoys success as a football quarterback, as an actor, and as editor of the *St. Regis' Tattler.* While a student at St. Regis' he meets and falls under the influence of Monsignor Thayer Darcy, who was once a romantic interest of Beatrice and who encourages both his philosophical and worldly ambitions. Amory decides to attend Princeton, which he describes to Darcy as "'lazy and good-looking and aristocratic.'"[5]

At Princeton, Amory becomes particular friends with brothers Kerry and Burne Holiday, young poet Thomas Parke D'Invilliers, and wealthy New Yorker Alec Connage. Amory writes for the theatrical group the Triangle Club and for the *Daily Princetonian,* and he is elected to the prestigious Cottage Club; much of his time is spent reading and discussing writers with his friends and pursuing his extracurricular activities. Amory becomes adept at the courtship game played with the new, liberated American girl: he finds it "rather fascinating to feel that any popular girl he met before eight he might quite possibly kiss before twelve."[6]

During Amory's sophomore year at Princeton he falls in love with debutante Isabelle Borgé, his first serious romantic involvement; his eventual break with her contributes to his failing an important exam, which in turn strips him of college leadership opportunities. When his father dies, Amory endures the additional blow of learning that the family fortune has dwindled, but he takes comfort in Monsignor Darcy's labeling him a "'personage'" who "'is never thought of apart from what he's done. . . . But remember, do the next thing!'"[7] In his final year at Princeton, Amory falls in love with his widowed third cousin, Clara Page, who will not marry him. Following graduation, he and his friends enter the military and serve in World War I, though no battles are described. During the war Beatrice dies, and Amory discovers that her estate is relatively small.

Book II: The Education of a Personage. Taking a job with an advertising agency, Amory shares a New York City apartment with Tom D'Invilliers, who is working for a weekly magazine called *The New Democracy,* and with Alec Connage, who has taken a position in his father's company. Amory falls in love with Alec's sister Rosalind, who is beautiful and independent but who refuses to marry him before he achieves success. Distressed by his loss of Rosalind, Amory quits his job and goes on a three-week binge. He laments to Tom their generation's apparent lack of faith in principles or individual acts of heroism: "'We *want* to believe. Young students try to believe in older authors, constituents try to believe in their Congressmen, countries try to believe in their statesmen, but they *can't.* . . . —And that is why I have sworn not to put pen to paper until my ideas either clarify or depart entirely. . . ."[8]

Amory visits a member of his family in Maryland. There he is attracted to Eleanor Savage, an atheist whose reckless, self-destructive behavior ends his romantic interest in her. In Atlantic City he encounters Alec Connage, who invites him to share his hotel suite. When a house detective observes Alec sneaking a young woman into his room, Amory protects his friend's name by claiming that the girl is with him. Back in New York a few days later, the news item about his alleged escapade in Atlantic City appears on the same page with the announcement of Rosalind Connage's engagement, he learns that his inheritance is gone, and he receives word that Monsignor Darcy has unexpectedly died. Destitute and alone, Amory sees life as meaningless. At Darcy's funeral, however, he discovers new purpose: "He found something that he wanted, had always wanted and always would want—not to be admired, as he had feared; not to be loved, as he had made himself believe; but to be necessary to people, to be indispensable; . . . Life opened up in one of its amazing bursts of radiance and Amory suddenly and permanently rejected an old epigram that had been playing listlessly in his mind: 'Very few things matter and nothing matters very much.'"[9]

Walking toward Princeton, Amory accepts a ride with a man who proves to be the father of one of his classmates who died in the war. Amory, arguing for socialism, declares, "'My whole generation is restless. I'm sick of a system where the richest man gets the most beautiful girl if he wants her, where the artist without an income has to sell his talents to a button manufacturer. . . . I and my sort would struggle against tradition; try, at least, to displace old cants with new ones.'"[10] Seeing the spires of Princeton, Amory feels "the spirit of the past brooding over a new generation . . . dedicated more than the last to the fear of poverty and the worship of success; grown up to find all Gods dead, all wars fought, all faiths in man shaken. . . ."[11] Yet, though he feels sorry for his generation, he does not pity himself; instead he vows, in the final lines of the novel, "to use to the utmost himself and his heritage from the personalities he had passed. . . . 'I know myself,' he cried, 'but that is all.'"[12]

THE BEAUTIFUL AND DAMNED, 1922

Book I. Anthony Comstock Patch is twenty-five in 1913, when the novel begins. The orphaned grandson of multimillionaire Adam J.

F. Scott and Zelda Sayre Fitzgerald, early 1920s

Patch, who is active in moral reform movements, Anthony lives in New York City, where he is supposedly writing a history of the Middle Ages but is in fact squandering time as he waits for his expected inheritance. He enjoys discussing philosophy and literature with his best friends and Harvard classmates, Maury Noble, a cynical man-about-town, and Richard Caramel, a writer who is working on his first novel.

Richard introduces Anthony to his beautiful cousin Gloria Gilbert. She confesses that she does not want to grow old or have responsibilities and that she likes men who are "'gracefully lazy.'"[13] Anthony—who "cherished all beauty and all illusion"[14]—is strongly attracted to her. During a dinner party that includes Richard, Maury, Anthony, and Jewish moviemaker Joseph Bloeckman, Gloria kisses Anthony but refuses to commit herself to him. Following a six-week period of separation, Gloria and Anthony confess their love for one another.

Book II. Married at Adam Patch's estate, Gloria and Anthony honeymoon for six months, during which time he discovers that she is "a girl of tremendous nervous tension and of the most high-handed selfishness," and she determines that he is "an utter coward toward any one of a million phantasms created by his imagination."[15] They rent a house near the country town of Marietta, where they spend a happy summer and fall. Caramel's first novel, *The Demon Lover*, has been a popular and critical success, but he is now writing unimportant stories for magazines, and Noble has gone into business. In November, Anthony and Gloria return to their New York City apartment.

Moving back to Marietta the next summer, the Patches are financially pinched, but Anthony rejects his grandfather's offer to support him as a foreign correspondent or bond salesman; similarly, Gloria decides not to do a screen test for Bloeckman. The Patches spend most of their time partying, often with frightening results: they drunkenly renew their lease on the Marietta house, though they can no longer afford it, and they have a nasty fight over whether or not she will go home alone from a party. At still another party, Gloria is terrified by one of their guests and flees into the night. Anthony, Maury, and Richard catch her at the railroad station, where Maury delivers an oration on the meaningless of life, which Gloria summarizes by saying, "'There's only one lesson to be learned from life . . . that there's no lesson to be learned from life.'"[16]

Adam Patch, who is outraged when he walks in on a drunken party at the younger Patches' house, disinherits Anthony. After Adam's death, Anthony contests the will and also tries unsuccessfully to write popular short stories for magazines. When the United States enters the war against Germany, Anthony is rejected for officers' training but is later drafted into the infantry. Adam Patch's will is upheld in court, but Gloria and Anthony file an appeal.

Book III. Gloria remains in New York to look after their court case while Anthony is stationed at a southern military base. He becomes romantically involved with a lower-class girl, Dot Raycroft. As Gloria's letters become cooler and less frequent, Anthony decides that he must break with Dot, telling her: "'Things are sweeter when they're lost. I know—because once I wanted something and got it. It was the only thing I ever wanted badly, Dot. And when I got it it turned to dust in my hands.'"[17] After his unit is transferred to New York, Anthony and Gloria are reunited at the Armistice Ball.

Gloria has remained faithful to Anthony during his absence, but after the war they are increasingly unhappy together: he is almost constantly drunk, and she complains about their severely reduced income. He cannot hold a job, and she fails a screen test arranged by Bloeckman. One afternoon Anthony meets Caramel, who has abandoned all artistic principles and who attacks "realism" such as that found in *This Side of Paradise*.[18] Later in the winter, completely out of money, a drunken and impoverished Anthony encounters Noble, who snubs him, and Bloeckman, who—insulted by Anthony—knocks him down and has him thrown into the street.

Three weeks later, while Richard and Gloria are in court awaiting the final verdict in the estate trial, Dot Raycroft arrives at the Patches' apartment and declares her love for Anthony, who blacks out. When Gloria and Richard return home to announce that Anthony has won his suit and is now worth $30 million, they find him deranged. In the novel's final scene the Patches are on an ocean liner, with a hard-looking Gloria garbed in a Russian sable coat and with Anthony engaged in a final—perhaps ironic—meditation: "Only a few months before people had been urging him to give in, to submit to mediocrity, to go to work. But he had known that he was justified in his way of life—and he had stuck it out stanchly. . . . 'I showed them,' he was saying. 'It was a hard fight, but I didn't give up and I came through!'"[19]

THE GREAT GATSBY, 1925

Chapter I. Narrator Nick Carraway begins his story with a retrospective meditation on the impossibility of reserving moral judgment. He then describes his coming east from the Midwest to enter the bond business in the spring of 1922 and his renting a small house on West Egg, Long Island, next door to a mansion owned by a man named Gatsby. One summer evening Nick attends a dinner party hosted by his distant cousin Daisy Fay Buchanan and her husband, Tom, with whom Carraway was acquainted at Yale. The wealthy Buchanans own an estate on fashionable East Egg, across the bay from West Egg. In the course of their evening together, Nick meets female champion golfer Jordan Baker, learns that Tom "has got some woman in New York,"[20] and discerns that Daisy is restless and unhappy. When Nick returns to his own house after dinner, he catches a glimpse of the mysterious Gatsby standing in his yard and gesturing across the bay.

Chapter II. When their train to New York City stops at the desolate "valley of ashes," Tom forces Nick to meet Myrtle Wilson, Buchanan's mistress, at the gas station/garage of her husband, George. Myrtle slips away to New York with Tom and Nick, and at the apartment Tom maintains for her, she, Buchanan, Carraway, a married couple from the apartment below, and Myrtle's sister have a drunken party. When Myrtle defies Tom by shouting Daisy's name, he breaks his mistress's nose.

Chapter III. Nick attends one of Gatsby's extravagant parties, and while searching for his host, he runs into Jordan. They hear sinister rumors about Gatsby, meet a man whom Nick calls Owl Eyes for his big glasses, and finally encounter Gatsby himself, who chats with Nick and asks to speak with Jordan privately. Following the party, which ends with squabbling guests and Owl Eyes wrecking his car, Nick begins casually dating Jordan, whom he finds attractive but "dishonest" and "careless."[21]

Chapter IV. Nick provides a catalogue of guests at Gatsby's parties. During a trip to New York City in his extraordinary yellow automobile, Gatsby gives Nick a highly romanticized account of his life: "'After that I lived like a young rajah in all the capitals of Europe . . . trying to forget something very sad that had happened to me long ago.'"[22] In the city Nick is introduced to Gatsby's shady business associate Meyer Wolfshiem. Later in the afternoon Jordan, after telling Carraway about the youthful romance of Gatsby and Daisy, relays his request that Nick arrange a reunion for the former lovers during a tea at his house.

Chapter V. Despite extreme nervousness on Gatsby's part, he and Daisy rekindle their romance when they meet in Nick's living room. Gatsby then insists that Nick and Daisy come to his house, where he displays his possessions for her and where "the colossal vitality of his illusion"[23] seems once again fulfilled by her.

Chapter VI. Nick tells the story of Gatsby's early life as James Gatz and of his association with millionaire adventurer Dan Cody. Carraway then recounts a Sunday afternoon visit of Tom and two of his friends to Gatsby's house, as well as the Buchanans' attendance shortly thereafter at one of his parties, the vulgarity of which offends Daisy. Following the party, Gatsby insists to Nick that one can repeat the past; through this statement Carraway understands that Gatsby has made regaining Daisy the crucial element of fulfilling his dream.

Chapter VII. Gatsby and Daisy spend secret afternoons at his house. At Daisy's invitation the Buchanans, Nick, Jordan, and Gatsby gather at Tom and Daisy's home on a hot Sunday afternoon, and Tom realizes that his wife and Gatsby are in love. Everybody then drives to the Plaza Hotel in New York City—Gatsby and Daisy in the Buchanans' car and Tom, Jordan, and Nick in Gatsby's car. Tom stops for gas at Wilson's garage, where he is observed by Myrtle, who assumes that Jordan is his wife and that the yellow car is his; Tom learns that Wilson, suspicious of Myrtle's fidelity, plans to take her away from the valley of ashes. It thus appears that Buchanan has lost both his wife and his mistress. At the Plaza Hotel, however, he regains partial control of the situation by forcing Daisy to confess that she has loved him and by frightening her with an account of Gatsby's criminal connections. Insisting that Daisy and Gatsby drive back together to East Egg in Gatsby's automobile, Tom follows later with Nick and Jordan in the Buchanans' car. Near Wilson's garage they come upon an accident scene and, stopping at the garage, learn that Myrtle has been killed, the victim of a hit-and-run accident, as she tried to stop a yellow automobile by running into its path. Tom assumes that Gatsby was at the wheel, but after Buchanan, Nick, and Jordan return to East Egg, Nick learns from Gatsby that Daisy was driving. Observing Tom and Daisy in their pantry apparently "conspiring together"[24] over a plate of cold chicken and bottles of ale, Nick leaves Gatsby standing vigil over Daisy's house: "standing there in the moonlight—watching over nothing."[25]

Chapter VIII. Before sunrise, Nick goes to Gatsby's house, where Gatsby reveals his real history, part of which Nick has already related in Chapter VI. Gatsby's account helps Nick fully grasp his neighbor's extraordinary idealization of Daisy and their love. Leaving Gatsby, Nick tells him he is better than the Buchanans and their crowd. The narrator next provides a flashback in which Michaelis, a friend of Wilson's, tries to comfort him following Myrtle's death but fails as Wilson begins his pursuit of his wife's murderer. As the chapter ends, Wilson shoots and kills Gatsby as he lies on a float in his swimming pool; Wilson then commits suicide.

Chapter IX. Nick assumes responsibility for making Gatsby's funeral arrangements. The Buchanans have abruptly left East Egg, Wolfshiem refuses to become involved, and of the multitudes of party guests, only Owl Eyes shows up to pass his benediction on Gatsby: "'The poor son-of-a-bitch.'"[26] Gatsby's father, Mr. Gatz, provides part of Gatsby's childhood history, and Wolfshiem, whom Nick seeks out in New York, confirms his own role in the making of Gatsby. After the funeral, in successive scenes, Nick breaks with Jordan and with Tom, who confesses that he had directed Wilson to Gatsby. In the novel's coda, Nick meditates upon the glory and tragedy of Gatsby and of all pursuers of the American dream.

TENDER IS THE NIGHT, 1934

Book I. Rosemary Hoyt, a nearly eighteen-year-old American actress, and her mother, Elsie Speers, arrive at Gausse's Hôtel des Etrangers on the French Riviera at Cap d'Antibes during June 1925. On the beach Rosemary meets American novelist Albert McKisco and his wife, Violet, and other members of their group: homosexuals Luis Campion and Royal Dumphry and middle-aged Mrs. Abrams, who recognizes the young actress from her movie, *Daddy's Girl.* Rosemary is more attracted to a group of tanned people sunbathing nearby, the leader of whom, Dick Diver, later awakens her when she falls asleep and risks sunburn. Rosemary immediately falls in love with Dick. Later in the week, again on the beach, Dick invites Rosemary to join his group, which includes his wife, Nicole; alcoholic composer Abe North and his wife, Mary; and half-French, half-American soldier-of-fortune Tommy Barban.

At their Riviera villa the Divers host a dinner party for the Diver and McKisco groups as well as Rosemary, her mother, and movie director Earl Brady. During the party Violet witnesses "a scene"[27] in an upstairs bathroom, which leads to a duel between Albert and Tommy, the latter of whom is trying to force Violet to stop talking about what she saw at the Divers' house. Neither man is hurt in the duel.

Rosemary becomes increasingly infatuated with Dick as she goes shopping with Nicole in Paris and visits the Beaumont Hamel battlefield with Abe and Dick, who delivers a moving oration on the "'century of middle-class love spent here. . . . the last love battle.'"[28] Rosemary confesses her love to Dick, who kisses her but who also explains that they cannot have an affair because his relationship with Nicole is extremely complex. The Divers, Mary, and Rosemary take Abe to the station so that he can return to America and work, but Abe fails to get on his train and instead goes on a bender.

The following evening, Dick, whose resistance to Rosemary is weakening, meets her at her hotel room. Abe also shows up at Rosemary's room with Jules Peterson, a black man who is in danger because he has become involved in one of Abe's drunken altercations. While Dick, Abe, and Rosemary are in Dick's room trying to decide how to help Peterson, he is murdered on Rosemary's bed. Dick drags the body out into the hallway and takes Rosemary's blood-stained bedding for Nicole to wash. Rosemary, who observes Nicole's hysterical response to the bloody bedspread, begins to understand that Violet had seen similarly deranged behavior in the Divers' Riviera bathroom.

Book II. This book begins with a flashback to 1917, when brilliant young Richard Diver—who has attended Yale, been a Rhodes Scholar, and studied medicine at Johns Hopkins University and in Vienna—arrives in Zürich to do further study in psychiatry. He serves in the U.S. army during World War I and then returns to Zürich in 1919. At a clinic there, he meets with his friend the Swiss psychiatrist Franz Gregorovious, who tells him that beautiful, wealthy mental patient Nicole Warren, from whom Dick has received letters, has been the victim of an incestuous episode with her father. Dick, who wants "'to be a good psychologist—maybe to be the greatest one that ever lived,'"[29] is romantically attracted to Nicole, but when both Franz and Nicole's psychiatrist object to the relationship, Dick reluctantly breaks with her. The couple is reunited during a chance meeting, and despite the objections of Baby Warren, Nicole's overbearing older sister, Dick and Nicole marry. Through a stream-of-consciousness narrative in chapter 10, Nicole recounts their early years together, the births of their two children, her mental breakdowns, and Dick's increasing reliance on Warren money. Her account ends with the arrival of Rosemary Hoyt on the Riviera during the summer of 1925 and thus functions as a bridge to the events occurring in Book I.

Following the murder of Peterson, the Divers return to the Villa Diana. They spend a skiing vacation in Gstaad, Switzerland, where Franz suggests that he and Dick operate a Swiss psychiatric clinic together; they form a partnership that lasts eighteen months. During this period, suspicious of her husband's fidelity and jealous of his attentions to his other patients, Nicole suffers a severe breakdown. When she recovers, Dick—exhausted and increasingly directionless—travels alone to Munich, where he learns from Tommy Barban that Abe North has been beaten to death in a New York City speakeasy. In Innsbruck Dick learns by way of a telegram that his minister father has died, news that leaves him "wishing he had always been as good as he had intended to be."[30] Following his burial of his father in Virginia, Dick returns to Europe, where in Rome he encounters Rosemary. They consummate their relationship, though Dick realizes he is no longer in love with her. He then goes out drinking, gets into a fight with a taxi driver, and is beaten and jailed by the Rome police. Dick is forced to ask Baby Warren to negotiate his release from jail. He is thus humiliated by his own inability to behave with integrity and purpose, which in turn requires him openly to draw on the Warrens' money and power: "It had been a hard night but she [Baby] had the satisfaction of feeling that, whatever Dick's previous record was, they now possessed a moral superiority over him for as long as he proved of any use."[31]

Book III. Back at the clinic, Dick's relationship with certain of his patients and with Franz Gregorovious grows strained, and the two psychiatrists decide to dissolve their partnership. The Divers return to the Riviera, where their relationship is clearly deteriorating, as are their friendships with others. They break with Mary North, who is now the Contessa di Minghetti; they encounter Tommy Barban at a yacht party where Dick behaves badly; and they once again meet Rosemary on the beach, where Dick unsuccessfully attempts to show off for her. When Rosemary remarks that he has changed, Dick confesses, "'The change came a long way back—but at first it didn't show. The manner remains intact for some time after the morale cracks.'"[32] Nicole, on the other hand, feels "new and happy," "cured," and "complete."[33] No longer needing her doctor husband, who, she believes, has planned her liberation from him, Nicole sleeps with Tommy at a Riviera hotel. But the following day, when Dick tells Nicole, "'I can't do anything for you any more. I'm trying to save myself,'" she replies, "'You're a coward! You've made a failure of your life, and you want to blame it on me.'"[34] Their break is complete, and when Tommy demands that Dick give Nicole a divorce, he agrees to do so. In the novel's last chapter the reader is told that Tommy and Nicole have married and that Dick is now unsuccessfully practicing general medicine in small upstate New York towns. The novel's brilliantly understated final sentence suggests the completeness of his fall from vast promise to anonymity and failure.

THE LOVE OF THE LAST TYCOON: A WESTERN (ORIGINALLY PUBLISHED AS THE LAST TYCOON, 1941)

Cecelia Brady, who narrates much of this unfinished novel, relates events that occurred five years before, during the mid 1930s. Flying home to Hollywood from Bennington College, Cecelia meets Wylie White, a screenwriter, and Mannie Schwartze, a former studio executive. Their plane is forced by bad weather to land in Nashville, Wylie's hometown. He takes Cecelia and Schwartze to Andrew Jackson's home, the Hermitage, where Schwartze commits suicide after Cecelia and Wylie have returned to the plane. There Cecelia has a conversation with the man she secretly loves, Monroe Stahr, a young Jewish producer who is a partner and rival of her father, producer Pat Brady. She learns that Schwartze has been rebuffed by Stahr, to whom he has sent a note warning about studio intrigues. Stahr, who is traveling under the name

"... He had flown up very high to see, on strong wings when he was young. And while he was up there he had looked on all the kingdoms, with the kind of eyes that can stare straight into the sun. Beating his wings tenaciously—finally frantically—and keeping on beating them he had stayed up there longer than most of us, and then, remembering all he had seen from his great height of how things were, he had settled gradually to earth. . . . this was where Stahr had come to earth after that extraordinary illuminating flight where he saw which way we were going, and how we looked doing it, and how much of it mattered. You could say that this was where an accidental wind blew him but I don't think so. I would rather think that in a 'long shot' he saw a new way of measuring our jerky hopes and graceful rogueries and awkward sorrows, and that he came here from choice to be with us to the end. Like the plane coming down into the Glendale airport, into the warm darkness."

Cecelia Brady on Monroe Stahr

From F. Scott Fitzgerald, *The Love of the Last Tycoon: A Western*, edited, with a preface and notes, by Matthew J. Bruccoli (New York: Scribner Paperback Fiction, 1994), pp. 20-21.

"Mr. Smith," spends time in the cockpit, where he gives the pilots advice on decision-making that defines his own practice as a producer: "'You've got to decide—on what basis? You can't test the best way—except by doing it. So you just do it.'"[35]

One month later the movie studio is shaken by an earthquake. Stahr and trouble-shooter "Robby" Robinson rescue two women who are floating on top of a large movie prop in the studio's flooded back lot. One of the women closely resembles Stahr's dead wife, actress Minna Davis. The morning after the flood, cameraman Pete Zavras breaks his arm when he tries to commit suicide by jumping off the balcony of one of the studio buildings. (It is later revealed that rumors have circulated about Zavras's going blind and that Stahr has arranged to have the cameraman's vision tested by a reputable oculist, which makes Zavras grateful to Stahr.) In the meanwhile, after asking Robinson to try to discover the identities of the two women on the studio lot the night before, Stahr goes through what Cecelia describes as "A Producer's Day." He instructs a British novelist on how to write for movies; he tries to comfort an impotent male star; he counsels writers, a director, and a studio functionary on the improvement of a screenplay that is about to go into production; he fires a director who cannot handle his tempestuous female star; and he takes a visitor, Prince Agge of Denmark, to a commissary luncheon with studio heads and then to the projection room, where they watch screen tests and the day's rushes and where Stahr labels himself "'the unity'"[36] in the studio.

Stahr meets Kathleen Moore, the Minna look-alike, and invites her to visit the studio. A week later he dances with her at a studio ball. During a date the following day, they make love at the unfinished house he is building at the beach. Afterward she tells him about a man with whom she had once lived, and they walk on the beach, where a conversation with a black fisherman inspires Stahr to rededicate himself to the making of quality movies. After he takes Kathleen home, he reads a letter that she had dropped in his car; the letter reveals that she plans to marry another man.

The next day Stahr has his weekly medical exam, during which his doctor reflects that overwork will probably soon cause a fatal strain on his weakened heart. That night Kathleen meets with Stahr and reveals further information about her commitments to her former lover and to her present fiancé. Stahr resists telling her that he wishes to make a life with her, and the following day she sends him a telegram announcing that she has gotten married.

Stahr asks Cecelia to arrange a meeting with Brimmer, a member of the Communist Party, which Stahr believes is exercising undue influence over his writers. In the course of the meeting the producer gets drunk, provokes a fight with the Communist, and is knocked down. After Brimmer leaves, Stahr asks Cecelia to accompany him to Douglas Fairbanks's ranch. The novel breaks off with her lines, "That's how the two weeks started that he and I went around together. It only took one of them for [gossip columnist] Louella [Parsons] to have us married."[37]

Although he had not completely developed the plot for his novel, Fitzgerald left an outline-plan which suggests that Stahr resumes his affair with Kathleen and then is blackmailed by Pat Brady. Discovering that Brady has arranged to have him murdered, Stahr plots Brady's death but then changes his mind while leaving Hollywood for the East Coast. He is unable to stop the murder, however, because his plane crashes and he is killed. At one point Fitzgerald had planned to end the novel with the plundering of the wrecked plane by children who are forever marked by the things they steal. He later apparently rejected this ending for a scene at Stahr's funeral in which the career of a has-been actor is revived when, as a result of a mistaken invitation, he serves as a pallbearer.

NOVELETTES

"May Day," *The Smart Set* (July 1920). Collected in *Tales of the Jazz Age* (1922).

This novelette is Fitzgerald's most successful experiment with literary naturalism. Its mock-heroic prelude, which describes both the triumphant return of American soldiers following World War I and the

Cover for the first magazine publication of Fitzgerald's satirical novelette (Matthew J. and Arlyn Bruccoli Collection of F. Scott Fitzgerald, Thomas Cooper Library, University of South Carolina)

materialism and dissipation of the "great city" they enter, brilliantly introduces the characters and theme of the novelette. May Day is traditionally a pagan celebration of spring, the commemoration day for the 1917 Russian Revolution, and the international distress call.

On 1 May 1919 impoverished would-be artist Gordon Sterrett, a Yale graduate, seeks out his well-to-do classmate Philip Dean at the Biltmore Hotel in New York City, where Dean is staying as he prepares for the Yale Gamma Psi dance to be held at Delmonico's hotel that evening. Sterrett begs Dean to lend him $300 so that he can pay blackmail to Jewel Hudson, his lower-class lover. Dean, who describes Sterrett as "'sort of bankrupt—morally as well as financially,'"[38] invites him to breakfast at the Yale Club and there reluctantly lends him only $80. At the same hour a pair of ignorant discharged soldiers, Carrol Key and Gus Rose, witness the beating of a Socialist orator and then decide to ask Key's brother, a waiter at Delmonico's, for liquor.

That evening, Sterrett's former girl-friend, Edith Bradin, who is attending the Yale dance with undergraduate Peter Himmel but who longs to see Sterrett again, is disgusted by his drunkenness and self-pity when he talks with her at Delmonico's. While Sterrett slumps in the stairway and Himmel drinks with Key and Rose in a side room at the hotel, Edith flees to the nearby office of her radical journalist brother, Henry Bradin. At the newspaper office Bradin and an associate are attacked by a mob of antisocialist rioters; Henry's leg is broken, and one of the mob's ringleaders, Carrol Key, is killed in a fall from a window. In the meantime Jewel Hudson has forced Sterrett to leave Delmonico's with her.

Before dawn on May 2 several of the novelette's principal characters—the addled Gus Rose; the pathetic Gordon Sterrett and manipulative Jewel Hudson; and the extremely intoxicated Peter Himmel and Philip Dean—gather at Childs' restaurant on Columbus Circle, where their conduct is ironically counterpointed by the heroic statue of Columbus outside. Himmel and Dean, who tuck "In" and "Out" signs into their shirt fronts and thus become "Mr. In and Mr. Out," drunkenly travel from Childs' to Delmonico's to the Commodore Hotel to the Biltmore. There they encounter Edith Bradin, who rebuffs them and identifies onlooker Gus Rose as one of the rioters who assaulted her brother. On the same morning Sterrett awakens in a sordid hotel room, remembers that he has married Jewel Hudson, and, returning to his small room on Twenty-seventh Street, commits suicide at his drawing desk.

"The Diamond as Big as the Ritz," *The Smart Set* (June 1922). Collected in *Tales of the Jazz Age*.

This novelette is one of Fitzgerald's earliest explorations of both the attractions and corrupting power of wealth. Protagonist John T. Unger leaves Hades, a small town on the Mississippi River, to attend St. Midas' School, the most expensive and exclusive prep school in the world. There he meets Percy Washington, who invites John to spend the summer with him at his Montana home built on a mountain made of diamond. Arriving at the desolate town of Fish, watched over by twelve apostle-like men who seem to have made a religious cult of observing the passing of the seven-o'clock train, the boys are transported by servants to the Washingtons' remote estate, where John discovers unimaginable luxury: "Sometimes the floor under their feet would flame in brilliant patterns from lighting below, patterns of barbaric clashing colors, of pastel delicacy, of sheer whiteness, or of subtle and intricate mosaic, surely from some mosque on the Adriatic Sea. Sometimes beneath layers of thick crystal he would see blue or green water swirling, inhabited by vivid fish and growths of rainbow foliage. Then they would be treading on furs of every texture and color or along corridors of palest ivory, unbroken as though carved complete from the gigantic tusks of dinosaurs extinct before the age of man. . . ."[39] John learns the history of the Washington family's discovery—and subsequent concealment—of the diamond mountain that has supplied their wealth. After breakfast, John accompanies Percy's father, Braddock Washington, on a visit to prisoners who have invaded the estate and who must be incarcerated to protect the Washingtons' secret.

The older Washington daughter, Jasmine, is a sentimental girl—"Her favorite books had to do with poor girls who kept house for widowed fathers"[40]—but John falls in love with the beautiful younger and preposterously romantic daughter, Kismine, who as the summer draws near its close inadvertently reveals that he, like all the Washingtons' guests, is to be killed. He flees to the neighboring mountain with Kismine and Jasmine, who mistakenly carry away rhinestones rather than diamonds, while the estate—betrayed by an escaped prisoner—is under aerial attack. In the course of the bombardment, John observes Braddock Washington arrogantly offering a bribe to God, who rejects it. Washington then leads his wife, son, and slaves through a trapdoor in the side of the wired diamond mountain and explodes everything—mountain, château, and aviator invaders. Only the girls, John, and what he calls "'the shabby gift of disillusion'"[41] survive.

"The Rich Boy," *The Red Book Magazine* (January and February 1926). Collected in *All the Sad Young Men* (1926).

This novelette is one of Fitzgerald's most complex examinations of how wealth influences character. Anson Hunter's story is told by an unnamed, partially involved narrator who had known Anson at Yale and who insists, as he begins his story, that he is analyzing an individual rich boy, not a type: "this is his and not his brothers' story."[42] The narrator then generalizes, however, that the very rich regard themselves as superior to other people and that this attitude makes them different.

The oldest son of a wealthy, distinguished New York family, Anson graduates from Yale, serves as a naval aviator during World War I, and then enters a New York brokerage house where he ultimately becomes a partner. While he is in the service, he falls in love with Paula Legendre, a beautiful heiress with whom he has long, serious conversations. They are informally engaged, but when Anson becomes helplessly drunk during one of their social engagements, Paula and her mother insist that they suspend their plans to marry. Reunited, Anson and Paula quarrel, break off their relationship, and then reconcile again, although his sense of superiority and of his power over her prevents him from proposing to her: "'No, let it wait—she is mine. . . .'"[43] Discouraged, Paula marries another man, and although Anson carries on with his normal duties and pleasures, "for three days, in any place, in any company, he would suddenly bend his head into his hands and cry like a child."[44]

Anson subsequently becomes involved with Dolly Karger, with whom he ultimately breaks because he cannot love her. He hears of Paula's divorce and remarriage but insists to the narrator that he no longer cares. He devotes himself to his brokerage firm, to advising

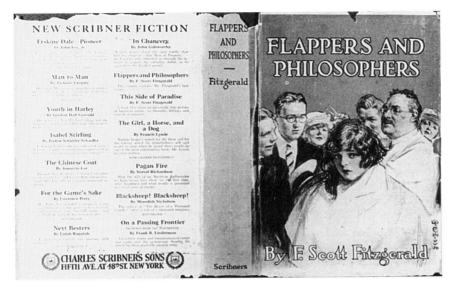

Dust jacket for Fitzgerald's first collection of stories (1920); the cover art by W. E. Hill illustrates "Bernice Bobs Her Hair," one of Fitzgerald's best-known stories about young people. (Matthew J. and Arlyn Bruccoli Collection of F. Scott Fitzgerald, Thomas Cooper Library, University of South Carolina)

young married friends about their problems, and to breaking up a disgraceful affair between his uncle's wife and a man-about-town. As time passes, however, he feels himself more and more alone: his friends and family seem no longer to depend on him, and he has no romantic prospects.

On a day when his situation seems particularly desperate, he encounters Paula, who is obviously pregnant and very happy with her second husband and family. Anson's sense of superiority is shattered when she declares herself in love "'at last'": "'I was infatuated with you, Anson—you could make me do anything you liked.'"[45] Following the reunion, Anson falls into depression and is encouraged to take a European vacation. Three days before his ship sails, Paula dies in childbirth.

The narrator, who is on board ship with Anson, reports that he shows no emotion at the news of Paula's death and that he restores his elevated sense of self by pursuing a pretty young passenger: "I was glad that he was himself again, or at least the self that I knew, . . . I don't think he was ever happy unless some one was in love with him, responding to him like filings to a magnet, helping him to explain himself, promising him something. . . . Perhaps they promised that there would always be women in the world who would spend their brightest, freshest, rarest hours to nurse and protect that superiority he cherished in his heart."[46]

CONTEMPORARY RECEPTION

Proper recognition of Fitzgerald as one of the major and enduring American fiction writers of the twentieth century came only after his death. Most contemporary reviewers judged his first novel, *This Side of Paradise,* as flawed but also as an auspicious beginning: ambitious, fresh, and exciting. In general, critics treated the succeeding novels published in Fitzgerald's lifetime—*The Beautiful and Damned, The Great Gatsby,* and *Tender Is the Night*—with respect, though they also tended to agree that the works fell short of their author's promise. In most cases reviewers praised Fitzgerald's final, unfinished novel—posthumously published under the title *The Last Tycoon*—though its incomplete state once more supported their contention that he had not fulfilled his talent. Fitzgerald's rather precarious contemporary reputation may have resulted in part from Scribners' publication of a collection of his short stories following each of the novels that appeared while he was living. Although reviewers usually applauded each collection, they often focused upon the purely commercial rather than the serious short fiction, thereby obscuring one of the writer's major achievements and confirming the suspicion that he was merely a skillful popular entertainer. Two more factors may have impaired Fitzgerald's contemporary critical reputation, though they were never directly raised by his reviewers: his image as a dissipated playboy of the 1920s destroyed by his own weaknesses in the 1930s, and the contrasting model of his friend and rival Ernest Hemingway, who, despite—or perhaps because of—his involvement in wars, African safaris, deep-sea fishing, and serial marriages, exuded artistic discipline and personal integrity.

When *This Side of Paradise* was published in March 1920, it was greeted with high praise—and some moral outrage. H. L. Mencken in *The Smart Set* proclaimed it the "best American novel that I have seen of late . . . a truly amazing first novel—original in structure, extremely sophisticated in manner, and adorned with a brilliancy that is as rare in American writing as honesty is in American statecraft." John Black in the *Brooklyn Daily Eagle* declared, "'This Side of Paradise' is the most independent, daring and challenging adventure in American fiction since Dreiser's early days." Yet, many reviewers correctly perceived that the novel lacked controlled structure and style: the writer for the *Philadelphia Sunday Press* found it "surcharged with a tremendous vitality, as yet not sufficiently restrained within the limits of a sure artistry"; Robert C. Benchley in the *New York Morning World* offered Fitzgerald "a crown of something very expensive" in spite of his novel's "immaturity, its ingenuousness and its many false notes"; and Edwin Francis Edgett in the *Boston Evening Transcript* noted the work's "boisterous exhibition of youthful though somewhat unregulated genius." Still other reviewers focused on its portrait of college men and their young women. Writers for campus magazines and newspapers—*The Harvard Crimson, The Dartmouth,* and *The Hamilton Literary Magazine*—provided firsthand support for Fitzgerald's vision of university life, and *The New York Times Book Review* called *This Side of Paradise* a "nearly perfect" picture of the experiences of college-age people with "the sexes . . . well-matched." Nevertheless, Heywood Broun in the *New York Tribune* complained that though the novel's portrayal of college men might be accurate, "the type is not interesting," and the reviewer for *The Independent* warned that the book's "picture of modern youth is so obviously founded on solid fact that Victorian mamas are likely to be quite upset by it." Indeed, the commentator for the Roman Catholic journal *America* provided the strongest expression of the conservative point of view: "The novel's central figure is an egotistic, unprincipled philandering youth, who seems to be a fair example of our non-Catholic college's output. . . . If the parties to Amory's various love-affairs are faithful portraits of the modern American girl, the country is going to the dogs rapidly."[47]

Many contemporary commentators on *This Side of Paradise,* including Burton Rascoe in the *Chicago Daily Tribune* and an unidentified writer for *The Nation,* concurred with the *St. Louis Post-Dispatch* reviewer that Fitzgerald was "an author of whom great things can be expected," yet by the time his first story collection, *Flappers and Philosophers,* appeared in September 1920, the young writer's reputation was under assault. Although Fanny Butcher in the *Chicago Sunday Tribune* predicted that "Bernice Bobs Her Hair" and "The Ice Palace" were "going to be classics some day" and Heywood Broun in the *New York Tribune* offered grudging admiration for "The Ice Palace," the majority of the reviewers defined the collection as diverting but unimportant. Sibyl Vane in *Publishers' Weekly* saw the stories as "clever light fiction done crisp"; the critic for the *San Francisco Chronicle* felt they were "the work of an artisan rather than an artist"; and the reviewer for *The New York Times Book Review and Magazine* regarded them as "the triumph of form over matter." Mencken asked in *The Smart Set:* "Will [Fitzgerald] proceed via the first part of 'This Side of Paradise' to the cold groves of beautiful letters, or will he proceed via 'Head and Shoulders' into the sunshine that warms [popular writers] Robert W. Chambers and Harold MacGrath?" *The Nation* concluded that he had already "proceeded to cultivate [dross] and to sell it to the *Saturday Evening Post*"; C. B. in the *Baltimore Evening Sun* wrote that "after the promise of 'This Side of Paradise' [the stories] are a terrible come down"; and I. W. L. in the *Boston Evening Transcript* declared that "the Fitzgerald vogue will pass."[48]

The Beautiful and Damned, published in March 1922, was the most widely reviewed of Fitzgerald's books because of the interest generated by *This Side of Paradise* two years before. Critics were sharply divided over whether this partially naturalistic story of Anthony and Gloria Patch, a young married couple who lead a life of dissipation while awaiting an inheritance, represented an advance over Fitzgerald's first novel. Reviewers who attacked the book charged that its ideas were either confused or simpleminded (Edwin Francis Edgett in the *Boston Evening Transcript,* Carl Van Doren in *The Nation,* and Burton Rascoe in *The Bookman,* for example) and that it lacked structure, design, and artistic control (Gilbert Seldes in *The Dial* and Phil A. Kinsley in the *Philadelphia Record*). Even those critics who admired the novel conceded its flaws: Harry Hansen in the *Chicago Daily News* praised its development of theme but also called it "at times superficial, ironical, grotesque, careless, disorderly"; Mencken in *The Smart Set* found in the novel signs that Fitzgerald had begun "to come into his maturity," though he also judged the book "not a complete success"; and Henry Seidel Canby in the *Literary Review of the New York Evening Post* noted "evidences of great and growing artistic power" and concluded, "[W]hen he is not showing off in pseudo-wit, or trying to shock the bourgeoisie, or discovering profound truths of philosophy which get muddled before he can grasp them, how this novelist can write!" Most contemporary reviewers were disappointed by Fitzgerald's writing in *The Beautiful and Damned,* though at least one, John V. A. Weaver in the *Brooklyn Daily Eagle,* predicted, "[W]hen he finally finds himself . . . he is going to be one of the really great figures of our native literature."[49]

Tales of the Jazz Age, published in September 1922, included eleven stories, a contents page with tongue-in-cheek annotations by Fitzgerald, and a dust jacket by popular cartoonist John Held Jr. The reviews were mostly favorable, though an unidentified writer for the

Minneapolis Journal declared: "There is not a well conceived story in the volume; not one that has any depth; and throughout the collection silliness is mistaken for comedy." Both John Farrar in the *New York Herald* and Edmund Wilson in *Vanity Fair* praised "The Diamond as Big as the Ritz," though Farrar compared it to work by Chambers, and Wilson evoked another "slick" writer, Frank Stockton. The reviewer for the *Philadelphia Evening Public Ledger* declared that "Diamond" "miss[ed] fire" and that Fitzgerald's other fine novelette in the collection, "May Day," was "readable without being wholly gripping"; Stephen Vincent Benét in the *New York Evening Post Literary Review* found the two novelettes neither "interesting" nor "superb." Mencken gave the collection only a brief notice in *The Smart Set* but observed that "The spread between Fitzgerald's best work and his worst is extraordinarily wide."[50]

Most reviewers of *The Great Gatsby*, published on 10 April 1925, regarded the novel as evidence of Fitzgerald's increasing artistic maturity but not as a masterpiece. Isabel Paterson in the *New York Herald Tribune Books* described *The Great Gatsby* as "beautifully and delicately balanced" but also as "neither profound nor durable . . . a book of the season only." The reviewer for the *St. Paul Pioneer Press*, while calling the novel "a distinct advance in the author's command of his medium," concluded that "the work in itself is not of the greatest importance." Mencken in the *Baltimore Evening Sun* praised "the charm and beauty of the writing" but labeled the story "unimportant," "a glorified anecdote." While commending the "sincerity of feeling" and the "delicacy of irony" in the novel, Laurence Stallings in the *New York World* confessed, "I do not think for one moment in reading this book that 'here is a great novel' or even, that 'here is a fine book.'" On the utterly negative side, Ruth Hale in the *Brooklyn Daily Eagle* could not find "one chemical trace of magic, life, irony, romance or mysticism" in *The Great Gatsby*, and Harvey Eagleton in the *Dallas Morning News* denounced the "characteristically unnecessary two-page list of the visitors to the Gatsby Long Island estate." On the other hand, in his *Saturday Review of Literature* essay, William Rose Benét praised not only the "thoroughly matured craftsmanship" but also the thematic profundity of the novel. Moreover, in a *Dial* review of writer and novel that perhaps most fully anticipated their standing in the late 1990s, Gilbert Seldes declared: "The question [of what Fitzgerald would do with his gifts as an author] has been answered in one of the finest of contemporary novels. Fitzgerald has more than matured; he has mastered his talents and gone soaring in a beautiful flight, leaving behind him everything dubious and tricky in his earlier work, and leaving even farther behind all the men of his own generation and most of his elders."[51]

All the Sad Young Men, now generally regarded as Fitzgerald's strongest short-story collection, was published in February 1926. Among the volume's nine stories were four major works: "The Rich Boy," "Winter Dreams," "Absolution," and "'The Sensible Thing.'" Although the unidentified reviewer for *The Dial* regarded the mood of the serious stories as strained and unbelievable, both Harry Hansen in the *Chicago Daily News* and E. C. Beckwith in the *Literary Review of the New York Evening Post* praised these works. Hansen and an unnamed writer for *The New York Times Book Review* also admired the variety of stories in the collection, and *The Bookman* provided a rave review: "As F. Scott Fitzgerald continues to publish books, it becomes apparent that he is head and shoulders better than any writer of his generation. 'All the Sad Young Men' contains several stories of compelling fineness, along with more conventional pieces of story telling that are sufficiently amusing with the old Fitzgerald talent. . . . 'All the Sad Young Men' is, it seems to me, by far the best book of short stories he has given us, and it contains some of his very best work."[52]

Tender Is the Night, Fitzgerald's fourth novel, was published in April 1934, nine years after *The Great Gatsby* and in the midst of the Great Depression. It has often been assumed that this story of wealthy American expatriates living on the Riviera in the 1920s was a critical failure in its time because it was attacked by leftist critics. Among major reviewers, however, only Philip Rahv in the Marxist newspaper *The Daily Worker* condemned it and its author for its alleged support of capitalism: "The truth is that Nicole [Diver] can be understood as a symbol of the entire crazy social system to which Fitzgerald has long been playing Dick Diver. . . . Dear Mr. Fitzgerald, you can't hide from a hurricane under a beach umbrella." Nor did critics complain about the novel's flashback structure. Instead, its very mixed reviews most frequently resulted from readers' high expectations for a book that had required such a long gestation period. Horace Gregory in the *New York Herald Tribune Books* described it as "not all that it should have been"; J. Donald Adams in *The New York Times Book Review* labeled it "a disappointment"; Hal Borland in the *Philadelphia Public Ledger* called it "not the important novel I had expected it to be"; and Clifton Fadiman in *The New Yorker* pronounced it not "the first-rate work of fiction we have been expecting from F. Scott Fitzgerald." At the heart of Fadiman's criticism were what he regarded as the "unconvincing" causes of Dr. Richard Diver's decline: "The events of the narrative, tragic as they are, are insufficient to motivate his downfall." Whether or not Diver's collapse was believable became the central issue for contemporary reviewers: Henry Seidel Canby in *The Saturday Review of Literature* and William Troy in *The Nation* found too many reasons for his decline; Adams in *The New York Times Book Review* regarded his fall as "contrived"; and an unnamed reviewer for the *Milwaukee Journal* lamented Diver's "all too sudden . . . physical, mental and moral disintegration." Nonetheless, John Chamberlain, who within a three-day period twice favorably reviewed the novel for *The New York Times,* defended Fitzgerald's handling of Diver's decline—"Compared to the motivation in Faulkner, it is logic personified"—and an unidentified writer for the *Journal of Nervous and Mental Disease* warmly recommended the novel to students of "the psychobiological sources of human behavior." Other reviewers found additional praiseworthy qualities in *Tender Is the Night.* Malcolm Cowley in *The New Republic* admired the novel's "richness of meaning and emotion"; the critic for the *Milwaukee Journal* called it Fitzgerald's "most mature work"; and Cameron Rogers in the *San Francisco Chronicle* viewed it as "a profoundly moving, beautifully written story, [which] should assure Fitzgerald's stature as an American writer." Most enthusiastically, Gilbert Seldes in the *New York Evening Journal* called *Tender Is the Night* Fitzgerald's "great novel" and declared that the author had "stepped again to his natural place at the head of the American writers of our time."[53]

Published in March 1935, *Taps at Reveille,* Fitzgerald's final collection to appear during his lifetime, included eighteen stories, five of them from his Basil Duke Lee series of 1928 and 1929 and three from his Josephine Perry series of 1930 and 1931. The volume also collected two of his acknowledged masterpieces, "The Last of the Belles" and "Babylon Revisited," neither of which drew particular attention from the reviewers, although Elizabeth Hart in *New York Herald Tribune Books* called the latter story "superb." Most of the contemporary critics, however, concurred with Edith H. Walton, who wrote in *The New York Times Book Review* that "Fitzgerald's material is rarely worthy of his talents" but who praised his "mastery of style" and "technical competence." T. S. Matthew in *The New Republic* accused the short-story writer of lack of depth—"His heroes have grown older but not riper"—and William Troy in *The Nation* declared that his moral vision was "vague and immature." John Chamberlain again played defender of Fitzgerald, arguing in *The New York Times* that his material and vision were at least as consequential as William Faulkner's, Marcel Proust's, Gustave Flaubert's, or Sinclair Lewis's.[54]

"The Last Tycoon is . . . , even in its imperfect state, Fitzgerald's most mature piece of work. It is marked off also from his other novels by the fact that it is the first to deal seriously with any profession or business. . . . Monroe Stahr, unlike any other of Scott Fitzgerald's heroes, is inextricably involved with an industry of which he has been one of the creators, and its fate will be implied by his tragedy. The moving-picture business in America has here been observed at a close range, studied with a careful attention and dramatized with a sharp wit such as are not to be found in combination in any of the other novels on the subject. The Last Tycoon is far and away the best novel we have had about Hollywood, and it is the only one which takes us inside."

Edmund Wilson

From the foreword to *The Last Tycoon*, edited by Wilson (New York: Scribners, 1941), p. x.

The Last Tycoon, Fitzgerald's final, unfinished novel, was published in October 1941, ten months after his death. Edited by Edmund Wilson, the volume included not only *The Last Tycoon* but also Fitzgerald's notes for the novel, five of his best-known short stories, and *The Great Gatsby*. Reviewers generally attempted to assess both the incomplete novel and Fitzgerald's career as a whole. W. M. R. in the *Kansas City Star* and John T. Appleby of the *Washington Post* saw little to praise in either the book or the reputation: Appleby, for example, declared that *The Last Tycoon* "demonstrate[d] conclusively the shallowness and the limitations of Fitzgerald's abilities." Even reviewers who admired the book and who felt that its author had abundant talent tended in many cases to doubt that Fitzgerald was much more than a writer bound by his times: J. Donald Adams in his front-page *New York Times Book Review* article guessed that the fiction writer would "be remembered [only] in his generation." Milton Rugoff in *New York Herald Tribune Books* more optimistically predicted that the best of Fitzgerald's work was "rich and rewarding enough to warrant the attention of another generation besides his own." Several reviewers—including Rugoff, Edward Weeks of *The Atlantic Monthly*, and Louis Nicholas of *The Philadelphia Record*—declared that Fitzgerald's portrait of movie producer Monroe Stahr and his Hollywood environment was superior to anything the author had produced before. Rugoff felt that "it held promise of being his best book"; Weeks called it "a book of great power, clarity, and characterization"; and Nicholas thought that it revealed Fitzgerald "on the verge of a new literary awakening." However, only Stephen Vincent Benét, writing in the *Saturday Review of Literature*, ventured an assessment of the book and of its author's career that approaches the judgment of readers and critics in the late 1990s. Of *The Last Tycoon* Benét wrote: "Had Fitzgerald been permitted to finish the book, I think there is no doubt that it would have added a major character and a major novel to American fiction." Of Fitzgerald as a writer, Benét declared: ". . . the evidence is in. You can take off your hats now, gentlemen, and I think perhaps you had better. This is not a legend, this is a reputation—

and, seen in perspective, it may well be one of the most secure reputations of our time."[55]

REVIVAL

The legend is that when Fitzgerald died in December 1940, all of his books were out of print. The truth is even more bitter. Six of his titles—*The Great Gatsby, Tender Is the Night, Flappers and Philosophers, Tales of the Jazz Age, All the Sad Young Men,* and *Taps at Reveille*—were in stock at Scribners but were not selling. Fitzgerald's final royalty statement in August 1940 showed total sales of forty copies of his books, including seven of *The Great Gatsby* and nine of *Tender Is the Night.* He earned $13.13 in royalties on these sales.

Fitzgerald's resurrection from forgotten writer to major literary figure is one of the great American success stories, though since it was a posthumous development, it carries a Fitzgeraldian poignancy. The revival began because of the efforts of writers who had known Fitzgerald and who recognized his brilliance, among them Edmund Wilson, John O'Hara, Dorothy Parker, Budd Schulberg, and Malcolm Cowley. The volumes that they produced attracted, first of all, a new and enthusiastic readership for Fitzgerald and, later, the attention of teachers and of literary scholars and critics. By 1960 Fitzgerald was ranked among the greatest American writers, and sales of his titles that year totaled 177,849 copies. In the late 1990s roughly 300,000 copies of *The Great Gatsby* were purchased each year, and in the years since Fitzgerald's death, at least fifteen million copies of his books have been sold by Scribners.

Wilson, who had been a friend of Fitzgerald's in college, was the key figure in the first stage of the revival. He edited Fitzgerald's unfinished last novel, which was published in 1941 as *The Last Tycoon* together with *The Great Gatsby* and five stories. Wilson also assembled the tributes to Fitzgerald by John Dos Passos, Glenway Wescott, John O'Hara, Budd Schulberg, and John Peale Bishop for the 17 February and 3 March 1941 issues of *The New Republic.* Though these publishing events were generally regarded as sentimental gestures, they were signs that other writers were not going to allow Fitzgerald's work to die.

In 1945, a key year for the revival, Wilson published *The Crack-Up,* which collected ten of Fitzgerald's autobiographical essays, selections from his notebooks and previously unpublished letters, and letters and tributes to him by such distinguished literary figures as Gertrude Stein, Edith Wharton, T. S. Eliot, Thomas Wolfe, John Dos Passos, and John Peale Bishop. *The Crack-Up,* which had a strong appeal for readers, has never gone out of print. Also during 1945 *The Great Gatsby* and other works by Fitzgerald became widely available and widely read: the Armed Services Editions distributed 150,000 copies each of *The Great Gatsby* and of another volume, *"The Diamond as Big as the Ritz" and Other Stories,* to Americans in service during World War II. That same year the first group of Bantam paperbacks included *The Great Gatsby* priced at twenty-five cents. *The Portable F. Scott Fitzgerald,* selected by Dorothy Parker and with an introduction by O'Hara, provided *The Great Gatsby, Tender Is the Night,* and nine stories.

In 1950 Fitzgerald's daughter, Scottie, donated his papers to Princeton, a gift that stimulated Fitzgerald scholarship. The following year Arthur Mizener published the first book-length biography, *The Far Side of Paradise,* which, together with Schulberg's novel based on Fitzgerald, *The Disenchanted* (1950), aroused interest in the writer's life. In 1951 literary historian Malcolm Cowley published an influential collection of twenty-eight Fitzgerald short stories and produced the so-called "Author's Final Version" of *Tender Is the Night,* which brought new readers to that masterpiece. Also in 1951 Alfred Kazin edited *F. Scott Fitzgerald: The Man and His Work,* the first major collection of critical essays on Fitzgerald by various authors. That same year Bantam added the original version of *Tender Is the Night* to its paperback line. The English publisher Penguin printed *The Great Gatsby* in paperback in 1950, adding the revised *Tender Is the Night* to its imprint in 1954 and *The Last Tycoon* in 1960. By the mid 1950s the Fitzgerald revival was well under way.

Fitzgerald's reputation continued to rise as his works, especially *The Great Gatsby,* became classroom standards and he achieved classic status. In 1957 Scribners produced its Student's Edition of *The Great Gatsby,* which was incorporated into the Scribner's Library editions in 1960 and thereafter became the most widely reprinted trade paperback among twentieth-century novels. During the 1960s and later, Fitzgerald scholarship and research resulted in major primary and secondary bibliographies; two journals (*The Fitzgerald Newsletter,* 1958–1968, and *The Fitzgerald-Hemingway Journal,* 1969–1979); more than twenty biographies; and in excess of fifty book-length critical studies. The Modern Language Association annual bibliography lists more than 1,300 entries, mostly articles and essays, published between 1963 and 1999. Since 1951, twenty-one collections of critical essays on Fitzgerald's life and work have been assembled. Since his death sixty-plus volumes of previously uncollected Fitzgerald writings—including five collections of his letters, seven volumes of his stories, his *Ledger,* his *Notebooks,* and facsimiles of his manuscripts, typescripts, and galley proofs—have been published.

Fitzgerald's work continues to attract diverse audiences: scholars, teachers, students, and readers for pleasure. For generation after generation of readers, his emotional intensity, warmth, style, and mastery of the storyteller's art have earned him a secure place among writers of genius.

ART IMITATING LIFE

Great fiction is often autobiographical since authors write most effectively about what they know. More than most other writers, Fitzgerald drew upon his own feelings and experiences for his novels and short stories. Yet, his fiction was never just thinly disguised autobiography; it was instead transmuted autobiography. None of the protagonists of his novels—Amory Blaine, Anthony Patch, Jay Gatsby, Dick Diver, or Monroe Stahr—can be fully identified with Fitzgerald, though he clearly assigned certain of his own emotions and experiences to them. In his best work, fictional elements provide artistic form and moral order that life rarely yields; autobiographical elements invest the work with an intensely "felt" quality, perhaps the most notable mark of Fitzgerald's greatest writing. Again and again he emphasized that his fiction had its origins in his feelings: "Taking things hard—from Genevra to Joe Mank—: That's stamp that goes into my books so that people can read it blind like brail,"[56] or "Whether it's something that happened twenty years ago or only yesterday, I must start out with an emotion—one that's close to me and that I can understand."[57]

Fitzgerald never wrote a roman à clef (a novel with a key), in which real people and events are slightly fictionalized, and much of the pleasure for readers comes through their ability to identify the prototypes for the characters and actions and to share what purports to be an insider's view of them. Fitzgerald drew upon his life, family, friends, and favorite locales for his novels and stories, but his purpose in doing so was not to expose real people and events but to re-create them in fictional forms capable of conveying truths as he saw them. Scottie Fitzgerald was the model for Honoria Wales in "Babylon Revisited," but the character is not simply a portrait of Scottie as an intelligent and charming child but is rather a vivid representation of all that her father, Charlie Wales, has lost through his irresponsible behavior.

F. Scott, Zelda, and Scottie Fitzgerald on the Riviera, mid 1920s

This Side of Paradise—as is frequently the case with first novels—is the most autobiographical of Fitzgerald's major works. Many of Amory Blaine's experiences are drawn from Fitzgerald's life. Amory spends part of his teenage years in Minneapolis/St. Paul, where Fitzgerald grew up. (Fitzgerald also called on childhood memories of St. Paul and of prep school for his eight Basil Duke Lee stories.) Amory, like his creator, attends prep school and Princeton (*Ha-Ha Hortense!* clearly echoes Fitzgerald's first Triangle Club musical, *Fie! Fie! Fi-Fi!*, and Amory's friend Thomas Parke D'Invilliers is based on Fitzgerald's friend John Peale Bishop). Amory's influential relationship with Monsignor Thayer Darcy recalls Fitzgerald's relationship with Father Cyril Sigourney Webster Fay (the young novelist, in fact, drew heavily on Fay's letters for Darcy's letter that appears in the Interlude between Book I and Book II of *This Side of Paradise*). Amory's unhappy romance with Isabelle Borgé parallels Fitzgerald's unsuccessful courtship of Ginevra King, and the protagonist's more serious involvement with and loss of Rosalind Connage is based on Fitzgerald's relationship with Zelda Sayre, whose unwillingness to commit herself to him before he achieved success both caused him distress and inspired him to finish

This Side of Paradise. (Zelda recognized herself in Rosalind and admired the character. In a 1923 interview she remarked, "I love Scott's books and heroines. I like the ones that are like me! That's why I love Rosalind. . . . I love [the heroines'] courage, their recklessness and spend-thriftness."[58] Most important, Amory's extraordinary ambitions replicate Fitzgerald's own.

The strongest autobiographical elements in Fitzgerald's second novel, *The Beautiful and Damned,* lie in its portrayal of a marriage both defined and strained by endless parties in New York City and its environs. Although Fitzgerald told Scottie in a 14 June 1940 letter that her mother was, in fact, a much more admirable person than Gloria Gilbert Patch,[59] the novel's major female character, Gloria and Zelda clearly shared a tendency toward reckless, irresponsible, selfish behavior. Anthony Patch reflects Fitzgerald's growing concern in the early 1920s that he was slipping into a life of dissipation, just as Richard Caramel illustrates Fitzgerald's fear that he was compromising his reputation as a serious artist by producing apparently unimportant popular literature. The Patches' cynical friend, Maury Noble, who late in the novel snubs Anthony, was based on the Fitzgeralds' friend George Jean Nathan, an influential drama critic and magazine editor.

Sheilah Graham, movie columnist and Fitzgerald's companion in Hollywood from 1937 to 1940; she was a model for Kathleen Moore in *The Love of the Last Tycoon.*

Between October 1922 and May 1924, the Fitzgeralds rented a house in Great Neck, Long Island, where they met and partied with well-to-do people, many of them in show business, and where Fitzgerald became a close friend of writer Ring Lardner. Lardner may have supplied a model for the enigmatic party guest Owl Eyes; Great Neck certainly provided the West Egg setting for Gatsby's extravagant parties, just as the Corona dump in the borough of Queens provided the valley of ashes setting for Wilson's garage. Gatsby's gambler friend Meyer Wolfshiem was loosely based on racketeer and gambler Arnold Rothstein, and Jordan Baker was modeled on amateur golf champion Edith

Cummings, who had gone to school with Ginevra King. In his "romantic readiness" and his belief in the American dream, Gatsby reflects his creator. But Fitzgerald drew some biographical data for the character from a Long Island neighbor, Max Gerlach, who was apparently a bootlegger and who, in a note to Fitzgerald on a newspaper clipping, used Gatsby's defining expression, "old sport."[60] Much of the material of Gatsby's life with Dan Cody was provided by Great Neck resident Robert Kerr, who in his youth had had a similar experience with a yachtsman benefactor. Fitzgerald's courtship of Zelda during the war and his desperation when she broke their engagement inspired Gatsby's feelings about Daisy, and Zelda's betrayal of Fitzgerald with Edouard Jozan during the summer of 1924 when the novel was being written fueled the sense of lost illusions in the novel.

The French and Swiss settings for *Tender Is the Night* were provided by the Fitzgeralds' extended stays in Paris, on the Riviera, and in Switzerland between May 1924 and September 1931. In the novel's earliest versions, the characters who ultimately evolved into Dick and Nicole Diver were based on Gerald and Sara Murphy, whose affluence, social grace, and charm were retained in the Divers. Finally, however, Dick became a reflection of Fitzgerald himself, as the writer examined both his growing sense of his emotional bankruptcy and his feelings about his wife's insanity, which is reflected in Nicole Diver. (There is, however, no evidence that Zelda had been a victim of incest, as was Nicole.) Abe North, the Divers' alcoholic composer friend, was drawn from Lardner, whose death and unfulfilled career Fitzgerald mourned.[61] Rosemary Hoyt was in part inspired by the young actress Lois Moran, whom the Fitzgeralds had met in Hollywood in 1927; the couple quarreled over Fitzgerald's attraction to Moran, who was a star of the 1925 silent movie *Stella Dallas,* on which Rosemary's movie *Daddy's Girl* was based. Tommy Barban was developed from several sources, among them Jozan, polo player and aviator Tommy Hitchcock, and, possibly, Ernest Hemingway.

The Love of the Last Tycoon is set in Hollywood, where Fitzgerald lived and worked between July 1937 and his death in December 1940. The novel's protagonist, Monroe Stahr, was based on the legendary movie producer Irving Thalberg, who was known for his quality movies, who opposed the leftist Screen Writers Guild, and who died young. More important, Stahr also emerged as a kind of wish-fulfillment for Fitzgerald himself: the failed screenwriter projecting himself into the role of movie mogul. This identification is supported by obvious parallels between Stahr's life and Fitzgerald's: Stahr's dead wife,

Minna Davis, reflects Zelda, who was by the late 1930s permanently lost to Fitzgerald, and the producer's new love, Kathleen Moore, is drawn from Sheilah Graham, Fitzgerald's companion in Hollywood. Cecelia Brady, the college girl/Hollywood insider who narrates *The Love of the Last Tycoon*, combined Scottie Fitzgerald with young screenwriter Budd Schulberg, who had been raised in Hollywood. Pat Brady, Cecelia's father and Stahr's duplicitous partner at the studio, was partially based on Louis B. Mayer, Thalberg's boss and competitor at Metro-Goldwyn-Mayer; George Boxley, English novelist turned screenwriter, was drawn from English novelist Aldous Huxley; and many of the other minor characters in the novel had their sources in actual Hollywood figures. Yet, the novel does not develop into a roman à clef since Stahr's personal life is different from Thalberg's and because the action of the novel is invented, not historical fact. It is important to note, also, that Pat Hobby, the protagonist of the seventeen Hollywood stories written by Fitzgerald for *Esquire* in 1939 and 1940, is in no way an autobiographical character. Fitzgerald was never a dishonest, illiterate hack like Hobby.

FITZGERALD AND THE MOVIES

Although Fitzgerald was an unsuccessful screenwriter, he was not, as legend has it, a pathetic, abused victim of the movie industry. During two of his three stays in Hollywood, he was given choice writing assignments and was paid well for his work.[62] That he failed as a screenwriter was largely the result of his fundamental distrust for the medium, which he regarded as a debased alternative to print. He felt that movies sacrificed individual vision by insisting on collaboration among screenwriters, and he was unwilling or unable to collaborate. In his 1936 essay "Pasting It Together" Fitzgerald stated:

> I saw that the novel, which at my maturity was the strongest and supplest medium for conveying thought and emotion from one human being to another, was becoming subordinated to a mechanical and communal art that, whether in the hands of Hollywood merchants or Russian idealists, was capable of reflecting only the tritest thought, the most obvious emotion. It was an art in which words were subordinate to images, where personality was worn down to the inevitable low gear of collaboration. As long past as 1930, I had a hunch that the talkies would make even the best selling novelist as archaic as silent pictures. . . . [T]here was a rankling indignity, that to me had

become almost an obsession, in seeing the power of the written word subordinated to another power, a more glittering, a grosser power. . . .[63]

Fitzgerald's negative attitude undoubtedly affected his screenwriting. In a 26 July 1937 letter to Anne Ober shortly after he began his third and final stay in Hollywood, he confessed that he found the work "hard as hell."[64] Some three years later, in a letter to Maxwell Perkins, he denigrated both screenwriting and his performance as a screenwriter: "I just couldn't make the grade as a hack—that, like everything else, requires a certain practised excellence—."[65] Although Fitzgerald—particularly during his last years in Hollywood—honestly tried to learn the art of screenwriting, he continued to believe that the movie medium was suitable for "none other than children's stories,"[66] as he told Scottie Fitzgerald in a winter 1939 letter. He simply could not master either the theoretical concepts or the idiom of writing for the movies.

Fitzgerald first went to Hollywood in January 1927 to write an original flapper comedy, "Lipstick," for United Artists. He was paid $3,500 in advance money and was to collect $12,500 on acceptance of his script. During their two months in California, the Fitzgeralds led an active social life. As he recalled to Scottie:

Hollywood made a big fuss over us. . . . I honestly believed that with no effort on my part I was a sort of magician with words—an odd delusion on my part when I had worked so desperately hard to develop a hard, colorful prose style.

Total result—a great time + no work. I was to be paid only a small amount unless they made my picture—they didn't.[67]

This brief stay in Hollywood had significant consequences, however, because Fitzgerald met two figures who would prove important to his later novels. Lois Moran, who charmed Fitzgerald and provoked resentment in Zelda, was a young actress who became a model for Rosemary Hoyt in *Tender Is the Night*. Irving Thalberg, who was the "boy genius" head of production at M-G-M and who impressed Fitzgerald "by the shrewdness of what he said—something more than shrewdness—by the largeness of what he thought"[68]—inspired the character Monroe Stahr in *The Love of the Last Tycoon*.

Fitzgerald only reluctantly agreed to his second Hollywood stay in November and December 1931. He and his wife had recently returned to America following Zelda Fitzgerald's discharge from a psychiatric hospital in Switzerland. When Thalberg and M-G-M offered him $1,200 a week to rewrite a screenplay based on Katherine Brush's novel *Red-Headed Woman,* Fitzgerald accepted. In Hollywood he quarreled with his collaborator, Marcel de Sano, and their completed screenplay was rejected as too somber a treatment of a woman who advances herself through sex. Fitzgerald later recalled in his July 1937 letter to Scottie: "I left with the money [$6,000], for this was a contract for weekly payments, but disillusioned and disgusted, vowing never to go back, tho they said it wasn't my fault + asked me to stay. . . . This was later interpreted as 'running out on them' + held against me."[69] During his 1931 stay, he attended a party hosted by Thalberg and his wife, actress Norma Shearer; in the course of the party Fitzgerald got drunk and sang a comic song. He drew on this material for one of his best-known Hollywood stories, "Crazy Sunday."[70]

In the summer of 1937 Fitzgerald again went on the M-G-M payroll. His July 1937 letter to Scottie recorded both his relief at finding a solution to his mounting financial difficulties and his determination to succeed at last in Hollywood: "I feel a certain excitement. The third Hollywood venture. Two failures behind me though one no fault of mine. . . . I want to profit by these two experiences—I must be very tactful but keep my hand on the wheel from the start—find out the key man among the bosses + the most malleable among the collaborators—then fight the rest tooth + nail until, in fact or in effect, I'm alone on the picture. That's the only way I can do my best work. Given a break I can make them double this contract in less than two years."[71] His original contract stipulated $1,000 per week for six months, with an option for an additional year at $1,250 per week—which he received. Among the working notes for *The Love of the Last Tycoon* is Fitzgerald's tongue-in-cheek assessment of the pay scale for screenwriters:

Junior writers $300

Minor poets—$500. a week.

Broken novelists –$850. – $1000.

One play dramatists – $1500.

Sucks –$2000. —Wits– $2500.[72]

Fitzgerald's first assignment under his 1937 M-G-M contract was to polish the screenplay for a college movie, *A Yank at Oxford;* his contributions were not extensive enough to earn him a credit—or listing on-screen as an author of the script—the means by which a movie writer's value is judged. Fitzgerald's only screen credit came with his next and most important assignment for M-G-M, the screenplay for

Three Comrades, Erich Maria Remarque's novel about post–World War I Germany. Fitzgerald expected to work alone, but his early partial draft proved too novelistic. He was then required to collaborate with E. E. Paramore, an experienced screenwriter whom Fitzgerald regarded as a hack and with whom he quarreled. The pair submitted six revisions of their screenplay between November 1937 and February 1938. When Joseph Mankiewicz, their producer, rewrote Fitzgerald's dialogue because the actors complained that their lines were too literary to be convincing, Fitzgerald was outraged and predicted that the movie would flop. Despite his dire predictions, *Three Comrades*—which starred Robert Taylor, Franchot Tone, Robert Young, and Margaret Sullavan—was a popular and critical success, ranking as one of the ten best movies of 1938. During the remainder of the year, Fitzgerald worked on M-G-M screenplays—"Infidelity," *Marie Antoinette, The Women,* and *Madame Curie*—which were either unproduced or reassigned to other writers.

When Fitzgerald's M-G-M contract expired in January 1939, it was not renewed. During his last weeks on the M-G-M payroll, he was loaned to Selznick International, where he briefly worked on *Gone with the Wind.* (He later claimed that he was let go by Selznick because he was unable to make Aunt Pitty sufficiently quaint.) In February 1939 United Artists teamed him with Budd Schulberg on *Winter Carnival,* but Fitzgerald was fired for drunkenness at Dartmouth College, an episode that provided material for Schulberg's 1950 novel *The Disenchanted.* Thereafter Fitzgerald freelanced at several studios—including Paramount, Universal, Goldwyn, and Twentieth Century-Fox—but his screenplays were not produced. His only Hollywood assignment to work on his own material came in 1940, when independent producer Lester Cowan hired him to write a screenplay for "Babylon Revisited." Fitzgerald invented a new plot for his adaptation, which he titled "Cosmopolitan"; although he produced a competent screenplay, he also sacrificed the complexity of his brilliant short story and replaced it with simple melodrama, which he believed was the standard of excellence for Hollywood movies. "Cosmopolitan" was not produced.

Though Fitzgerald never achieved success in the movie studios, the industry treated him well. During his last years in Hollywood, M-G-M kept him on the payroll for eighteen months, enabling him to pay off most of his debts and to provide for himself and his family. After he was let go by M-G-M, he continued to be assigned to quality projects by other major studios. Most important, Hollywood rewarded Fitzgerald in another, more enduring way. He used his experiences in the studios as material for *The Love of the Last Tycoon,* which was about 60 percent written when Fitzgerald died. Even in its incomplete, work-in-progress state, it is regarded as the best of the many Hollywood novels.

MOVIE-WRITING ASSIGNMENTS

This list does not include scenarios and synopses Fitzgerald wrote on speculation. For this material, see the entry on Hollywood in Mary Jo Tate's *F. Scott Fitzgerald A to Z* and the "Movie Projects" section of her primary bibliography.

Grit. Film Guild, 1924. Original story by Fitzgerald, who provided the "source" but did not write the scenario.

"Lipstick." United Artists, 1927. Unproduced. Published in *Fitzgerald/ Hemingway Annual 1978,* pp. 5–33.

Red-Headed Woman. M-G-M, 1931. Fitzgerald's screenplay was rejected.

A Yank at Oxford. M-G-M, 1937. Fitzgerald polished the screenplay but did not receive screen credit.

Three Comrades. M-G-M, 1937–1938. Fitzgerald shared screen credit with E. E. Paramore. Fitzgerald's original version—without Paramore's and Mankiewicz's revisions—has been published. Carbondale & Edwardsville: Southern Illinois University Press, 1978.

"Infidelity." M-G-M, 1938. Unproduced. Published in *Esquire,* 80 (December 1973): 193–200, 290–304.

Marie Antoinette. M-G-M, 1938. Fitzgerald's screenplay was rejected.

The Women. M-G-M, 1938. The screenplay by Fitzgerald and Donald Ogden Stewart was rejected.

Madame Curie. M-G-M, 1938–1939. Fitzgerald's screenplay was rejected.

Gone with the Wind. Selznick International, 1939. Fitzgerald polished the screenplay but did not receive screen credit.

Winter Carnival. United Artists (Walter Wanger), 1939. Fitzgerald worked on the screenplay with Budd Schulberg but was fired.

"Air Raid," Paramount, 1939. Unproduced. Fitzgerald worked on the screenplay with Donald Ogden Stewart.

"Open That Door." Universal, 1939. Unproduced. Fitzgerald worked on the screenplay for one week.

Raffles. Goldwyn, 1939. Fitzgerald worked on the screenplay for one week but did not receive screen credit.

"Cosmopolitan" ("Babylon Revisited"). Columbia (Lester Cowan), 1940. Unproduced. Published as *Babylon Revisited: The Screenplay*, introduction by Schulberg, afterword by Matthew J. Bruccoli. New York: Carroll & Graf, 1993.

Life Begins at Eight-Thirty. Twentieth Century-Fox, 1940. Fitzgerald's screenplay was rejected.

ADAPTATIONS OF FITZGERALD'S WORK

The motion-picture adaptations of Fitzgerald's novels have been disappointing, although the 1962 *Tender Is the Night* and the 1974 *Great Gatsby* were big-budget productions. He was a storyteller with an intensely personal manner. The camera cannot reproduce Fitzgerald's style: his point of view, tone, warmth, and wit.

MOVIES

The Chorus Girl's Romance (based on "Head and Shoulders"), Metro, 1920. Scenario by Percy Heath; directed by William P. Dowlan.

The Husband Hunter (based on "Myra Meets His Family"), Fox, 1920. Scenario by Joseph F. Poland; directed by Howard M. Mitchell.

The Offshore Pirate, Metro, 1921. Directed by Dallas M. Fitzgerald.

The Beautiful and Damned, Warner Brothers, 1922. Adapted by Olga Printzlau; directed by William Seiter.

Conductor 1492 (based on "The Camel's Back"), Warner Brothers, 1924. Story by Johnny Hines; directed by Charles and Frank Hines.

The Great Gatsby (from the Owen Davis play), Famous Players, 1926. Script by Becky Gardiner; adaptation by Elizabeth Meehan; directed by Herbert Brenon.

The Pusher-in-the-Face, Paramount–Famous Players–Lasky, 1928.

The Great Gatsby, Paramount, 1949. Screenplay by Cyril Hume and Richard Maibaum; directed by Elliott Nugent.

The Last Time I Saw Paris (based on "Babylon Revisited"), M-G-M, 1954. Screenplay by Philip G. Epstein, Julius J. Epstein, and Richard Brooks; directed by Brooks.

Tender Is the Night, Twentieth Century-Fox, 1962. Screenplay by Ivan Moffat; directed by Henry King.

The Great Gatsby, Paramount, 1974. Screenplay by Francis Ford Coppola; directed by Jack Clayton.

The Last Tycoon, Paramount, 1976. Screenplay by Harold Pinter; directed by Elia Kazan.

PLAYS

The Great Gatsby, by Owen Davis. An unpublished typescript is at the Library of Congress.

The Young and Beautiful, by Sally Benson (based on the Josephine Perry stories). New York: S. French, 1956.

Three Hours Between Planes, by Elihu Winer. New York: S. French, 1958.

Bernice Bobs Her Hair, by D. D. Brooke. Chicago: The Dramatic Publishing Company, 1982.

TELEVISION PRODUCTIONS

The Great Gatsby, NBC—*Robert Montgomery Presents,* 9 May 1955. Written by Albert Sapinsley.

The Great Gatsby, CBS—*Playhouse 90,* 6 June 1958. Written by David Shaw.

The Last of the Belles, A Herbert Brodkin production, 1974. Written by James Costigan.

Bernice Bobs Her Hair, Learning in Focus, 1977. Written and directed by Joan Micklin Silver.

Tender Is the Night, Showtime/BBC, 1985. Written by Dennis Potter; directed by Robert Knights.

Under the Biltmore Clock (based on "Myra Meets His Family"), American Playhouse, Rubicon Film Productions, 1985. Written by Ilene Cooper and Neal Miller; directed by Miller.

Tales from the Hollywood Hills: Pat Hobby Teamed with Genius (based on several Pat Hobby stories), Zenith Productions/PBS, 1987. Written and directed by Robert C. Thompson.

"The Sensible Thing," Empathy Films/KTEH, San Jose Public Television, 1996. Produced by Elise Robertson and T. Reid Norton; written and directed by Robertson.

BALLET

The Great Gatsby, The Pittsburgh Ballet, premiered 25 April 1996. Scenario and choreography by Bruce Wells; original music by Michael Moricz; scenery and costume design by Peter Farmer.

OPERA

The Great Gatsby, The Metropolitan Opera, premiered 20 December 1999. Words and music by John Harbison; song lyrics by Murray Horwitz. The libretto has been published, New York: Schirmer, 1999.

NOTES

1. For first periodical appearances of stories, poems, essays, reviews, plays, and interviews by F. Scott Fitzgerald, see Matthew J. Bruccoli, *F. Scott Fitzgerald: A Descriptive Bibliography,* revised and augmented edition. Pittsburgh: University of Pittsburgh Press, 1987.

2. For first periodical appearances of articles and stories by Zelda Fitzgerald, see Bruccoli, *F. Scott Fitzgerald: A Descriptive Bibliography.*

3. Fitzgerald, *This Side of Paradise* (New York: Scribners, 1998), p. 25.

4. Ibid., p. 25.

5. Ibid., p. 33.

6. Ibid., p. 66.

7. Ibid., pp. 108–09.

8. Ibid., pp. 217–18.

9. Ibid., p. 269.

10. Ibid., pp. 280–81.

11. Ibid., p. 284.

12. Ibid., p. 285.

13. *The Beautiful and Damned* (New York: Scribners/The Scribner Library, [1964]), pp. 65–66.

14. Ibid., p. 73.

15. Ibid., p. 157.

16. Ibid., p. 255.

17. Ibid., p. 341.

18. Ibid., p. 421.

19. Ibid., p. 449.

20. Fitzgerald, *The Great Gatsby,* preface and notes by Matthew J. Bruccoli (New York: Collier Books-Scribner Classic, 1992), p. 19.

21. Ibid., p. 63.

22. Ibid., p. 70.

23. Ibid., p. 101.

24. Ibid., p. 153.

25. Ibid., p. 153.

26. Ibid., p. 183.

27. Fitzgerald, *Tender Is The Night: A Romance,* text established by Bruccoli (London: Everyman, 1996), p. 40.

28. Ibid., p. 62.

29. Ibid., p. 183.

30. Ibid., p. 212.

31. Ibid., p. 243.

32. Ibid., p. 291.

33. Ibid., p. 294.

34. Ibid., p. 306.

35. Fitzgerald, *The Love of the Last Tycoon: A Western,* edited, with a preface and notes, by Bruccoli (New York: Scribner Paperback Fiction, 1994), p. 20.

36. Ibid., p. 58.

37. Ibid., p. 129.

38. Fitzgerald, *The Short Stories of F. Scott Fitzgerald,* edited, with a preface, by Bruccoli (New York: Scribners, 1989), p. 102.

39. Ibid., p. 189.

40. Ibid., p. 202.

41. Ibid., p. 216.

42. Ibid., p. 318.

43. Ibid., p. 327.

44. Ibid., p. 328.

45. Ibid., p. 346.

46. Ibid., p. 349.

47. H. L. Mencken, *Smart Set,* 62 (August 1920): 140—reprinted in *F. Scott Fitzgerald: The Critical Reception,* edited by Jackson R. Bryer (New York: Burt Franklin, 1978), p. 28; John Black, "A Good First Novel: Vigorous, Amusing and Independent," *Brooklyn Daily Eagle,* 10 April 1920, p. 5 (*Critical Reception,* pp. 8–9); N. B. C., "Old and New Standards in First Novels," *Philadelphia Sunday Press,* 4 April 1920, sec. 2, p. 7 (*Critical Reception,* pp. 6–7); Robert C. Benchley, "Books and Other Things," *New York Morning World,* 21 April 1920, p. 10 (*Critical Reception,* pp. 14–15); Edwin Francis Edgett, "A Young Novelist Defies Tradition," *Boston Evening Transcript,* 12 May 1920, part 3, p. 4 (*Critical Reception,* pp. 21–22); David W. Bailey, "A Novel About Flappers for Philosophers," *Harvard Crimson,* 1 May 1920, p. 3 (*Critical Reception,* pp. 19–20); R. F. McPartlin, "Princeton Scene of Novel—'This Side of Paradise' Is True-to-Life Novel," *Dartmouth,* 24 April 1920, p. 2 (*Critical Reception,* p. 16); Strafford P. Riggs, *Hamilton Literary Magazine,* 55 (November 1920): 53 (*Critical Reception,* p. 31); "With College Men," *New York Times Book Review,* 9 May 1920, p.

240 (*Critical Reception*, p. 21); Heywood Broun, "Paradise and Princeton," *New York Tribune*, 11 April 1920, sec. 7, p. 9 (*Critical Reception*, pp. 9–11); "Youth Will Be Served," *Independent*, 103 (10 July 1920): 53–54 (*Critical Reception*, pp. 27–28); *America*, 23 (29 May 1920): 139 (*Critical Reception*, p. 25).

48. Burton Rascoe, "A Youth in the Saddle," *Chicago Daily Tribune*, 3 April 1920, p. 11 (*Critical Reception*, pp. 3–5); "Reforms and Beginnings," *Nation*, 110 (24 April 1920): 557–558 (*Critical Reception*, pp. 16–17); "Good Afternoon! Have You a Little P.D. in Your Home?" *St. Louis Post-Dispatch*, 1 April 1920, p. 29 (*Critical Reception*, pp. 2–3); Fanny Butcher, *Chicago Sunday Tribune*, 26 September 1920, part 1, p. 9 (*Critical Reception*, pp. 38–39); Broun, "Books," *New York Tribune*, 1 November 1920, p. 10 (*Critical Reception*, pp. 45–46); Sibyl Vane, "Flappers and Philosophers," *Publishers' Weekly*, 98 (18 September 1920): 661–662 (*Critical Reception*, p. 35); "Youth Insurgent," *San Francisco Chronicle*, 23 January 1921, p. 2E (*Critical Reception*, pp. 51–52); "Flappers," *New York Times Book Review and Magazine*, 26 September 1920, p. 24 (*Critical Reception*, pp. 39–40); Mencken, *Smart Set*, 63 (December 1920): 140 (*Critical Reception*, p. 48); "Sic Transit," *Nation*, 111 (18 September 1920): 329–330 (*Critical Reception*, pp. 35–36); C. B., "Fitzgerald's New Book Is Disappointing," *Baltimore Evening Sun*, 23 October 1920, p. 8 (*Critical Reception*, p. 42); I. W. L., "Flappers and Others," *Boston Evening Transcript*, 6 November 1920, part 4, p. 4 (*Critical Reception*, pp. 46–47).

49. Edgett, "The Beautiful and Damned," *Boston Evening Transcript*, 11 March 1922, part 3, p. 10 (*Critical Reception*, pp. 81–82); Carl Van Doren, "The Roving Critic," *Nation*, 114 (15 March 1922): 318 (*Critical Reception*, pp. 92–93); Rascoe, "Novels from the Younger Set," *Bookman*, 55 (May 1922): 304–305 (*Critical Reception*, p. 121); Gilbert Seldes, as Vivian Shaw, "This Side of Innocence," *Dial*, 72 (April 1922): 419–421 (*Critical Reception*, pp. 107–109); Phil A. Kinsley, "Two in Swift Descent on Life's Toboggan," *Philadelphia Record*, 12 March 1922, part 7, p. 7 (*Critical Reception*, pp. 87–89); Harry Hansen, "'The Beautiful and Damned,'" *Chicago Daily News*, 15 March 1922, p. 12 (*Critical Reception*, pp. 90–92); Mencken, "Fitzgerald and Others," *Smart Set*, 67 (April 1922): 140–141 (*Critical Reception*, pp. 106–107); Henry Seidel Canby, "The Flapper's Tragedy," *Literary Review of the New York Evening Post*, 4 March 1922, p. 463 (*Critical Reception*, pp. 63–65); John V. A. Weaver, "Better than 'This Side of Paradise,'" *Brooklyn Daily Eagle*, 4 March 1922, p. 3 (*Critical Reception*, pp. 68–70).

50. "Too Much Fire Water," *Minneapolis Journal*, 10 December 1922, women's sec., p. 12 (*Critical Reception*, pp. 162–63); John Farrar, *New York Herald*, 8 October 1922, sec. 7, pp. 12, 13 (*Critical Reception*, pp. 141–142); Edmund Wilson, "The Jazz King Again," *Vanity Fair*, 19 (November 1922): 24 (*Critical Reception*, pp. 152–153); "F. Scott Fitzgerald Puffs as Jazz Age Outpaces Him," *Philadelphia Evening Public Ledger*, 28 November 1922, p. 30 (*Critical Reception*, p. 157); Stephen Vincent Benét, "Plotting an Author's Curve," *New York Evening Post Literary Review*, 18 November 1922, p. 219 (*Critical Reception*, pp. 155–156); Mencken, *Smart Set*, 71 (July 1923): 141 (*Critical Reception*, p. 163).

51. Paterson, "Up to the Minute," *New York Herald Tribune Books*, 19 April 1925, p. 6 (*Critical Reception*, pp. 200–202); *St. Paul Pioneer Press*, 19 April 1925, sec. 3, p. 7 (*Critical Reception*, p. 203); Mencken, "As H. L. M. Sees It," *Baltimore Evening Sun*, 2 May 1925, p. 9 (*Critical Reception*, pp. 211–214); Laurence Stallings, "The First Reader—Great Scott," *New York World*, 22 April 1925, p. 13 (*Critical Reception*, pp. 203–205); Ruth Hale, "The Paper Knife," *Brooklyn Daily Eagle*, 18 April 1925, p. 5 (*Critical Reception*, p. 197); Harvey Eagleton, "Prophets of the New Age—III. F. Scott Fitzgerald," *Dallas Morning News*, 10 May 1925, part 3, p. 9 (*Critical Reception*, pp. 222–224); Benét, "An Admirable Novel," *Saturday Review of Literature*, 1

(9 May 1925): 739–740 (*Critical Reception*, pp. 219–221); Seldes, "Spring Flight," *Dial*, 79 (August 1925): 162–164 (*Critical Reception*, pp. 239–241).

52. *Dial*, 80 (June 1926): 521 (*Critical Reception*, pp. 274–275); Hansen, "The Boy Grows Older," *Chicago Daily News*, 3 March 1926, p. 16 (*Critical Reception*, pp. 255–256); E. C. Beckwith, "Volume of F. Scott Fitzgerald Stories in Which 'Absolution' Reigns Supreme," *Literary Review of the New York Evening Post*, 13 March 1926, p. 4 (*Critical Reception*, pp. 260–261); "Scott Fitzgerald Turns a Corner," *New York Times Book Review*, 7 March 1926, p. 9 (*Critical Reception*, pp. 257–258); "The Best of His Time," *Bookman*, 63 (May 1926): 348–349 (*Critical Reception*, p. 27).

53. Philip Rahv, "You Can't Duck Hurricane Under a Beach Umbrella," *Daily Worker*, 5 May 1934, p. 7 (*Critical Reception*, pp. 315–317); Horace Gregory, "A Generation Riding to Romantic Death," *New York Herald Tribune Books*, 15 April 1934, p. 5 (*Critical Reception*, pp. 306–308); J. Donald Adams, "Scott Fitzgerald's Return to the Novel," *New York Times Book Review*, 15 April 1934, p. 7 (*Critical Reception*, pp. 304–306); Hal Borland, "'Of Making Many Books—,'" *Philadelphia Public Ledger*, 13 April 1934, p. 9 (*Critical Reception*, pp. 293–294); Clifton Fadiman, "F. Scott Fitzgerald," *New Yorker*, 10 (14 April 1934): 112–115 (*Critical Reception*, pp. 301–303); Canby, "In the Second Era of Demoralization," *Saturday Review of Literature*, 10 (14 April 1934): 630–631 (*Critical Reception*, pp. 300–301); William Troy, "The Worm i' the Bud," *Nation*, 138 (9 May 1934): 539–540 (*Critical Reception*, pp. 318–320); "Scott Fitzgerald Essays Return to Novel Writing," *Milwaukee Journal*, 22 April 1934, sec. 5, p. 3 (*Critical Reception*, pp. 313–315); John Chamberlain, "Books of The Times," *New York Times*, 16 April 1934, p. 15 (*Critical Reception*, pp. 311–312); *Journal of Nervous and Mental Disease*, 82 (July 1935): 115–117 (*Critical Reception*, pp. 331–332); Malcolm Cowley, "Breakdown," *New Republic*, 79 (6 June 1934): 105–106 (*Critical Reception*, pp. 323–325); Cameron Rogers, "Fitzgerald's Novel a Masterpiece," *San Francisco Chronicle*, 15 April 1934, p. 4D (*Critical Reception*, pp. 309–310); Seldes, "True to Type—Scott Fitzgerald Writes Superb Tragic Novel," *New York Evening Journal*, 12 April 1934, p. 23 (*Critical Reception*, pp. 292–293). See also Bruccoli, "*Tender Is the Night* and the Reviewers," *Modern Fiction Studies*, 7 (Spring 1961): 49–54.

54. Elizabeth Hart, "F. Scott Fitzgerald, Looking Backward," *New York Herald Tribune Books*, 31 March 1935, p. 4 (*Critical Reception*, pp. 342–343); Edith H. Walton, "Scott Fitzgerald's Tales," *New York Times Book Review*, 31 March 1935, p. 7 (*Critical Reception*, pp. 344–345); T. S. Matthews, *New Republic*, 82 (10 April 1935): 262 (*Critical Reception*, p. 347); Troy, "The Perfect Life," *Nation*, 140 (17 April 1935): 454–456 (*Critical Reception*, pp. 347–349); Chamberlain, "Books of The Times," *New York Times*, 27 March 1935, p. 19 (*Critical Reception*, pp. 340–342).

55. W. M. R., "Fitzgerald's Tragedy of Hollywood," *Kansas City Star*, 8 November 1941, p. 14 (*Critical Reception*, pp. 364–366); John T. Appleby, "Post-Mortem Findings," *Washington Post*, 16 November 1941, sec. 6, p. 12 (*Critical Reception*, pp. 369–371); Adams, "Scott Fitzgerald's Last Novel," *New York Times Book Review*, 9 November 1941, p. 1 (*Critical Reception*, pp. 366–368); Milton Rugoff, *New York Herald Tribune Books*, 26 October 1941, p. 18 (*Critical Reception*, pp. 356–358); Edward Weeks, *Atlantic Monthly*, 169 (January 1942): [n.pag.] (*Critical Reception*, pp. 377–379); Louis Nicholas, "F. Scott Fitzgerald's Novel an Anatomy of Hollywood," *Philadelphia Record*, 16 November 1941, p. 16M (*Critical Reception*, pp. 371–372); Benét, "Fitzgerald's Unfinished Symphony," *Saturday Review of Literature*, 24 (6 December 1941): 10 (*Critical Reception*, pp. 374–376).

56. Fitzgerald, *The Notebooks of F. Scott Fitzgerald*, edited by Bruccoli (New York: Harcourt Brace Jovanovich/Bruccoli Clark, 1978), p. 1072.

57. Fitzgerald, "One Hundred False Alarms," in *Afternoon of an Author: A Selection of Uncollected Stories and Essays,* introduction and notes by Arthur Mizener (New York: Scribners, 1957), p. 132.

58. Zelda Fitzgerald, "What a 'Flapper Novelist' Thinks of His Wife," *Baltimore Sun,* 7 October 1923; reprinted in *F. Scott Fitzgerald in His Own Time,* edited by Bruccoli and Jackson R. Bryer (Kent, Ohio: Kent State University Press, 1971), p. 259.

59. Fitzgerald, *Correspondence of F. Scott Fitzgerald,* edited by Bruccoli and Margaret M. Duggan (New York: Random House, 1980), p. 600.

60. Scrapbook, Princeton University Library; the clipping is reproduced in *Fitzgerald/Hemingway Annual 1976,* p. 108.

61. See Fitzgerald, "Ring," in *The Crack-Up,* edited by Edmund Wilson (New York: New Directions, 1945), pp. 34–40.

62. For a detailed discussion of Fitzgerald and the movies, see Alan Margolies, "F. Scott Fitzgerald's Work in the Film Studios," *Princeton University Library Chronicle,* 32 (Winter 1971): 81–110.

63. Fitzgerald, "Handle with Care," in *The Crack-Up,* p. 78.

64. Fitzgerald, *As Ever, Scott Fitz—: Letters Between F. Scott Fitzgerald and His Literary Agent Harold Ober, 1919–1940,* edited by Bruccoli, foreword by Scottie Fitzgerald Smith (Philadelphia & New York: Lippincott, 1972), p. 330.

65. Fitzgerald, *F. Scott Fitzgerald: A Life in Letters,* edited by Bruccoli, with Judith S. Baughman (New York: Scribners, 1994), p. 445.

66. Ibid., p. 384.

67. Ibid., p. 330.

68. Fitzgerald, introduction to *The Love of the Last Tycoon: A Western,* edited, with a preface and notes, by Bruccoli (New York: Scribner Paperback Fiction, 1994), p. xviii.

69. Fitzgerald, *A Life in Letters,* p. 330.

70. *The American Mercury,* 27 (October 1932): 209–220.

71. Fitzgerald, *A Life in Letters,* pp. 330–331.

72. Princeton University Library; printed in *The Love of the Last Tycoon,* p. 176.

FITZGERALD ON FITZGERALD
AND ON WRITING

In his novels and short fiction, Fitzgerald wrote artistically transformed autobiography. His correspondence, *Ledger,* and *Notebooks* were more overtly autobiographical, the work of a self-historiographer who painstakingly documented his life, opinions, and work. Fitzgerald's personal essays, notably those posthumously collected in *The Crack-Up,* analyze his experience and career in terms of his American identity. He saw himself as a representative or exemplary American figure: as a participant in and storyteller about his times. Fitzgerald's comments on his life and on the profession of authorship reveal his commitment both to honest self-exploration and to the art of fiction.

From the *Ledger* for September 1918–August 1919

The most important year of life. Every emotion and my life work decided. Miserable and exstatic but a great success.[1]

From a letter to Maxwell Perkins, 18 September 1919

Of course I was delighted to get your letter and I've been in a sort of trance all day; not that I doubted you'd take it[2] but at last I have something to show people. It has enough advertisement in St. Paul already to sell several thousand copies + I think Princeton will buy it (I've been a periodical, local Great-Expectations for some time in both places.)

Terms ect I leave to you but one thing I can't relinquish without at least a slight struggle. Would it be utterly impossible for you to publish the book Xmas—or say by February? I have so many things dependent on its success—including of course a girl[3]—not that I expect it to make me a fortune but it will have a psychological effect on me and all my surroundings and besides open up new fields. I'm in that stage where every month counts

Monthly	Expenditure	1923		
TAXES	200.00			
RENT	300.00	TRIPS, PLEASURE + PARTIES		
FOOD	200.00	HOUSE LIQUOR	80 00	(apportioned per 1 m
COAL+WOOD	35 00	PLAZA	26 50	"
ICE	8 50	ALABAMA	133 00	"
GAS	27 00	ATLANTIC CITY	10 00	"
LIGHT	14 50	THEATRE	20 00	"
PHONE	25 00	BARBER	10 00	"
WATER	5 00	HAIR DRESSING	15 00	"
		CHARITY	4 00	"
SERVANTS	295.00	WILD PARTIES	100 00	"
		Taxis	15 00	
DOCTORS	42 50	Gambling	33 00	"
DRUG STORE	32 50	LUNCHES (N.Y)	25 00	"
CLUB	105 50	SUBWAY (ect)	29 00	"
		Miscellaneous Cash	276 00	"
NEWSPAPERS	5 00			
BOOKS	14 50	MISS		
FLOWERS	9 00			
AUTO	23 00			
PLUMBER	13 50			
ELECTRIC	1 50			
COMUTATION	4 00			
SCOTT'S CLOTHES	33 00			
Zelda's CLOTHES	100 00			
BABY'S CLOTHES	25 00			
HOUSEHOLD	81 00		785 60	
AND MISSCLFINEUS			1620.40	
CHARGES	12 00			
TYPING	1620.40		2396.00	

Fitzgerald attempted to manage his money by recording his monthly expenses, which, in 1923, included not only "WILD PARTIES" but also the faint notation "MISSING $1000.00" (Matthew J. and Arlyn Bruccoli Collection of F. Scott Fitzgerald, Thomas Cooper Library, University of South Carolina)

frantically and seems a cudgel in a fight for happiness against time. Will you let me know more exactly how that difference in time of publication influences the sale + what you mean by "early Spring"?[4]

From "The Author's Apology," 1920

I don't want to talk about myself because I'll admit I did that somewhat in this book. In fact, to write it took three months; to conceive it—three minutes; to collect the data in it—all my life. The idea of writing it came on the first of last July: it was a substitute form of dissipation.[5]

My whole theory of writing I can sum up in one sentence. An author ought to write for the youth of his own generation, the critics of the next, and the schoolmasters of ever afterward.[6]

From "Contemporary Writers and Their Work, a Series of Autobiographical Letters—F. Scott Fitzgerald," 1920

. . . I felt I could work out a tale ["The Ice Palace"] about some person or group of persons of Anglo-Saxon birth living for generations in a very cold climate. I already had one atmosphere detail—the first wisps of snow weaving like advance-guard ghosts up the street.

At the end of two weeks I was in Montgomery, Alabama, and while out walking with a girl[7] I wandered into a graveyard. She told me I could never understand how she felt about the Confederate graves, and I told her I understood so well that I could put it on paper. Next day on my way back to St. Paul it came to me that it was all one story—the contrast between Alabama and Minnesota. When I reached home I had

(1) The idea of this contrast.

(2) The natural sequence of the girl visiting in the north.

(3) The idea that some phase of the cold should prey on her mind.

(4) That this phase should be an ice palace—I had the idea of using an ice palace in a story since several months before when my mother told me about one they had in St. Paul in the eighties.

(5) A detail about snow in the vestibule of a railway train.[8]

From "Who's Who—and Why," 1920

The history of my life is the history of the struggle between an overwhelming urge to write and a combination of circumstances bent on keeping me from it.

When I lived in St. Paul and was about twelve I wrote all through every class in school in the back of my geography book and first year Latin and on the margins of themes and declensions and mathematics problems. Two years later a family congress decided that the only way to force me to study was to send me to boarding school. This was a mistake. It took my mind off my writing. I decided to play football, to smoke, to go to college, to do all sorts of irrelevant things that had nothing to do with the real business of life, which, of course, was the proper mixture of description and dialogue in the short story.

· · ·

Near the end of my last year at school I came across a new musical-comedy score lying on top of the piano. It was a show called *His Honor the Sultan,* and the title furnished the information that it had been presented by the Triangle Club of Princeton University.

That was enough for me. From then on the university question was settled. I was bound for Princeton.

I spent my entire Freshman year writing an operetta for the Triangle Club. To do this I failed in algebra, trigonometry, coördinate geometry and hygiene. . . .

The next year, 1916–17, found me back in college, but by this time I had decided that poetry was the only thing worth while, so with my head ringing with the meters of Swinburne and the matters of Rupert Brooke[9] I spent the spring doing sonnets, ballads and rondels into the small hours. I had read somewhere that every great poet had written great poetry before he was twenty-one. I had only a year and, besides, war was impending. I must publish a book of startling verse before I was engulfed.

By autumn I was in an infantry officers' training camp at Fort Leavenworth, with poetry in the discard and a brand-new ambition—I was writing an immortal novel. Every evening, concealing my pad behind *Small Problems for Infantry,*[10] I wrote paragraph after paragraph on a somewhat edited history of me and my imagination. The outline of twenty-two chapters, four of them in verse, was made, two chapters were completed; and then I was detected and the game was up. I could write no more during study period.

This was a distinct complication. I had only three months to live—in those days all infantry officers thought they had only three months to live—and I had left no mark on the world. But such consuming ambition was not to be thwarted by a mere war. Every Saturday at one o'clock when the week's work was over I hurried to the Officers' Club, and there, in a corner of a roomful of smoke, conversation and rattling newspapers, I wrote a one-hundred-and-twenty-thousand-word novel on the consecutive week-ends of three months. There was no revising; there was no time for it. As I finished each chapter I sent it to a typist in Princeton.

Meanwhile I lived in its smeary pencil pages. The drills, marches, and *Small Problems for Infantry* were a shadowy dream. My whole heart was concentrated upon my book. . . .[11]

"In his final conception of the genteel romantic hero, Fitzgerald demonstrated with greater clarity and depth than ever before why, in no small way, he was an original. In the genteel American literature of Fitzgerald's youth, the romantic hero devoted his talents to the plutocrats, to the class that ruled because of wealth. Fitzgerald tore this figure down and in his major novels re-created him. His romantic heroes, resembling the genteel stereotype in all outward aspects, gave their loyalties to an aristocratic sense of virtue that seemed once to have existed in an older America. They were visionaries of a moral order that the American past made available to them, even if an imaginary one; and the tragedy and pathos of their individual lives bound them essentially to the nation's destiny."

Robert Sklar

From *F. Scott Fitzgerald: The Last Laocoön* (New York: Oxford University Press, 1967), p. 341.

From "What I Was Advised to Do—and Didn't," 1922

"Good morning, Mr. Fitzgerald," said the man with horn-rimmed spectacles, "I was asked to come down to the copy department and speak to you about writing. I understand that you received $30 for a story.[12] Now I have had five stories in the *Saturday Evening Post* during the last ten years and I know the game from A to Z. There's nothing in it. It's all right for picking up a little spare cash, but as for making a living at it, it won't do. You're dreaming. It would take ten years before you'd even begin to get a start. In the meanwhile, you'd starve. Take my advice, give up writing and stay at your job."

I didn't![13]

From a letter to Maxwell Perkins, mid July 1922

. . . I want to write something <u>new</u>—something extraordinary and beautiful and simple + intricately patterned.[14]

From a letter to Maxwell Perkins, ca. 10 April 1924

. . . While I have every hope + plan of finishing my novel in June you know how those things often come out.[15] And even if it takes me 10 times that long I cannot let it go out unless it has the very best I'm capable of in it or even as I feel sometimes, something better than I'm capable of. Much of what I wrote last summer was good but it was so interrupted that it was ragged + in approaching it from a new angle I've had to discard a lot of it—in one case 18,000 words (part of which will appear in the Mercury as a short story).[16] It is only in the last four months that I've realized how much I've—well, almost <u>deteriorated</u> in the three years since I finished the Beautiful and Damned. The last four months of course I've worked but in the two years—over two years—before that, I produced exactly <u>one</u> play, <u>half a dozen</u> short stories and three or four articles—an average of about <u>one hundred</u> words a day. If I'd spent this time reading or travelling or doing anything—even staying healthy—it'd be different but I spent it uselessly, niether in study nor in contemplation but only in drinking and raising hell generally. If I'd written the B. + D. at the rate of 100 words a day it would have taken me <u>4 years</u> so you can imagine the moral effect the whole chasm had on me.

. . .

I feel I have an enormous power in me now, more than I've ever had in a way but it works so fitfully and with so many bogeys because I've <u>talked so much</u> and not lived enough within myself to delelop the nessessary self reliance. Also I don't know anyone who has used up so [torn]sonel experience as I have at 27. Copperfield[17] + Pendennis[18] were written at past forty while This Side of Paradise was three books + the B. + D. was two. So in my new novel I'm thrown directly on purely creative work—not trashy imaginings as in my stories but the sustained imagination of a sincere and yet radiant world. So I tread slowly and carefully + at times in considerable distress. The book will be a consciously artistic achievment + must depend on that as the 1st books did not.

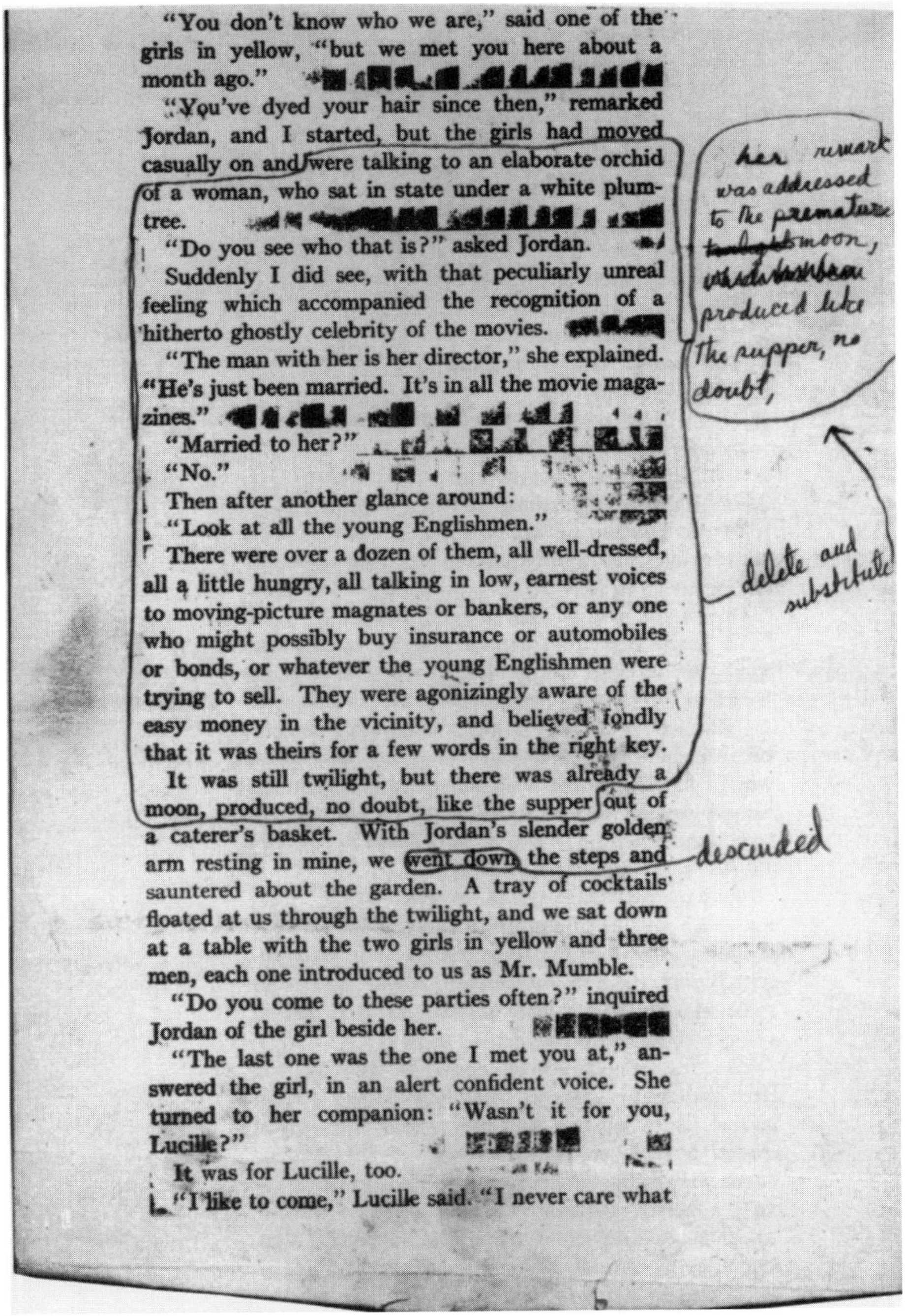

"You don't know who we are," said one of the girls in yellow, "but we met you here about a month ago."

"You've dyed your hair since then," remarked Jordan, and I started, but the girls had moved casually on and were talking to an elaborate orchid of a woman, who sat in state under a white plum-tree.

"Do you see who that is?" asked Jordan.

Suddenly I did see, with that peculiarly unreal feeling which accompanied the recognition of a hitherto ghostly celebrity of the movies.

"The man with her is her director," she explained. "He's just been married. It's in all the movie magazines."

"Married to her?"

"No."

Then after another glance around:

"Look at all the young Englishmen."

There were over a dozen of them, all well-dressed, all a little hungry, all talking in low, earnest voices to moving-picture magnates or bankers, or any one who might possibly buy insurance or automobiles or bonds, or whatever the young Englishmen were trying to sell. They were agonizingly aware of the easy money in the vicinity, and believed fondly that it was theirs for a few words in the right key.

It was still twilight, but there was already a moon, produced, no doubt, like the supper out of a caterer's basket. With Jordan's slender golden arm resting in mine, we went down the steps and sauntered about the garden. A tray of cocktails floated at us through the twilight, and we sat down at a table with the two girls in yellow and three men, each one introduced to us as Mr. Mumble.

"Do you come to these parties often?" inquired Jordan of the girl beside her.

"The last one was the one I met you at," answered the girl, in an alert confident voice. She turned to her companion: "Wasn't it for you, Lucille?"

It was for Lucille, too.

"I like to come," Lucille said. "I never care what

her remark was addressed to the premature ~~twilight~~ moon, produced like the supper, no doubt,
delete and substitute
descended

Fitzgerald's revising and rewriting of the novel in galleys made *The Great Gatsby* a masterpiece.

If I ever win the right to any liesure again I will assuredly not waste it as I wasted this past time. Please believe me when I say that now I'm doing the best I can.[19]

From a letter to Maxwell Perkins, ca. 24 April 1925

In all events I have a book of good stories for the fall.[20] Now I shall write some cheap ones until I've accumulated enough for my my next novel. When that is finished and published I'll wait and see. If it will support me with no more intervals of trash I'll go on as a novelist. If not I'm going to quit, come home, go to Hollywood and learn the movie business. I can't reduce our scale of living and I can't stand this financial insecurity. Anyhow there's no point in trying to be an artist if you can't do your best. I had my chance back in 1920 to start my life on a sensible scale and I lost it and so I'll have to pay the penalty. Then perhaps at 40 I can start writing again without this constant worry and interruption.[21]

From a letter to H. L. Mencken, 4 May 1925

I think the book[22] is so far a commercial failure—at least it was two weeks after publication—hadn't reached 20,000 yet. So I rather regret (but not violently) the fact that I turned down $15,000.00 for the serial rights. However I have all the money I need and was growing rather tired of being a popular author. My trash for the Post grows worse and worse as there is less and less heart in it—strange to say my whole heart was in my first trash. I thought that the <u>Offshore Pirate</u> was quite as good as <u>Benediction</u>.[23] I never really "wrote down" until after the failure of the <u>Vegetable</u> and that was to make this book possible. I would have written down long ago if it had been profitable—I tried it unsuccessfully for the movies. People don't seem to realize that for an intelligent man writing down is about the hardest thing in the world. . . .[24]

From a letter to Maxwell Perkins, ca. 22 May 1925

. . . I think all the reviews[25] I've seen, except two, have been absolutely stupid and lowsy. Some day they'll eat grass, by God! This thing, both the effort and the result have hardened me and I think now that I'm much better than any of the young Americans without exception.[26]

From a letter to Maxwell Perkins, ca. 27 December 1925

I write to you from the depths of one of my unholy depressions. The book[27] is wonderful—I honestly think that when its published I shall be the best American novelist (which isn't saying a lot) but the end seems far away. When its finished I'm coming home for awhile anyhow though the thought revolts me as much as the thought of remaining in France. I wish I were twenty-two again with only my dramatic and feverishly enjoyed miseries. You remember I used to say I wanted to die at thirty— well, I'm now twenty-nine and the prospect is still welcome. My work is the only thing that makes me happy—except to be a little tight—and for those two indulgences I pay a big price in mental and physical hangovers.[28]

From a letter to Harold Ober, received 13 May 1930

. . . I know you're losing faith in me + Max too but God knows one has to rely in the end on one's own judgement. I could have published four lowsy, half baked books in the last five years + people would have thought I was at least a worthy young man not drinking myself to pieces in the south seas—but I'd be dead as Michael Arlen,[29] Bromfield,[30] Tom Boyd,[31] Callaghan[32] + the others who think they can trick the world with the hurried and the second rate. These Post stories in the Post are at least not any spot on me—they're honest and if their form is stereotyped people know what to expect when they pick up the Post. The novel is another thing—if, after four years I published the Basil Lee stories as a book I might as well get tickets for Hollywood immediately.[33]

From a letter to Maxwell Perkins, ca. 30 April 1932

. . . If you like it[34] please don't wire her [Zelda Fitzgerald] congratulations, and please keep whatever praise you may see fit to give on the staid side—I mean, as you naturally would, rather than yield to a tendency one has with invalids to be extra nice to cheer them up. This seems a nuance but it is rather important at present to the doctors that Zelda does not feel that the acceptance (always granted you like it) means immediate fame and money. I'm afraid all our critical tendencies in the last decade got bullish; we discovered one Hemingway to a dozen Callaghans and Caldwells[35] (I think the latter is a washout) + probably created a lot of spoiled geniuses who might have been good workmen. Not that I regret it—if the last five years uncovered Ernest,[36] Tom Wolfe + Faulkner[37] it would have been worth while, but I'm not certain enough of Zelda's present stability of character to expose her to any superlatives. If she has a success coming she must associate it with work done in a workmanlike manner for its own sake, + part of it done fatigued and uninspired, and part of it done when even to remember the original inspiration and impetus is a psychological trick. She is not twenty-one and she is not strong, and she must not try to follow the pattern of my trail which is of course blazed distinctly on her mind.[38]

From a letter to Maxwell Perkins, 19 January 1933

. . . Am going on the water-wagon from the first of February to the first of April but don't tell Ernest because he has long convinced himself that I am an incurable alcoholic, due to the fact that we almost always meet on parties. I am <u>his</u> alcoholic just like Ring[39] is mine and do not want to disillusion him, tho even Post stories must be done in a state of sobriety. . . .[40]

From "One Hundred False Starts," 1933

I am thirty-six years old. For eighteen years, save for a short space during the war, writing has been my chief interest in life, and I am in every sense a professional.[41]

From the *Ledger* for September 1933–September 1934

<u>Zelda breaks, the novel finished. Hard times begin for me, slow but sure. Ill Health Throughout</u>[42]

From a letter to Egbert S. Oliver,[43] 7 January 1934

The first help I ever had in writing in my life was from my father who read an utterly imitative Sherlock Holmes story of mine and pretended to like it.[44]

But after that I received the most invaluable aid from one Mr. C. N. B. Wheeler then headmaster of the St. Paul Academy now the St. Paul Country Day School in St. Paul, Minnesota. 2. From Mr. Hume, the co-headmaster of the Newman School and now headmaster of the Canterbury School. 3. From Courtland Van Winkle in freshman year at Princeton—now professor of literature at Yale (he gave us the book of Job to read and I don't think any of our preceptorial group ever quite recovered from it.) After that comes a lapse. Most of the professors seemed to me old and uninspired, or perhaps it was just that I was getting under way in my own field.[45]

From a letter to Maxwell Perkins, 4 March 1934

. . . After all, Max, I am a plodder. One time I had a talk with Ernest Hemingway, and I told him, against all the logic that was then current, that I was the tortoise and he was the hare, and that's the truth of the matter, that everything that I have ever attained has been through long and persistent struggle while it is Ernest who has a touch of genius which enables him to bring off extraordinary things with facility. I have no facility. I have a facility for being cheap, if I wanted to indulge that. I can do cheap things. I changed Clark Gable's act at the moving picture theatre here the other day. I can do that kind of thing as quickly as anybody but when I decided to be a serious man, I tried to struggle over every point until I have made myself into a slow-moving behemoth (if that is the correct spelling), and so there I am for the rest of my life. . . . [46]

From a letter to H. L. Mencken, 23 April 1934

. . . I would rather impress my image (even though an image the size of a nickel) upon the soul of a people than be known,

"Jubal the impossible came up with an air of possession, and Basil's heart went bobbing off around the ballroom in a pink silk dress. Lost again in a fog of indecision, he walked out on the veranda. There was a flurry of premature snow in the air and the stars looked cold. Staring up at them he saw that they were his stars as always—symbols of ambition, struggle and glory. The wind blew through them, trumpeting that high white note for which he always listened, and the thin-blown clouds, stripped for battle, passed in review. The scene was of an unparalleled brightness and magnificence, and only the practiced eye of the commander saw that one star was no longer there."

F. Scott Fitzgerald

An example of Fitzgerald's stylistic versatility from "Basil and Cleopatra" (1929), in *The Short Stories of F. Scott Fitzgerald,* edited, with a preface, by Matthew J. Bruccoli (New York: Scribners, 1989), pp. 447–448.

except in so far as I have my natural obligation to my family—to provide for them. I would as soon be as anonymous as Rimbaud,[47] if I could feel that I had accomplished that purpose—and that is no sentimental yapping about being disinterested. It is simply that having once found the intensity of art, nothing else that can happen in life can ever again seem as important as the creative process.[48]

From a letter to Ernest Hemingway, 1 June 1934

To go back to my theme song, the second technical point that might be of interest to you concerns direct steals from an idea of yours, an idea of Conrad's and a few lines out of David-into-Fox-Garnett.[49] The theory back of it I got from Conrad's preface to The Nigger,[50] that the purpose of a work of fiction is to appeal to the lingering after-effects in the reader's mind as differing from, say, the purpose of oratory or philosophy which leave respectively leave people in a fighting or thoughtful mood. . . . I imitated it [the dying fall in Garnett's book] as accurately as it is humanly decent in my own ending of Tender, telling the reader in the last pages that, after all, this is just a casual event, and trying to let him come to bat for me rather than going out to shake his nerves, whoop him up, then leaving him rather in a condition of a frustrated woman in bed. . . .[51]

From a letter to Maxwell Perkins, 11 March 1935

. . . It has become increasingly plain to me that the very excellent organization of a long book or the finest perceptions and judgment in time of revision do not go well with liquor. A short story can be written on a bottle, but for a novel you need the mental speed that enables you to keep the whole pattern in your head and ruthlessly sacrifice the sideshows as Ernest did in "A Farewell to Arms." If a mind is slowed up ever so little it lives in the individual part of a book rather than in a book as a whole; memory is dulled. I would give anything if I hadn't had to write Part III of "Tender is the Night" entirely on stimulant. If I had one more crack at it cold sober I believe it might have made a great difference. Even Ernest commented on sections that were needlessly included and as an artist he is as near as I know for a final reference. . . .[52]

Statement on Huckleberry Finn, 30 November 1935

Huckleberry Finn took the first journey <u>back</u>. He was the first to look <u>back</u> at the republic from the perspective of the west. His eyes were the first eyes that ever looked at us objectively that were not eyes from overseas. There were mountains at the frontier but he wanted more than mountains to look at with his restless eyes—he wanted to find out about men and how they lived together. And because he turned back we have him forever.[53]

From "The Crack-Up," 1936

. . . It seemed a romantic business to be a successful literary man—you were not ever going to be as famous as a movie star but what note you had was probably longer-lived—you were never going to have the power of a man of strong political or religious convictions but you were certainly more independent. Of course within the practice of your trade you were forever unsatisfied—but I, for one, would not have chosen any other.[54]

From "Pasting It Together," 1936

. . . in a real dark night of the soul it is always three o'clock in the morning, day after day. . . .[55]

From "Early Success," 1937

The compensation of a very early success is a conviction that life is a romantic matter. In the best sense one stays young. When the primary objects of love and money could be taken for granted and a shaky eminence had lost its fascination, I had fair years to waste, years that I can't honestly regret, in seeking the eternal Carnival by the Sea. Once in the middle twenties I was driving along the High Corniche Road through the twilight with the whole French Riviera twinkling on the sea below. As far ahead as I could see was Monte Carlo, and though it was out of season and there were no Grand Dukes left to gamble and E. Phillips Oppenheim[56] was a fat industrious man in my hotel, who lived in a bathrobe—the very name was so incorrigibly enchanting that I could only stop the car and like the Chinese whisper: "Ah me! Ah me!" It was not Monte Carlo I was looking at. It was back into the mind of the young man with cardboard soles who had walked the streets of New York. I was him again—for an instant I had the good fortune to share his dreams, I who had no more dreams of my own. And there are still times when I creep up on him, surprise him on an autumn morning in New York or a spring night in Carolina when it is so quiet that you can hear a dog barking in the next county. But never again as during that all too short period when he and I were one person, when the fulfilled future and the wistful past were mingled in a single gorgeous moment—when life was literally a dream.[57]

From a letter to Scottie Fitzgerald, Spring 1938

About <u>adjectives</u>: all fine prose is based on the verbs carrying the sentences. They make sentences move. Probably the finest technical poem in English is Keats' <u>Eve of Saint Agnes</u>. A line like:

The Hare limped trembling through the frozen grass, is so alive that you race through it, scarcely noticing it, yet it has colored the whole poem with its movement—the limping, trembling, and freezing is going on before your own eyes. . . .[58]

From a letter to Kenneth Littauer,[59] late July? 1939

Here's another Hollywood story.[60] It is absolutely true to Hollywood as I see it. Asking you to read it I want to get two things clear. First, that it isn't particularly likely that I'll write a great many more stories about young love. I was tagged with that by my first writings up to 1925. Since then I have written stories about young love. They have been done with increasing difficulty and increasing insincerity. I would either be a miracle man or a hack if I could go on turning out an identical product for three decades.

I know that is what's expected of me, but in that direction the well is pretty dry and I think I am much wiser in not trying to strain for it but rather to open up a new well, a new vein. You see, I not only announced the birth of my young illusions in "This Side of Paradise" but pretty much the death of them in some of my last <u>Post</u> stories like "Babylon Revisited." Lorrimer[61] seemed to understand this in a way. Nevertheless, an overwhelming number of editors continue to associate me with an absorbing interest in young girls—an interest that at my age would probably land me behind the bars.[62]

From a letter to Zelda Fitzgerald, 18 May 1940

It's hard to explain about the Saturday Evening Post matter. It isn't that I haven't tried, but the trouble with them goes back to the time of Lorimer's retirement in 1935. I wrote them three stories that year and sent them about three others which they didn't like. The last story they bought they published last in the issue and my friend, Adelaide Neil on the staff, implied to me that they didn't want to pay that big price for stories unless they could use them in the beginning of the issue. . . .

As you should know from your own attempts, high priced commercial writing for the magazines is a very definite trick. The rather special things that I brought to it, the intelligence and the good writing and even the radicalism all appealed to old Lorimer who had been a writer himself and liked style. The man who runs the magazine now[63] is an up and coming young Republican who gives not a damn about literature and who publishes almost nothing except escape stories about the brave frontiersmen, etc., or fishing, or football captains—nothing that would even faintly shock or disturb the reactionary bourgeois. Well, I simply can't do it and, as I say, I've tried not once but twenty times.

As soon as I feel I am writing to a cheap specification my pen freezes and my talent vanishes over the hill and I honestly don't blame them for not taking the things that I've offered to them from time to time in the past three or four years. An explanation of their new attitude is that you no longer have a chance of selling a story with an unhappy ending (in the old days many of mine <u>did</u> have unhappy endings—if you remember.) In fact the standard of writing from the best movies, like Rebecca,[64] is, believe it or not, much higher at present than that in the commercial magazines such as Colliers and the Post.[65]

From a letter to Maxwell Perkins, 20 May 1940

Professionally, I know, the next move must come from me. Would the 25 cent press keep <u>Gatsby</u> in the public eye—or <u>is the book unpopular</u>. Has it <u>had</u> its chance? Would a popular reissue in that series with a preface <u>not</u> by me but by one of its admirers—I can maybe pick one—make it a favorite with class rooms, profs, lovers of English prose—anybody. But to die, so completely and unjustly after having given so much. Even now there is little published in American fiction that doesn't slightly bare my stamp—in a <u>small</u> way I was an original. . . .[66]

From a letter to Scottie Fitzgerald, 5 October 1940

. . . Once one is caught up into the material world not one person in ten thousand finds the time to form literary taste, to examine the validity of philosophic concepts for himself, or to form what, for lack of a better phrase, I might call the wise and tragic sense of life.

By this I mean the thing that lies behind all great careers, from Shakespeare's to Abraham Lincoln's, and as far back as there are books to read—the sense that life is essentially a cheat and its conditions are those of defeat, and that the redeeming things are not "happiness and pleasure" but the deeper satisfactions that come out of struggle. Having learned this in theory from the lives and conclusions of great men, you can get a hell of a lot more enjoyment out of whatever bright things come your way.[67]

From *The Love of the Last Tycoon,* 1941

Schwartze looked toward me as toward a jury.

"There's a writer for you," he said. "Knows everything and at the same time he knows nothing."

"What's that?" said Wylie, indignant.

It was my first inkling that he was a writer. And while I like writers—because if you ask a writer anything you usually get an answer—still it belittled him in my eyes. Writers aren't people exactly. Or, if they're any good, they're a whole *lot* of people trying so hard to be one person. It's like actors, who try so pathetically not to look in mirrors. Who lean *back*ward trying—only to see their faces in the reflecting chandeliers.[68]

From *The Notebooks of F. Scott Fitzgerald,* 1978

You don't write because you want to say something; you write because you've got something to say. (#330)

Genius is the ability to put into effect what is in your mind. There's no other definition of it. (#332)

Books are like brothers. I am an only child. Gatsby my imaginary eldest brother, Amory my younger, Anthony my worry. Dick my comparatively good brother but all of them far from home. When I have the courage to put the old white light on the home of my heart, then— (#1025)

There never was a good biography of a good novelist. There couldn't be. He is too many people if he's any good. (#1037)

My sometimes reading my own books for advice. How much I know sometimes—how little at others. (#1275)

I didn't have the two top things—great animal magnetism or money. I had the two second things, tho', good looks and intelligence. So I always got the top girl. (#1378)

In a short story, you have only so much money to buy just one costume. Not the parts of many. One mistake in the shoes or tie, and you're gone. (#1765)

As a novelist I reach out to the end of all man's variance, all man's villainy—as a man I do not go that far. I cannot claim honor—but even the knights of the Holy Grail were only striving for it, as I remember. (#1973)

The purpose of a fiction story is to create passionate curiosity and then to gratify it unexpectedly, orgasmically. Isn't that what we expect from all contacts? (#2038)

I want to write scenes that are frightening and inimitable. I don't want to be as intelligible to my contemporaries as Ernest who as Gertrude Stein said, is bound for the Museums.[69] I am sure I am far enough ahead to have some small immortality if I can keep well. (#2068)

NOTES

1. F. Scott Fitzgerald, *F. Scott Fitzgerald's Ledger: A Facsimile,* introduction by Matthew J. Bruccoli (Washington, D.C.: NCR Microcard Editions, 1972), p. 173.

2. *This Side of Paradise.*

3. Fitzgerald and Zelda Sayre were married eight days after the publication of *This Side of Paradise.*

4. Fitzgerald, *F. Scott Fitzgerald: A Life in Letters,* edited by Bruccoli with Judith S. Baughman (New York: Scribners, 1994), p. 32.

5. Enforcement of Prohibition had begun on 1 July 1919.

6. Statement inserted in copies of *This Side of Paradise* distributed at a meeting of the American Booksellers Association; *F. Scott Fitzgerald In His Own Time*, edited by Bruccoli and Jackson R. Bryer (Kent, Ohio: Kent State University, 1971), p. 164.

7. Zelda Sayre.

8. "Contemporary Writers and Their Work, a Series of Autobiographical Letters—F. Scott Fitzgerald," *Editor*, 53 (Second July Number 1920): 121–122; reprinted in *F. Scott Fitzgerald on Authorship*, edited by Bruccoli with Baughman (Columbia: University of South Carolina Press, 1996), p. 36.

9. English poet (1887–1915) who died in World War I; Fitzgerald drew the title of *This Side of Paradise* from Brooke's "Tiare Tahiti" (1914): "Well this side of Paradise! . . . / There's little comfort in the wise."

10. This 1917 textbook by Alfred William Bjornstad was used in officer training classes.

11. "Who's Who—and Why," *Saturday Evening Post*, 193 (18 September 1920): 42, 61; reprinted in *F. Scott Fitzgerald on Authorship*, pp. 38–39.

12. "Babes in the Woods," Fitzgerald's first story sold to a magazine; it was published in the September 1919 issue of *The Smart Set*.

13. "What I Was Advised to Do—and Didn't," *Philadelphia Public Ledger*, 22 April 1922, p. 11; reprinted in *F. Scott Fitzgerald In His Own Time*, p. 166.

14. Fitzgerald, *A Life in Letters*, [iv]; he was beginning to work on the novel that would develop into *The Great Gatsby*.

15. *The Great Gatsby* was completed in summer 1924.

16. "Absolution" (June 1924).

17. *David Copperfield* (1850), by Charles Dickens.

18. *Pendennis* (1850), by William Makepeace Thackeray.

19. Fitzgerald, *A Life in Letters*, pp. 65, 67.

20. *All the Sad Young Men* was published in February 1926.

21. Fitzgerald, *A Life in Letters*, p. 107.

22. *The Great Gatsby* was published in April 1925.

23. "The Offshore Pirate" had been published in the 29 May 1920 *Saturday Evening Post* and "Benediction" in the February 1920 *Smart Set*, edited by H. L. Mencken; both were collected in *Flappers and Philosophers* (1920).

24. Fitzgerald, *A Life in Letters*, p. 111.

25. Reviews of *The Great Gatsby*.

26. Fitzgerald, *A Life in Letters*, p. 113.

27. Fitzgerald was beginning work on the novel that became *Tender Is the Night*.

28. Fitzgerald, *A Life in Letters*, p. 131.

29. British novelist chiefly remembered for his best-selling novel *The Green Hat* (1924).

30. Louis Bromfield, American novelist.

31. St. Paul novelist whom Fitzgerald brought to Scribners.

32. Morley Callaghan, Canadian novelist published by Scribners.

33. Fitzgerald, *A Life in Letters,* p. 182–83.

34. Zelda Fitzgerald's novel, *Save Me the Waltz* (1932).

35. American novelist Erskine Caldwell, two of whose books were published by Scribners.

36. Ernest Hemingway.

37. American novelist William Faulkner.

38. Fitzgerald, *A Life in Letters,* p. 217.

39. Ring Lardner.

40. Fitzgerald, *A Life in Letters,* p. 226.

41. "One Hundred False Starts," *Saturday Evening Post,* 205 (4 March 1933): 13, 65–66; reprinted in Fitzgerald, *Afternoon of an Author,* edited by Arthur Mizener (New York: Scribners, 1957), p. 131.

42. Fitzgerald, *Ledger,* p. 188.

43. Of Willamette University, Salem, Oregon.

44. Probably "The Mystery of the Raymond Mortgage," *St. Paul Academy Now and Then* (February 1910).

45. Fitzgerald, *A Life in Letters,* p. 243.

46. Ibid., pp. 248–249.

47. Nineteenth-century French symbolist poet.

48. Fitzgerald, *A Life in Letters,* p. 256.

49. British novelist David Garnett, whose best-known work was *Lady into Fox* (1922).

50. *The Nigger of the "Narcissus,"* Conrad's 1898 novel.

51. Fitzgerald, *A Life in Letters,* pp. 263–264.

52. Ibid., pp. 277–278.

53. Fitzgerald, *In His Own Time,* p. 176 (Matthew J. and Arlyn Bruccoli Collection of F. Scott Fitzgerald, Thomas Cooper Library, University of South Carolina).

54. Fitzgerald, "The Crack-Up," in *The Crack-Up,* edited by Edmund Wilson (New York: New Directions, 1945), pp. 69–70.

55. Ibid., p. 75.

56. English author of best-selling spy novels.

57. Fitzgerald, "Early Success," *American Cavalcade* (October 1937); reprinted in *The Crack-Up,* pp. 89–90.

58. Fitzgerald, *A Life in Letters,* p. 357.

59. Fiction editor at *Collier's.*

60. Probably "Last Kiss," declined by Littauer in 1939 but published—after Fitzgerald's death—by *Collier's* in its 16 April 1949 issue and awarded a $1,000 bonus as the best story in that issue.

61. George Horace Lorimer, editor of *The Saturday Evening Post.*

62. Fitzgerald, *A Life in Letters,* p. 402.

63. Wesley Winans Stout.

64. *Rebecca,* the 1940 movie produced by David O. Selznick and directed by Alfred Hitchcock, was based on the 1938 novel by English writer Daphne du Maurier.

65. Fitzgerald, *A Life in Letters,* pp. 443–444.

66. Ibid., p. 445.

67. Ibid., p. 465.

68. Fitzgerald, *The Love of The Last Tycoon: A Western,* edited, with a preface and notes, by Bruccoli (New York: Scribner Paperback Fiction, 1994), p. 12.

69. In *The Autobiography of Alice B. Toklas* (1933).

FITZGERALD AS STUDIED

INFLUENCES AND READING

The influence of F. Scott Fitzgerald's writing on other authors is misunderstood. Fitzgerald wrote like nobody else. Nobody else wrote like Fitzgerald. Many writers have acknowledged their admiration of his style, but no writer has successfully imitated him. Imitations of Fitzgerald turn into parodies because his tone and his emotional investment in his material are lacking in imitators. In 1949 John O'Hara—Fitzgerald's staunchest admirer among major writers—informed John Steinbeck that "Fitzgerald was a better just plain writer than all of us put together. Just words writing."[1]

Critics—including those who knew Fitzgerald, such as Edmund Wilson—were responsible for the deprecating image of him as a scarcely educated "natural" who wrote masterpieces without knowing much about literature. Fitzgerald, a Princeton dropout, was better educated than Ernest Hemingway or William Faulkner. He read widely and knew more about English and American literature than most graduate students of English. The reading lists and letters of instruction he sent to his daughter and the curriculum of the "College of One" he prepared for Sheilah Graham document the extent of his postcollege self-education efforts. Fitzgerald's correspondence and interviews provide evidence of his familiarity with major literature and his sharp critical judgments. For a long time his favorite novel was Joseph Conrad's *Nostromo* (1904), but he ranked James Joyce's *Ulysses* (1922) as the greatest novel in the English language. Fitzgerald admired the novels of Edith Wharton and Willa Cather. He recommended the early Henry James but sensibly avoided the later novels. He praised Fyodor Dostoyevsky (*The Brothers Karamazov*, 1879–1880) and Marcel Proust (*Remembrance of Things Past*, 1913–1927).

Young writers are shaped by their reading, even though they often outgrow their early enthusiasms. Always keenly interested in history, Fitzgerald read during his boyhood the English historical novels of George Alfred Henty and American counterparts such as the Young Kentuckian series. He described his first novel, *This Side of Paradise,* as "A Romance and a Reading List";[2] it mentions ninety-eight writers and sixty-four titles—evidence of the books that he read instead of studying while at prep school and college. The novelists Fitzgerald admired during his literary apprenticeship at Princeton were H. G. Wells (*The Research Magnificent,* 1915) and Compton Mackenzie (*Sinister Street,* 1913–1914)—British authors of what he called "quest novels"—whose influence is evident in *This Side of Paradise.* These novels trace the development or apprenticeship of an ambitious youth seeking to fulfill his talent or genius. Fitzgerald also read Oscar Wilde's *Picture of Dorian Gray* (1891) and the English poets. During his early years Francis Palgrave's *Golden Treasury* (1861–1897) was his preferred anthology. John Keats, Fitzgerald's favorite poet, inspired his use of sensory language and rich imagery. The verse of nineteenth-century English poets Percy Bysshe Shelley and Algernon Charles Swinburne also impressed Fitzgerald during his Princeton years. Fitzgerald read relatively little American fiction in prep school and college: Booth Tarkington, Owen Johnson's *Stover at Yale* (1912), and some Theodore Dreiser—probably *Sister Carrie* (1900) and *Jennie Gerhardt* (1911). Tarkington was a particular favorite of the young Fitzgerald, as a realist, a stylist, and a humorist. One of the putative reasons for Fitzgerald's choice of Princeton was Tarkington's connection with the Triangle Club. In his 1922 review of that year's *Gentle Julia* Fitzgerald identified Tarkington as "our best humorist since Mark Twain."[3] Honesty or truth to life was Fitzgerald's chief test of fiction; in the same review he scored Tarkington's gentility: "It is a pity that the man who writes better prose than any other living American was brought up in a generation that considered it a crime to tell the truth."[4]

During his early years as a professional, in 1920–1921, Fitzgerald experienced a temporary conversion to the American naturalistic fiction writers—the realists who portrayed characters as victims of deterministic forces. These writers included Frank Norris and his now-forgotten brother Charles, both of whose novels Fitzgerald admired. In his 1921 review of Charles Norris's novel *Brass* (1921), Fitzgerald ranked Norris's earlier *Salt* (1918) high among the achievements in American fiction: "A novel interests me on one of two counts: either it is something entirely new and fresh and profoundly felt, as, for instance, 'The Red Badge of Courage' or 'Salt,' or else it is a tour de force by a man of exceptional talent, a Mark Twain or a Tarkington. A great book is both these things. . . ."[5] The impetus toward naturalism was triggered by Fitzgerald's respect for H. L. Mencken, editor of *The Smart Set,* who was the most forceful American literary and social critic during the 1920s. They remained friends after Fitzgerald outgrew Mencken's influence. The effects of Fitzgerald's exposure to naturalism are evident in "May Day" and in *The Beautiful and Damned.* Mencken, a strong advocate of Conrad's work, may have recommended it to Fitzgerald, whose reading of Conrad influenced his structure and point of view in *The Great Gatsby.*

CONTEMPORARY BEST-SELLERS AND AWARD-WINNERS

It is instructive to consider writers who were praised during the time Fitzgerald was refining his technical skills and mastering his craft. One of the lessons to be learned from literary history is that most authors' reputations while they are publishing tend to be wrong. In many cases the higher the contemporary praise, the deeper the fall. In the 1920s the now-unread romantic novels of James Branch Cabell and Joseph Hergesheimer were accorded respect, and their authors were ranked above Fitzgerald. In the 1930s proletarian writers such as John Steinbeck and James T. Farrell were regarded as more "serious" than Fitzgerald.

Literary prizes are unreliable as gauges of merit, but they indicate something about the taste and literary politics of an era. These novels won the Pulitzer Prize[6] during the two decades when Fitzgerald was writing: 1921, *The Age of Innocence,* by Wharton; 1922, *Alice Adams,* by Tarkington; 1923, *One of Ours,* by Cather; 1924, *The Able McLaughlins,* by Margaret Wilson; 1925, *So Big,* by Edna Ferber; 1926, *Arrowsmith,* by Sinclair Lewis; 1927, *Early Autumn,* by Louis Bromfield; 1928, *The Bridge of San Luis Rey,* by Thornton Wilder; 1929, *Scarlet Sister Mary,* by Julia Peterkin; 1930, *Laughing Boy,* by Oliver La Farge; 1931, *Years of Grace,* by Margaret Ayre Barnes; 1932, *The Good Earth,* by Pearl S. Buck; 1933, *The Store,* by T. S. Stribling; 1934, *Lamb in His Bosom,* by Caroline Miller; 1935, *Now in November,* by Josephine W. Johnson; 1936,

"10 BEST BOOKS I HAVE READ," 1923

Samuel Butler's *Note Books.* The mind and heart of my favorite Victorian.

The Philosophy of Friedrich Nietzsche (H. L. Mencken). A keen, hard intelligence interpreting the Great Modern Philosopher.

Portrait of the Artist as a Young Man (James Joyce). Because James Joyce is to be the most profound literary influence in the next fifty years.

Zuleika Dobson (Max Beerbohm). For the sheer delight of its exquisite snobbery.

The Mysterious Stranger (Mark Twain). Mark Twain in his most sincere mood. A book and a startling revelation.

Nostromo (Joseph Conrad). The great novel of the past fifty years, as Ulysses is the great novel of the future.

Vanity Fair (Thackeray). No explanation required.

The Oxford Book of English Verse. This seems to me a better collection than Palgrave's.

Thais (Anatole France). The great book of the man who is Wells and Shaw together.

Seventeen (Booth Tarkington). The funniest book I've ever read.—

F. Scott Fitzgerald

From *Jersey City Evening Journal,* 24 April 1923, p. 9; syndicated by the North American Newspaper Alliance; reprinted in *F. Scott Fitzgerald on Authorship,* edited by Matthew J. Bruccoli with Judith S. Baughman (Columbia: University of South Carolina Press, 1996), p. 86.

Honey in the Horn, by Harold L. Davis; 1937, *Gone With the Wind,* by Margaret Mitchell; 1938, *The Late George Apley,* by J. P. Marquand; 1939, *The Yearling,* by Marjorie Kinnan Rawlings; 1940, *The Grapes of Wrath,* by Steinbeck; 1941, prize denied to *For Whom the Bell Tolls,* by Ernest Hemingway. The awards present a mixture of meritorious novels that are still read and forgotten novels. The Pulitzer judges had a batting average of .500—superb for baseball, but poor for literary judgment. In the year after the publication of *The Great Gatsby* the prize went to *Arrowsmith* (and was declined by Lewis); in the year after the publication of *Tender Is the Night* it went to *Now in November.* Two American novelists won the Nobel Prize in literature during this period: Lewis in 1930 (the first award to an American) and Buck in 1938 (no comment seems possible).

The best-sellers lists provide another measure of contemporary taste: the gauge of crowd-pleasing. Fitzgerald never had a real best-seller, although *This Side of Paradise* and *The Beautiful and Damned* briefly appeared at the bottom of some lists. In 1925 the top ten novels were A. Hamilton Gibbs, *Soundings;* Margaret Kennedy, *The Constant Nymph;* Gene Stratton Porter, *The Keeper of the Bees;* E. Barrington, *Glorious Apollo;* Michael Arlen, *The Green Hat;* Ann Douglas Sedgwick, *The Little French Girl;* Lewis, *Arrowsmith;* Anne Parish, *The Perennial Bachelor;* Rafael Sabatini, *The Carolinian;* and A. S. M. Hutchinson, *One Increasing Purpose.* One of these books, *Arrowsmith,* is still read. The crop was better in 1934—the year of *Tender Is the Night*—with Hervey Allen's *Anthony Adverse;* James Hilton's *Good-Bye, Mr. Chips;* and Isak Dinesen's *Seven Gothic Tales.*

A Sinclair Lewis novel was published in each year that a Fitzgerald novel appeared: 1920—*This Side of Paradise* and *Main Street;* 1922—*The Beautiful and Damned* and *Babbitt;* 1925—*The Great Gatsby* and *Arrowsmith;* 1934—*Tender Is the Night* and *Work of Art.* Lewis's novels surpassed Fitzgerald's in sales and critical recognition. While Lewis was regarded as a major American literary figure and enjoyed international prestige, Fitzgerald was patronized as a once-promising writer who had sold out to the magazines.

SOCIAL REALISM

Fitzgerald is thought of as a romantic—meaning an imaginative and emotional—writer, but he combined these qualities with realism, meaning accuracy of observation and characterization. *This Side of Paradise* was read as a realistic account of Princeton undergraduate experience. *Tender Is the Night,* subtitled "A Romance," provides a convincing account of expatriate life and a profound examination of character deterioration.

Fitzgerald properly belongs with the American social realists and social historians, the line that extends from Wharton, Dreiser, Tarkington, and Norris through Lewis, O'Hara, James Gould Cozzens, and the proletarian writers. He was one of the few American novelists who wrote seriously about the effects of money on character. To the requirement of telling truthfully what happened, Fitzgerald added his defining qualities of lyricism and sensitivity in order to evoke how life felt at that place and at that moment. He was the poet of time. He explicated the function and purpose of social realism in a letter to his daughter, Scottie: "But when in a freak moment you will want to give the low-down, not the scandal, not the merely <u>reported</u> but the <u>profound</u> essence of what happened at a prom or after it, perhaps that honesty will come to you—and then you will understand how it is possible to make even a forlorn Laplander <u>feel</u> the importance of a trip to Cartiers!"[7]

Fitzgerald recorded social history by means of selected evocative details, usually in descriptions of place: Chicago's Union Station, the Paris Ritz, or the Princeton campus, for example. He did not load his fiction with documentation or reportage, as did Dreiser. Fitzgerald tried to get the details right, even though he committed factual blunders: his Manhattan and Paris geography is shaky; in *The Great Gatsby* the Queensboro Bridge incorrectly links Manhattan and Astoria. Fitzgerald also knew when to omit details. The make of Gatsby's gorgeous car is not provided because no actual car would do: it was a Gatsbymobile.

John O'Hara, the master of depicting social stratification in fiction, explicated the function of Fitzgerald's technique to produce verisimilitude:

He always knew what he was writing about, which is so, so untrue of so, so many writers. It may not seem like much in 1945, when it is done all the time, but twenty-five years ago it was delightful to find a writer who would come right out and say Locomobile instead of high-powered motor car, Shanley's instead of gay cabaret, and George, instead of François, the *chasseur* at the Paris Ritz. These touches guaranteed that the writer knew what he was talking about and was not getting his information from Mr. Carnegie's local contribution to culture. . . . Scott Fitzgerald had the correct impressions because, quite apart from his gifts, the impressions were not those of a man who's never been there. As we used to say, he knew the forks.[8]

Fitzgerald's type of social realism focusing on the American upper classes became unfashionable in the 1930s. The lower classes and proletarian causes did not move him, and he did not try to write about them.

Fitzgerald (left) and fiction writer John O'Hara
in California, late 1938 or early 1939
(Photo by Belle O'Hara)

Fitzgerald's reputation, readership, and earnings declined sharply during the Depression as he came to be regarded as an anachronism after the tastemakers and opinion-makers underwent conversions to the political Left. Fitzgerald observed in his *Notebooks* that "In thirty-four and thirty-five the party line crept into everything except the Sears Roebuck Catalogue."[9] Nonetheless, he was aware of the political movements of his time and made a study of marxism. In the planning stages of *Tender Is the Night,* Fitzgerald considered having Diver send his son to the U.S.S.R. for his education. Fitzgerald's only novel set in the 1930s, *The Love of the Last Tycoon,* portrays an heroic business figure—a movie producer with taste and artistic standards—who opposes the unionization of Hollywood writers.

The proletarian writers were social novelists. John Dos Passos had been a radical in the 1920s. His *U.S.A.* trilogy (*The 42nd Parallel,* 1930; *1919,* 1932; *The Big Money,* 1936) was deservedly admired in the early 1930s, but his reputation was downgraded after he turned against communism. Steinbeck was highly praised for his treatment of dispossessed and victimized characters in *Of Mice and Men* (1937) and *The Grapes of Wrath* (1939). Fitzgerald, who rarely attacked other writers, expressed strong antipathy to Steinbeck's work. In a Spring 1939 letter to John Biggs, Fitzgerald called Steinbeck a "cheap blatant imitation of D. H. Lawrence. A book club return of the public to its own vomit."[10] Writing to his "intellectual conscience," Edmund Wilson, in 1940, Fitzgerald characterized Steinbeck as "a rather cagey cribber" from Frank Norris:

> Most of us begin as imitators but it is something else for a man of his years and reputation to steal a whole scene as he did in "Mice and Men". . . . I've always encouraged young writers—I put Max Perkins on to Caldwell, Callaghan and God knows how many others but Steinbeck bothers me. I suppose he cribs for the glory of the party.[11]

The hard-boiled or tough-guy writers who wrote crime fiction were allied with the proletarian school. These crime writers originally wrote for the pulp magazines of the 1920s and achieved literary status with the emergence of Dashiell Hammett as a novelist in 1929. They included James M. Cain, Horace McCoy, and Raymond Chandler. Fitzgerald was on friendly terms with Hammett and McCoy in Hollywood, but he provided no critical observations on their work. It appears that his unsuccessful "Count of Darkness" stories, written in 1935–1936, were attempts to place hard-boiled speech in a medieval setting.

At one time O'Hara was mispositioned among the hard-boiled writers because of his objectivity and accurate use of American speech. He and Fitzgerald became friends when O'Hara was writing *Appointment in Samarra* (1934) and Fitzgerald was writing *Tender Is the Night*. Fitzgerald recognized O'Hara's literary gifts but had reservations about his "glooms." In his *Notebooks* Fitzgerald observed that "The queer slanting effect of the substantive, the future imperfect, a matter of intuition or ear to O'Hara, is unknown to careful writers like Bunny [Wilson] and John [Peale Bishop]."[12] But he also observed that "John O'Hara is in a perpetual state of just having discovered that it's a lousy world."[13] Fitzgerald provided an endorsement for *Appointment in Samarra*: "John O'Hara's novel indicates the tremendous strides that American writers have taken since the war."[14] Reviewers detected Fitzgerald's influence on *Apointment in Samarra*. Fitzgerald pasted several of these reviews in his scrapbook, captioned "The Cross of John O'Hara."[15]

THE MATERIAL OF AMERICAN FICTION

Fitzgerald's comments on writing—his own and other writers'—merit close attention. He did not practice literary criticism as such and wrote few book reviews. Most of his comments on his contemporaries are in letters. His review of Hemingway's *In Our Time* (1925), headed "How to Waste Material—A Note on My Generation," addresses the matter of writers' finding authentic American subjects and characters: "For one Dreiser who made a single minded and irreproachable choice there have been a dozen like Henry James who have stupid-got with worry over the matter, and yet another dozen who, blinded by the fading tail of Walt Whitman's comet, have botched their books by the insincere compulsion to write 'significantly' about America."[16]

Fitzgerald's fullest attack on the revival of the American farm novel came in his letter to Maxwell Perkins responding to Thomas Boyd's novel *Samuel Drummond* (1925):

All this is preparatory to saying that his new book sounds utterly lowsy—Shiela Kaye-Smith[17] has used the stuff about the farmer having girls instead of boys and being broken up about it. The characters you mention have every one, become stock-props in the last ten years—"Christy, the quaint old hired man" after a season in such stuff as Owen Davis' Ice Bound[18] must be almost ready for the burlesque circuit.

History of the Simple Inarticulate Farmer and his Hired Man Christy

(Both guaranteed to be utterly full of the Feel of the Soil)

1st Period

1855—English Peasant discovered by Geo. Elliot in Mill on the Floss, Silas Marner ect.

1888—Given intellectual interpretation by Hardy in Jude and Tess

1890—Found in France by Zola in Germinal

1900—Crowds of Scandanavians, Hamsun, Bojer[19] ect, tear him bodily from the Russian, and after a peep at Hardy, Hamlin Garland[20] finds him in the middle west.

————

Most of that, however, was literature. It was something pulled by the individual out of life and only partly with the aid of models in other literatures.

2nd Period

1914—Shiela Kaye-Smith frankly imitates Hardy, produces two good books + then begins to imitate herself.

1915—Brett Young[21] discovers him in the coal country

1916—Robert Frost discovers him in New England

1917—Sherwood Anderson discovers him in Ohio

1918—Willa Cather turns him Swede

1920—Eugene O'Niell puts him on the boards in Different + Beyond Horizon

1922—Ruth Suckow[22] gets in before the door closes

These people were all good second raters (except Anderson) Each of them brought something to the business—but they exhausted the ground, the type was set. All was over.

————

3rd Period

The Cheapskates discover him—Bad critics and novelists ect.

1923 Homer Croy[23] writes <u>West of the Water Tower</u>

1924 Edna Ferber turns from her flip jewish saleswoman for a strong silent earthy carrot grower and—the Great Soul of Charley Towne[24] thrills to her passionately. Real and Earthy Struggle

1924 <u>Ice Bound</u> by the author of <u>Nellie the Beautiful Cloak Model</u> wins Pulitzer Prize

<u>The Able Mcgloughlins</u> wins $10,000 prize + is forgotten the following wk.

1925 <u>The Apple of the Eye</u>[25] pronounced a masterpiece

<u>1926</u>—TOM, BOYD, WRITES, NOVEL, ABOUT, INARTICU-LATE, FARMER WHO, IS, CLOSE, TO SOIL, AND, HIS, HIRED, MAN CHRISTY!

"STRONG! VITAL! REAL!"

As a matter of fact the American peasant as "real" material scarcely exists. He is scarcely 10% of the population, isn't bound to the soil at all as the English + Russian peasants were—and, if has any sensitivity whatsoever (except a most sentimental conception of himself, which our writers persistently shut their eyes to) he is in the towns before he's twenty. Either Lewis, Lardner and myself have been badly fooled, or else using him as typical American material is simply <u>a stubborn seeking for the static in a world that for almost a hundred years has simply not been static</u>. Isn't it a 4th rate imagination that can find only that old property farmer in all this amazing time and land? And anything that ten people a year can do well enough to pass muster has become so easy that it isn't worth the doing.[26]

MODERNISM

Because of Fitzgerald's residence in France during the 1920s he is usually grouped with the American expatriates who flourished in Paris and experimented with the literary techniques classified as modernism. Yet he did not participate in the expatriate literary life—apart from his discovery of Hemingway—and did not write for the Paris-based little magazines and small presses. Fitzgerald was an established and successful writer before he went to France for financial reasons and remained for social reasons. The expatriates left America as an expression of their rejection of American culture. Fitzgerald remained intensely American. He was an American writer living abroad, not an expatriate. *The Great Gatsby* was written in Southern France in 1924, but it was not an experimental work and owed nothing to France.

The now-legendary American expatriates in Paris—Gertrude Stein, Ezra Pound, and Hemingway—fostered the movement that came to be called modernism. These writers experimented with new forms of literature, new uses of language, new ways of rendering experience; they experimented with the presentation of time and consciousness. Fitzgerald became a twentieth-century novelist with his third novel, *The Great Gatsby,* in which he mastered point of view and the techniques of reordering time and structuring narrative. The technical advances in the novel were influenced by the work of Conrad, not by the Paris expatriate crowd. Fitzgerald eschewed experiments with language, speech, sentence structure, or typography. There are no Joycean compounds and neologisms in Fitzgerald. Many writers embraced the stream-of-consciousness technique after Joyce's *Ulysses,* but Fitzgerald did not make significant use of it until *Tender Is the Night,* where Nicole Diver's internal monologue in Book II, chapter 10, bridges present-time narrative and flashback time. He inscribed a copy of *The Great Gatsby* to modernist poet T. S. Eliot as "the greatest of living poets"[27] and probably took the symbolic name "Valley of Ashes" from Eliot's *The Waste Land* (1922).

Although he was on friendly terms with Stein and hailed the genius of Joyce, Fitzgerald was not influenced by modernism because his style and technique were formed before he arrived in France. Not even his admiration for Hemingway altered Fitzgerald's writing. Nonetheless, Fitzgerald's residence in Europe provided him with material. He wrote brilliantly about Paris and Americans abroad in "Babylon Revisited," "One Trip Abroad," and *Tender Is the Night.* Yet Fitzgerald does not extol the virtues of expatriation: his Americans undergo a process of deterioration in Europe. Unlike Henry James's Americans, who are corrupted or defeated by European values, Fitzgerald's characters are spoiled by their own idleness and their choice of Europe as a place where money buys more than it does in America.

Fitzgerald rejected the concept of a postwar "lost generation" of war survivors given currency by Hemingway's *The Sun Also Rises* (1926) and generally espoused by the expatriates. According to this notion, the people who had experienced World War I—male and female—were permanent casualties unable to return to postwar life. In his 1929 story "The

passenger was through at the window. When she turned they both

and
started; he saw it was the girl.

going
"Oh, hello," she cried " I'm glad you're along. I was

great
just asking when the pool opened. The thing about this ship

is that you can always get a swim."

"Why do you like to swim?" he demanded.

She smiled laughed.
"You always ask me that." she smiled.

had dinner:
"Perhaps you'd tell me, if we dine together to-night."

left
But when he lift her he knew that she could never tell

or another.
him, she was another. France was a land, England a people, but
was
America, was the graves at Shiloh and the tired, drawn nervous

faces of its great men, and g

dieing
And the country boys in the Argonne for a phrase that
bodies
was empty before their body withered. It was a willingness

of the heart.

having about it still that quality of the
idea, was harder to letter — it was

The revised typescript of the coda to his 1929 story "The Swimmers" shows
Fitzgerald achieving eloquence through revision. (Matthew J. and Arlyn Bruccoli Collection of
F. Scott Fitzgerald, Thomas Cooper Library, University of South Carolina)

In his photo inscription Hemingway derisively linked Fitzgerald with another Princetonian, travel-writer Richard Halliburton. (Matthew J. and Arlyn Bruccoli Collection of F. Scott Fitzgerald, Thomas Cooper Library, University of South Carolina)

Swimmers" Fitzgerald redefines "lost generation" and proclaims the moral worth of America:

> . . . he had a sense of overwhelming gratitude and of gladness that America was there, that under the ugly débris of industry the rich land still pushed up, incorrigibly lavish and fertile, and that in the heart of the leaderless people the old generosities and devotions fought on, breaking out sometimes in fanaticism and

excess, but indomitable and undefeated. There was a lost generation in the saddle at the moment, but it seemed to him that the men coming on, the men of the war, were better; and all his old feeling that America was a bizarre accident, a sort of historical sport, had gone forever. The best of America was the best of the world.[28]

Fitzgerald's best stories set in Europe are anti-expatriatism stories.

FITZGERALD AND HEMINGWAY

Fitzgerald's friendship with Hemingway is the most celebrated and distorted friendship in American literature. What has become the defining anecdote about them—reported as gospel—never happened. Fitzgerald did not tell Hemingway, "The very rich are different from you and me." Hemingway did not reply, "Yeah—they have more money." Academic types particularly like this phantom exchange and repeat it in classrooms to convince their students that Fitzgerald was trivial and materialistic in comparison to the serious, tough-minded Hemingway.

This is what happened: In his 1936 *Esquire* story "The Snows of Kilimanjaro" Hemingway remarks that the protagonist "remembered poor Scott Fitzgerald and his romantic awe of them [the rich] and how he had started a story once that began, 'The very rich are different from you and me.' And how someone had said to Scott, Yes, they have more money. But that was not humorous to Scott. He thought they were a special glamorous race and when he found they weren't it wrecked him just as much as any other thing that wrecked him."[29] The Fitzgerald story referred to is "The Rich Boy" (1926), which includes this superb opening: "Let me tell you about the very rich. They are different from you and me. . . . They think, deep in their hearts, that they are better than we are. . . ."[30] No romantic awe there.

Hemingway's use of Fitzgerald's words to denigrate him resulted from an encounter in which Hemingway—not Fitzgerald—was the goat. In conversation with Scribners editor Maxwell Perkins and critic Mary Colum, Hemingway had said, "I am getting to know the rich." Colum responded, "The only difference between the rich and other people is that the rich have more money."[31] She was wrong, but Hemingway dealt with the embarrassment of her put-down by making Fitzgerald the victim and himself the presumed victor. Hemingway rationalized his brutal conduct by claiming that Fitzgerald's confessional articles in *Esquire* (later collected in *The Crack-Up*) were contemptible and made him fair game.

"... This is to tell you about a young man named Ernest Hemmingway, who lives in Paris, (an American) writes for the transatlantic Review + has a brilliant future. Ezra Pount published a a collection of his short pieces in Paris, at some place like the Egotist Press. I havn't it hear now but its remarkable + I'd look him up right away. He's the real thing."

F. Scott Fitzgerald

From a letter to Maxwell Perkins, ca. 10 October 1924, in *F. Scott Fitzgerald: A Life in Letters,* edited by Matthew J. Bruccoli with Judith S. Baughman (New York: Scribners, 1994), p. 82.

Hemingway had a compulsion to turn on writers and others to whom he was obligated. Fitzgerald had recognized Hemingway's genius in 1924 on the basis of his Paris publications—before Hemingway had an American publisher—and recommended him to Perkins in a letter that year.[32] Hemingway's posthumously published memoir of his Paris apprenticeship in the 1920s, *A Moveable Feast* (1964), ridicules Fitzgerald as a drunk, a fool, a wife-dominated weakling, and an irresponsible writer.[33] This was Hemingway's method of discharging his personal and professional debts to Fitzgerald, who had assiduously promoted Hemingway's career.

There was no cross-fertilization between Fitzgerald's and Hemingway's writings because their material and styles were so different. However, Fitzgerald served as volunteer editor for *The Sun Also Rises,* providing advice on cutting the opening, which Hemingway acted on.[34] Hemingway subsequently rejected Fitzgerald's advice on *A Farewell to Arms* (1929) and dismissed the worth of his literary judgment. Nonetheless, Hemingway, an excellent judge of writing, described the brilliance of Fitzgerald's prose—but in a disparaging manner:

> *His talent was as natural as the pattern that was made by the dust on a butterfly's wings. At one time he understood it no more than the butterfly did and he did not know when it was brushed or marred. Later he became conscious of his damaged wings and of their construction and he learned to think and could not fly any more because the love of flight was gone and he could only remember when it had been effortless.*[35]

Hemingway praised *The Great Gatsby* but thought Fitzgerald could do better. Hemingway's initial response to *Tender Is the Night* was mixed, complaining that the Divers were not convincing, but providing professional advice:

> You see, Bo, you're not a tragic character. Neither am I. All we are is writers and what we should do is write. Of all people on earth you needed discipline in your work and instead you marry someone who is jealous of your work, wants to compete with you and ruins you. It's not as simple as that and I thought Zelda was crazy the first time I met her and you complicated it even

more by being in love with her and, of course you're a rummy. But you're no more a rummy than Joyce is and most good writers are. But Scott good writers always come back. Always. You are twice as good now as you were at the time you think you were so marvellous. You know I never thought so much of Gatsby at the time. You can write twice as well now as you ever could. All you need to do is write truly and not care about what the fate of it is.[36]

Five years later Hemingway wrote Perkins after rereading *Tender Is the Night:*

It's amazing how <u>excellent</u> much of it is. If he had integrated it better it would have been a fine novel (as it is) much of it is better than anything else he ever wrote. How I wish he would have kept on writing. Is it really all over or will he write again? If you write him give him my great affection. (I always had a very stupid little boy feeling of superiority about Scott—like a tough little boy sneering at a delicate but talented little boy.) But reading that novel much of it was so good it was frightening.[37]

Fitzgerald summarized this painful friendship in his *Notebooks:* "I talk with the authority of failure—Ernest with the authority of success. We could never sit across the table again."[38] Fitzgerald's self-proclaimed failure no longer seems failure—except in terms of what might have been. His achievements are extraordinary. It is worth noting that Fitzgerald's literary output between 1920 and 1940 matched Hemingway's.

FITZGERALD AND WOLFE

Thomas Wolfe, the third member of Perkins's triumvirate of young geniuses, elicited Fitzgerald's scrupulous criticism. After hailing the publication of *Look Homeward, Angel* in 1929, Fitzgerald wrote Perkins: "You have a great find in him—what he'll do is incalculable. He has a deeper culture than Ernest and more vitality, if he is slightly less of a poet that goes with the immense surface he wants to cover. . . . John Bishop told me he needed advice about cutting ect, but after reading his book I thought that was nonsense. He strikes me as a man who should be let alone as to length, if he has to be published in five volumes."[39] Fitzgerald recognized Wolfe's genius and potential but complained about his self-indulgence. They engaged in an epistolary debate about the putter-inners (Zola and Wolfe) and the leaver-outers (Flaubert and Fitzgerald).[40] Although Fitzgerald continued to praise Wolfe's command of language he became distrustful of Wolfe's self-indulgence after *Of Time and the River* was published in 1935. That same year Fitzgerald sent Perkins an analysis of Wolfe's weaknesses:

Reading Tom Wolfe's story in the current *Modern Monthly*[41] makes me wish he was the sort of person you could talk to about his stuff. It has all his faults and virtues. It seems to me that with any sense of humor he could see the Dreiserian absurdities of how the circus people "ate the cod, bass, mackerel, halibut, clams and oysters of the New England coast, the terrapin of Maryland, the fat beeves, porks and cereals of the middle west," etc., etc., down to "the pink meated lobsters that grope their way along the sea-floors of America." And then (after one of his fine paragraphs which sounds a note to be expanded later) he remarks that they leave nothing behind except "the droppings of the camel and the elephant in Illinois." A few pages further on his redundance ruined some paragraphs (see the last complete paragraph on page 103) that might have been gorgeous. I sympathize with his use of repetition, of Joyce-like words, endless metaphor, but I wish he could have seen the disgust in Edmund Wilson's face when I once tried to interpolate part of a rhymed sonnet in the middle of a novel, disguised as prose. How he can put side by side such a mess as "With chitterling tricker fast-fluttering skirrs of sound the palmy honied birderies came" and such fine phrases as "tongue-trilling chirrs, plum-bellied smoothness, sweet lucidity" I don't know. He who has such infinite power of suggestion and delicacy has absolutely no right to glut people on whole meals of caviar. I hope to Christ he isn't taking all these emasculated paeans to his vitality very seriously. I'd hate to see such an exquisite talent turn into one of those muscle-bound and useless giants seen in a circus. Athletes have got to learn their games; they shouldn't just be content to tense their muscles, and if they do they suddenly find when called upon to bring off a necessary effect they are simply liable to hurl the shot into the crowd and not break any records at all. The metaphor is mixed but I think you will understand what I mean, and that he would too—save for his tendency to almost feminine horror if he thinks anyone is going to lay hands on his precious talent. I think his lack of humility is his most difficult characteristic, a lack oddly enough which I associate only with second or third rate writers. He was badly taught by bad teachers and now he hates learning.

There is another side of him that I find myself doubting, but this is something that no one could ever teach or tell him. His lack of feeling of other people's passions, the lyrical value of Eugene Gant's love affair with the universe—is that going to last through a whole saga? God, I wish he could discipline himself and really plan a novel.[42]

Fitzgerald wrote Scottie after reading Wolfe's *You Can't Go Home Again* (1940) that "The stuff about the GREAT VITAL HEART OF AMERICA is simply corny."[43]

When Fitzgerald read a book that excited him, he wanted others to know about it and read it. This true anecdote (most literary anecdotes are apocryphal) defines his feeling about books and authors: when he discovered that there were no copies of *Look Homeward, Angel* in the public library of Wolfe's hometown, Asheville, North Carolina, Fitzgerald bought copies and insisted that they be shelved.

HIS CONTEMPORARIES ON FITZGERALD

The phrase "a writer's writer" is generally utilized to alibi a writer whose books are not widely read or whose work is so difficult that it requires an indoctrinated readership. During his lifetime and after, Fitzgerald was and is a writer's writer, but not in any apologetic sense. Writers have always recognized that Fitzgerald could do things they could not do. When he was being disparaged by critics—who are rarely real writers themselves—good writers recognized his skills. Sixty years after his death characters in novels praise Fitzgerald and his work; his name or the name Gatsby frequently appear in books and titles.

The following excerpts from statements by serious writers of Fitzgerald's time document the respect and admiration accorded to him by members of his craft.

Gertrude Stein, 22 May 1925

Here we are and have read your book *[The Great Gatsby]* and it is a good book. I like the melody of your dedication it shows that you have a background of beauty and tenderness and that is a comfort. The next good thing is that you write naturally in sentences and that too is a comfort. You write naturally in sentences and one can read all of them and that among other things is a comfort. You are creating the contemporary world much as Thackery did his in Pendennis and Vanity Fair and this isn't a bad compliment. You make a modern world and a modern orgy strangely enough it was never done until you did it in This Side of Paradise. My belief in This Side of Paradise was alright. This is as good a book and different and older and that is what one does, one does not get better but different and older and that is always a pleasure. . . .[44]

T. S. Eliot, 31 December 1925

When I have time I should like to write to you more fully and tell you exactly why it [The Great Gatsby] seems to me such a remarkable book. In fact it seems to me to be the first step that American fiction has taken since Henry James. . . .[45]

Eliot never elaborated on his statement.

John O'Hara, "In Memory of Scott Fitzgerald: Certain Aspects" (1941)

F. Scott Fitzgerald was a *right* writer, and it's going to be a damned shame if the generation after mine (I am thirty-six) and the one after that don't get to know him. I had the good luck to read "This Side of Paradise" when it first came out, twenty years ago, and I've read it practically annually since then. He was the first novelist to make me say, "Hot dog! Some writer, I'll say." I was younger than his people in "This Side of Paradise," but I was precocious. Amory Blaine's mother's maiden name was Beatrice O'Hara, and I was in love with a girl named Beatrice then, a coincidence that became less important page by page. The people were right, the talk was right, the clothes, the cars were real, and the mysticism was a kind of challenge. But the time "The Beautiful and Damned" and "The Great Gatsby" appeared, the man could do no wrong. In a burst of enthusiasm I once said to Dorothy Parker, "This guy just can't write a bad piece." And again she was right. She said: "No. He can write a bad piece, but he can't write badly." He sent me the page proofs of "Tender Is the Night," which was a major honor in my life. I read it three times then, but only twice since, for that fine book is not to be read just any time. It's a dangerous book to encounter during some of the moods that come over you after you're thirty. You don't like to think of yourself, lone, wandering and lost, like

Richard Diver, going from town to town in bleak upstate New York, with All That behind you.[46]

Archibald MacLeish on *Tender Is the Night*, 1934

Great God Scott You can write. You can write better than ever. You are a fine writer. Believe it. Believe It—not me[47]

Robert Benchley, 29 April 1934

Honestly, Scott, I think that it *[Tender Is the Night]* is a beautiful piece of work, not only technically, but emotionally. I haven't had a book get hold of me like that for years. As a journeyman writer, I can not even conceive of anyone's being able to do that scene in the Guaranty Trust, just from the point of view of sheer manipulation of words, to say nothing of the observation contained in it. And the feeling of the whole book is so strong upon me, even now, that I am oppressed by a not-quite-vague-enough fear that several people I am fond of are very unhappy.[48]

Thomas Wolfe, March? 1934

Scott, I want to tell you how glad I am that your book *[Tender Is the Night]* is being published next month, and also what a fine book it is. I read it as it came out in Scribner's Magazine and even read the proofs of the last two installments. I tell you this because I got the jump on most readers in this way. I thought you'd be interested to know that the people in the book are even more real and living now than they were at the time I read it. It seems to me you've gone deeper in this book than in anything you ever wrote. . . . I think it's the best work you've done so far, and I know you'll understand what I mean and won't mind if I get a kind of selfish hope and joy out of your own success. . . ."[49]

John Dos Passos, "A Note on Fitzgerald" (1945)

The fact that at the end of a life of brilliant worldly successes and crushing disasters Scott Fitzgerald was engaged so ably in a work of such importance proves him to have been the first-rate novelist his friends believed him to be. In *The Last Tycoon* he was managing to invent a set of people seen really in the round instead of lit by an envious spotlight from above or below. *The Great Gatsby* remains a perfect example of this sort of treatment at an earlier, more anecdotic, more bas relief stage, but in the fragments of *The Last Tycoon*, you can see the beginning of a real grand style. Even in their unfinished state these fragments, I believe, are of sufficient dimensions to raise the level of American fiction to follow in some such way as Marlowe's blank verse line raised the whole level of Elizabethan verse.[50]

LATER WRITERS ON FITZGERALD

Subsequent generations of writers have expressed their sense of Fitzgerald's work as an inspiration and gauge for writers.

Richard Yates

No single book made me decide to be a writer; that decision came as a consequence of boyhood and had little to do with books at all. But it was F. Scott Fitzgerald's *The Great Gatsby,* which I read for the first time at 22, that persuaded me to quit fooling around and get to work. The purity of that novel, the grace and the swiftly gathering power of it, showed me what a high, fine thing writing could be—and suggested too, as if in whispers, how much it might cost.[51]

J. D. Salinger, *The Catcher in the Rye,* (1951)

I still don't see how he [Holden's brother] could like a phony book like [Hemingway's *A Farewell to Arms*] and still like that one by Ring Lardner or that other one he's so crazy about, *The Great Gatsby.* . . . I was crazy about *The Great Gatsby.* Old Gatsby. Old sport. That killed me.[52]

Salinger, letter to Elizabeth Murray

Re-read a lot of Scott Fitzgerald's work this week. God, I love that man. Damn fool critics are forever calling writers geniuses for their idiosyncracies—Hemingway for his reticent dialogue, Wolfe for his gargantuan energy, and so on. Fitzgerald's only idiosyncrasy was his pure brilliance.[53]

The following authorial tributes were provided for the Fitzgerald Centenary Celebration at the University of South Carolina in 1996:[54]

Paul Auster

I first read *The Great Gatsby* as a high school student more than thirty years ago, and even now I don't think I have fully recovered from the experience. Fitzgerald's book is not like other books. It does more than just tell a story—it cuts to the heart of storytelling itself—and the result is a work of such simplicity, power, and beauty that one is marked by it forever. I realize that I am not alone in my opinion, but I can't think of another twentieth-century American novel that has meant as much to me.

Richard Bausch

I reread Fitzgerald perhaps more often than any other writer, and one of the saddest things I know of is the letter to Perkins, when he speaks of himself in the past tense: "In my own way I was an original." My God, that always makes me hurt. How much he would have reveled in the history of his work, though, and *Gatsby* stands right up there with the best of everything. This slender volume that manages to be inclusive, and to express the peculiarly cruel effects of our oddly materialistic brand of optimism, better than so many tomes, so many roundhouse attempts to be as big as the country. I hope there is a writers' heaven, and that he's sitting on a bar stool there, toasting, as he would be, everybody who sold him short.

Thomas Berger

The Great Gatsby is as nearly perfect as a novel can be, with not a word, not an emotion, not an idea in excess or lacking or misplaced or corrupted. On each rereading I am prepared to find on almost every page gems previously overlooked or perhaps once noticed but temporarily forgotten: e.g., the character Klipspringer, a career houseguest, who after Gatsby's death telephones the house not to ask when to come for the funeral but rather to request that his tennis shoes be forwarded to the address of his new host—I had only half-recalled that his first name (Ewing) is as wondrously right as the last, but until recently I had, unaccountably, mislaid all memory of the mixture of the comic and the touching in the scene in which Klipspringer is summoned by Gatsby to play the piano for Daisy on her tour of the mansion, and the song he performs on

Gatsby's special request is "Ain't We Got Fun," a vivacious tune with somewhat cynical lyrics that, though I was an infant when the novel was published, was still around when I was old enough to listen to it during the Great Depression that, so to speak, put paid to the era with which Fitzgerald is peculiarly associated, the one towards which, having been born just before its midpoint, I feel proprietary. . . .

James Dickey

. . . [Fitzgerald's] principal emphasis is on the social scene, both in itself—its ethos—and in the individuals who make it up. To these preoccupations he brought great originality and insight, conveyed by means of what I should be inclined to call a kind of *lyric* penetration, more akin to poetry than to any fiction other than Fitzgerald's. ". . . I became aware of the old island here that flowered once for Dutch sailors' eyes . . . for a transitory enchanted moment man must have held his breath in the presence of this continent, compelled into an aesthetic contemplation he neither understood nor desired, face to face for the last time in history with something commensurate to his capacity for wonder."

These qualities are unique, and made Fitzgerald a truer spokesman for his generation than did his tales of flappers and diamonds as big as the Ritz. They advanced him into an overview, an original kind of intimacy that took in not only the 1920s but all of existence, the feeling of life itself, given an intensity that we could not summon without him. He understood, through his age, the Ages. He was our Perseus: craft against petrifaction, the wild secret revelation against the standard response, life against death. . . .

George Garrett

I have known many writers for whom Fitzgerald is not, by any means, the primary model or influence of their own work. But I have yet to meet a writer who does not take Fitzgerald as an undeniable influence and a vital example. His direct influence is, then, wider and deeper than it might seem. It is an influence that has been beneficial to a whole generation of American writers. You can always learn from the finest works of Fitzgerald. It is awesome (as they say), but it is also encouraging. . . .

George V. Higgins

After many seasons of occasional reflection it begins increasingly to seem to me that the power of Fitzgerald's work to fascinate is the product of the destructive paradox that *The Great Gatsby* captures so nearly perfectly. The only means Gatsby has to create the grand illusion of his shining romance with Daisy is his loot, its origin as corrupt as the carefree world where she lives with Tom. The existence of the romance requires first the corruption that creates the wealth, and then the denial that the corruption took place—which assures the demolition of the romance.

The enduring congruent power of Fitzgerald's life to fascinate, and sadden, is the result of his disastrous insistence upon making it a looking-glass of the lethal paradox he wrote about, so that if his life was to reflect truly the romance he wished to live, it too had to be destroyed. He was too good an artist for his own good; he saw the necessity for the fatal symmetry, however reluctantly or imperfectly, and he attended to it.

John le Carré

Fitzgerald is the writer's ultimate writer. You know the trick, you watch him perform it, and all of a sudden you don't know how it's done any more. How did he get there from here? How does he keep the light on in the dark? Why do I know that when he never told me? How does he make a rainbow out of black and white? I go back to him when I want to be revived. Or better perhaps, reassured that words can be made to do anything in the right hands.

Norman Mailer

What would any of us have been without Fitzgerald? A little less, for certain. Literary pleasures of the most special sort would have been withheld, and some of his errors in life, God bless him, would soon have been ours.

Budd Schulberg

In the last year of his life Scott Fitzgerald often talked of his dilemma at finding himself thrust aside by a new generation of critics and readers who seemed to prefer the new gods of the 30s,

John Steinbeck, James T. Farrell, Clifford Odets. . . . Still clinging to his faith in his own talent, he persisted in the face of Job-like discouragements.

But, like Edmund Wilson, Stephen Vincent Benét, and other Eastern litterateurs, there was an informed circle of friends and admirers of Stanley Rose's Book Store on Hollywood Boulevard who didn't need half a century of hindsight to recognize his stature. Drinking and talking together in the back room, Dorothy Parker, Dashiell Hammett, John O'Hara, Nathanael West, and a dozen other lesser-known writers toiling in the studios were ardent believers in the genius of Fitzgerald.

Mary Lee Settle

We learned from Fitzgerald's clear clean prose visions more than from any other modern writer. He wrote the American dream, why it survives, and, too often, where the naiveté ends. He was the dreamer who woke, and sang with a voice as clear as a boy, as wise as a sage in an age that smothers truth with the soft, accepted sentiment of fake courage and fake passion. There are the blithe, astonished eyes of Fitzgerald, who saw so clearly, judged so little, and wrote with such Mozartian joy and sadness.

Other writers have made Fitzgerald and *The Great Gatsby* a source for their own fiction. Budd Schulberg's *The Disenchanted* (1950) is a novelized recounting of their disastrous movie collaboration. The Canadian-born novelist Kenneth Millar (1915–1983), who wrote as Ross Macdonald, was deeply involved with Fitzgerald's work. His 1966 novel *Black Money* is an updated retelling of the Gatsby saga: a poor boy idealizes a woman from a higher class, illegally makes the money that he believes will win her, and is betrayed by his corrupt goddess. From Millar's notebooks:

I think when Fitzgerald said he was the last for a time, he may have had in mind the fact that he was the last writer to embody the national fate, the last who swallowed whole the vast Platonic hubris of the Romantics, (Gatsby is said to have "drunk the Platonic milk of wonder"), the last who saw himself as a kind of dizzy philosopher-king at the apex of society, the last who projected his subjective life in fiction as a kind of tragic legend for his age and for future time. He suffered it out in his mind and ego—his personal self and his own fate central to all his fiction—and died as he wrote it.[55]

NOTES

1. John O'Hara, 2 or 3 June 1949, in *Selected Letters of John O'Hara*, edited Matthew J. Bruccoli (New York: Random House, 1978), p. 224.

2. F. Scott Fitzgerald, *The Notebooks of F. Scott Fitzgerald*, edited by Bruccoli (New York: Harcourt Brace Jovanovich/Bruccoli Clark, 1978), # 1021.

3. *St. Paul Daily News*, 11 May 1922, feature section, p. 6; reprinted in *F. Scott Fitzgerald In His Own Time*, edited by Bruccoli and Jackson R. Bryer (Kent, Ohio: Kent State University Press, 1971), p. 131.

4. Fitzgerald, *In His Own Time*, pp. 131–132.

5. Fitzgerald, "Poor Old Marriage," *Bookman*, 54 (November 1921), 253–254; reprinted in *In His Own Time*, p. 127.

6. The prize is awarded to a novel published in the preceding year.

7. Fitzgerald, *The Letters of F. Scott Fitzgerald*, edited by Andrew Turnbull (New York: Scribners, 1963), p. 101.

8. O'Hara, introduction to *The Portable F. Scott Fitzgerald*, selected by Dorothy Parker (New York: Viking, 1945), p. xii.

9. Fitzgerald, *Notebooks*, # 1826.

10. Fitzgerald, *F. Scott Fitzgerald: A Life in Letters*, edited by Bruccoli with Judith S. Baughman (New York: Scribners, 1994), p. 389.

11. Fitzgerald, *Correspondence of F. Scott Fitzgerald*, edited by Bruccoli and Margaret M. Duggan (New York: Random House, 1980), pp. 612–613.

12. Fitzgerald, *Notebooks*, # 1062.

13. Ibid., # 1901.

14. Bruccoli, *The O'Hara Concern: A Biography of John O'Hara* (Pittsburgh: University of Pittsburgh Press, 1995), p. 111.

15. *The Romantic Egoists: Scott and Zelda Fitzgerald*, edited by Scottie Fitzgerald Smith, Bruccoli, and Joan P. Kerr (New York: Scribners, 1974), p. 204.

16. Fitzgerald, "How to Waste Material—A Note on My Generation," *Bookman*, 63 (May 1926): 262–265; reprinted in *In His Own Time*, p. 145.

17. British novelist.

18. Play that won the 1923 Pulitzer Prize for drama.

19. Knut Hamsun and Johan Bojer, Norwegian novelists.

20. American naturalistic writer.

21. Francis Brett Young, British novelist.

22. Midwestern fiction writer.

23. Midwestern novelist and humorist.

24. Charles H. Towne, journalist and editor.

25. 1924 novel by American fiction writer Glenway Wescott.

26. Fitzgerald, *A Life in Letters*, pp. 117–119.

27. Fitzgerald, *Correspondence*, p. 180.

28. Fitzgerald, *The Short Stories of F. Scott Fitzgerald,* edited, with a preface, by Bruccoli (New York: Scribners, 1989), p. 512.

29. Ernest Hemingway, "The Snows of Kilimanjaro," *Esquire* (August 1936): 200.

30. Fitzgerald, *The Short Stories of F. Scott Fitzgerald,* p. 318.

31. Bruccoli, *Fitzgerald and Hemingway: A Dangerous Friendship* (New York: Carroll & Graf, 1994), pp. 191–192.

32. Fitzgerald, ca. 10 October 1924, *A Life in Letters,* p. 82.

33. Hemingway, "Scott Fitzgerald," "Hawks Do Not Share," "A Matter of Measurements," in *A Moveable Feast* (New York: Scribners, 1964), 147–193.

34. Fitzgerald, *Correspondence,* pp. 193–196.

35. Hemingway, *A Moveable Feast,* p. [145].

36. Hemingway, 28 May 1934, *Fitzgerald and Hemingway,* p. 172.

37. Ibid., p. 201.

38. Fitzgerald, *Notebooks,* # 1915.

39. Fitzgerald, *A Life in Letters,* pp. 199–200.

40. Fitzgerald to Thomas Wolfe, mid July 1937, in *A Life in Letters,* p. 332; Wolfe to Fitzgerald, 26 July 1937, in Fitzgerald, *The Crack-Up,* edited by Edmund Wilson (New York: New Directions, 1945), pp. 312–316.

41. "Circus at Dawn."

42. Fitzgerald, 17 April 1935, in *Dear Scott/Dear Max: The Fitzgerald–Perkins Correspondence,* edited by John Kuehl and Bryer (New York: Scribners, 1971), pp. 220–221.

43. Fitzgerald, 29 November 1940, in *A Life in Letters,* p. 472.

44. Gertrude Stein, in *Correspondence,* p. 164.

45. T. S. Eliot, in *The Crack-Up,* p. 310.

46. O'Hara, *New Republic,* 104 (3 March 1941): 311.

47. Archibald MacLeish, in *Romantic Egoists,* p. 200.

48. Robert Benchley, in *Romantic Egoists,* p. 203.

49. Wolfe, in *Romantic Egoists,* p. 203.

50. John Dos Passos, "A Note on Fitzgerald," in *The Crack-Up,* p. 343.

51. Richard Yates, *New York Times Book Review,* 25 November 1979, pp. 82–83.

52. J. D. Salinger, *The Catcher in the Rye* (Boston: Little, Brown, 1951), pp. 182–183.

53. Letter to Elizabeth Murray, *Seventy* (New York: House of El Dieff, 1970), item # 78; reprinted in *Profile of F. Scott Fitzgerald,* compiled by Bruccoli (Columbus, Ohio: Merrill, 1971), [vi].

54. *Tributes* (Columbia, S.C.: Thomas Cooper Society, 1996).

55. Ross Macdonald, *Self-Portrait: Ceaselessly Into the Past,* edited, with an afterword, by Ralph B. Sipper, foreword by Eudora Welty (Santa Barbara: Capra Press, 1981), p. 123.

RESOURCES FOR STUDY OF
F. SCOTT FITZGERALD

STUDY QUESTIONS

1. In a June 1925 letter to Maxwell Perkins, Fitzgerald called "Winter Dreams" "A sort of 1st draft of the Gatsby idea." Focusing on characterization and theme, discuss the accuracy of Fitzgerald's appraisal.

2. Fitzgerald often treated the "New Woman" who emerged in the 1920s. Define this term. Choose three of his female characters—two from short stories and one from a novel—and discuss how each embodies characteristics of the "New Woman."

3. Discuss the causes and possible solutions for the "crack-up" that Fitzgerald describes in the three *Crack-Up* essays: "The Crack-Up," "Pasting It Together," and "Handle with Care."

4. Fitzgerald fell in love with and married a southern girl, Zelda Sayre. Using three of his short stories—"The Ice Palace," "The Jelly Bean," and "The Last of the Belles"—define his vision of the South and of the young women it produced.

5. Analyze Nicole Diver's stream-of-consciousness account (in Book II, chapter 10 of *Tender Is the Night*) of her relationship with Dick Diver. Show how it defines and foreshadows the stages of Diver's disintegration.

6. Unlike many writers who tend to handle the subject with condescension, Fitzgerald seriously treats the concerns of young people. Choose three of the following stories—"Bernice Bobs Her Hair," "The Offshore Pirate," "The Jelly Bean," "The Captured Shadow," "First Blood," "The Hotel Child"—and discuss the concerns of youth that Fitzgerald addresses.

7. *This Side of Paradise* is often described as a quest novel. Define the objects of Amory Blaine's quest. How successful is he in achieving his goals?

8. Monroe Stahr in *The Love of the Last Tycoon* has been called the protagonist in Fitzgerald's novels who achieves the greatest success. In

what ways does he succeed? Does his character reveal qualities that will lead to his defeat?

9. Choosing two of the eight Basil Duke Lee stories and two of the five Josephine Perry stories, discuss the ways in which these figures are different from or similar to each other in character and aspirations.

10. Fitzgerald often used evocative titles for his fiction. Focusing upon theme, symbolism, and/or characterization, show how two of the following are appropriately titled: "May Day," "The Diamond as Big as the Ritz," "Winter Dreams," "Absolution," "Emotional Bankruptcy," "Babylon Revisited."

11. In many of his best works, Fitzgerald examines the influence of wealth upon character. Define how affluence determines, for better or worse, the actions of two of the following characters: Tom Buchanan in *The Great Gatsby*, Anson Hunter in "The Rich Boy," Dick Diver in *Tender Is the Night*, Braddock Washington in "The Diamond as Big as the Ritz."

12. Nick Carraway says of Gatsby that he possessed "some heightened sensitivity to the promises of life" (6). Focusing on two of the following characters—Basil Duke Lee in "Basil and Cleopatra," Rudolph Miller in "Absolution," Dexter Green in "Winter Dreams," George O'Kelly in "'The Sensible Thing'"—show to what extent each embodies the sensitivity attributed to Gatsby.

13. When "May Day" was collected in *Tales of the Jazz Age*, Fitzgerald commented: "I have tried . . . to weave them [the events of the novelette] into a pattern." Focusing upon characterization of the major figures in the story, identify the pattern that emerges.

14. Fitzgerald's female characters are, in general, less idealistic and more practical than his male characters. Discuss how their concerns for the realities of their world dictate the actions of two of the following characters: Rosalind Connage in *This Side of Paradise*, Daisy Buchanan in *The Great Gatsby*, Jonquil Cary in "'The Sensible Thing,'" Paula Legendre in "The Rich Boy," Julia Ross in "A New Leaf."

15. Dexter Green in "Winter Dreams," George O'Kelly in "'The Sensible Thing,'" and Jay Gatsby in *The Great Gatsby* are all poor boys who pursue rich girls with greater or lesser success. Discuss what each learns in the course of his pursuit.

16. Fitzgerald, like all good writers, wrote what is called "transmuted autobiography"—that is, fiction that reflects events and relationships in his own life. Relating two of the following stories to the biographi-

cal and thematic sections of this book, discuss how these stories reflect Fitzgerald's personal concerns: "Two Wrongs," "What a Handsome Pair!," "Financing Finnegan," "One Trip Abroad."

17. Abe North in *Tender Is the Night* is an attractive and affectionately treated alcoholic. Discuss ways in which Abe functions both as a lure and a warning for Dick Diver.

18. Romanticism is defined as a literary movement that celebrates imagination, individualism, and striving for the ideal. Choosing one of the following—Amory Blaine in *This Side of Paradise,* Anthony Patch in *The Beautiful and Damned,* Jay Gatsby in *The Great Gatsby,* Dick Diver in *Tender Is the Night,* Monroe Stahr in *The Love of the Last Tycoon*—discuss how the character is or is not a Romantic.

19. In his *Notebooks* Fitzgerald wrote: "The two basic stories of all times are Cinderella and Jack the Giant Killer—the charm of women and the courage of men" (# 1071). Discuss how this motif is developed in two of Fitzgerald's stories.

20. As a realist Fitzgerald was the master of selective detail. Choose two of the following stories and show how the author used selective detail to reveal a character or setting in each story: "The Last of the Belles," "Babylon Revisited," "The Captured Shadow," "The Ice Palace," "One Trip Abroad."

GLOSSARY OF TERMS

Allegory A narrative in which characters, actions, or objects are employed as representatives of something beyond the narration itself. Thus, a character might represent Love or Pride or Gluttony, and a journey might represent human beings' movement from birth to death. Fitzgerald's "The Diamond as Big as the Ritz" has allegorical elements as the protagonist travels from Hades through Fish (a Christian symbol) with its twelve men (suggesting the Apostles of Christ) to the apparent paradise of the Washingtons' estate, which proves to be a false paradise.

Allusion A reference to a well-known historical or literary figure or event or to another literary source. At the beginning of chapter 6 of *The Great Gatsby,* Nick Carraway speaks of Gatsby's "Platonic conception of himself" (104); Carraway alludes to the belief of fourth-century B.C. Greek philosopher Plato in the possibility of ideal forms. Fitzgerald's title *This Side of Paradise* is drawn from Rupert Brooke's "Tiare Tahiti," and *Tender Is the Night* comes from John Keats's "Ode to a Nightingale."

Cluster Stories Short stories in which Fitzgerald tested themes, characters, and/or scenes that he later developed in novels. Among the cluster stories for *The Great Gatsby* are "Winter Dreams," "Absolution," "'The Sensible Thing,'" and "The Diamond as Big as the Ritz." "The Rich Boy," which examines the effects of wealth on character, is a post–*The Great Gatsby* cluster novelette. *Tender Is the Night* has at least thirty-seven cluster stories, the most important of which are "Babylon Revisited" and "One Trip Abroad."

Conflict The struggle of opposing forces in a narrative, the resolution of which usually reveals the theme or themes of the work. Four basic kinds of conflicts may exist in a literary work: 1) a central figure may struggle against another central figure; 2) a central figure may struggle against himself or herself; 3) a central figure may struggle against natural forces; 4) a central figure may struggle against social forces. Most complex literature includes more than one of these conflicts. In *The Great Gatsby,* for example, Gatsby is in conflict with Tom Buchanan for Daisy, but, more important, he struggles against the social system that makes the Buchanans' wealth "better"—that is, more powerful—than his own. In *Tender Is the Night* Dick Diver tries to maintain his integrity against the forces of the Warren money; his most difficult struggle, however, pits his desire to fulfill his genius against his desire to give pleasure to himself and others.

Dialogue Conversation between characters that advances the plot of a novel or story and that reveals traits of the speakers. The dialogue in chapter 1 of *The Great Gatsby* suggests the distinct natures of four major characters: Tom Buchanan, Daisy Fay Buchanan, Jordan Baker, and Nick Carraway; it also introduces major plot devices:

Tom's infidelity, Daisy's unhappiness, and the presence of Gatsby across the bay.

Emotional Bankruptcy Fitzgerald employed financial metaphors to develop a theme that pervades his work: the idea that human beings have a fixed amount of emotional capital and that when this capital is recklessly expended, it cannot be replaced. The theme is most obviously explored in "Emotional Bankruptcy," "Babylon Revisited," *Tender Is the Night,* and the three *Crack-Up* essays: "The Crack-Up," "Pasting It Together," and "Handle with Care."

Eponym A name of a person or literary figure so closely associated with a particular time, place, or characteristic that the name functions as a symbol for that time, place, or characteristic. Gatsby has become an eponym for the extravagance of the Jazz Age.

Facsimile An exact copy—often photographic or xerographic—of a document or text. Many of Fitzgerald's works have been published in facsimile, including the manuscript for *The Great Gatsby* (1973); Fitzgerald's *Ledger* (1973); manuscripts, revised typescripts and carbons, and revised proofs for his novels, stories, articles, and play (18 volumes, 1990–1991); musical score and acting script for *Fie! Fie! Fi-Fi!* (1996); and uncorrected galley proofs for *Trimalchio* (2000), which Fitzgerald rewrote and revised as *The Great Gatsby.* See **Fitzgerald's Works** for a complete listing of facsimile volumes.

Galley Proofs Set from an author's typescript, these long printed pages were a stage at which editors read for typos and an author usually corrected typographical errors or made minor stylistic improvements. Fitzgerald radically rewrote and revised the galley proofs for *The Great Gatsby.*

Genre The general category, usually determined by form or technique, into which a literary work fits. Major literary genres include fiction, nonfic-

tion, poetry, and drama. These genres are frequently divided into subgenres. Fiction includes the novel, the novelette, and the short story. Fitzgerald produced work in all these subgenres as well as some twenty-eight short-short stories (1,100–2,250 words apiece) for *Esquire* from 1935 through 1940.

Irony A literary device through which words, actions, or situations convey a meaning opposite from the meaning they seem to convey. In "Babylon Revisited," for example, Paul the bartender and Charlie Wales understand the phrase "Selling short" in entirely different ways, Paul interpreting it in its financial sense and Charlie interpreting it in its moral sense.

Jazz Age Name—for which Fitzgerald claimed credit—for the decade of the 1920s. Also known as the Roaring Twenties, the Boom, and the Age of Wonderful Nonsense, the decade dramatically ended with the stock market crash in October 1929, which was followed by the Great Depression of the 1930s.

Manuscript A handwritten document. Fitzgerald composed his stories and novels in manuscript, which he then turned over to secretaries who produced typescripts and carbon copies (copies that resulted from placing blue or black carbon sheets between sheets of typing paper).

Metaphor A figure of speech through which one object is equated—using the word *is* or *was*—with another, apparently dissimilar object. At the end of chapter 5 of *The Great Gatsby,* Nick says of Daisy, "that voice was a deathless song" (101). Fitzgerald repeatedly used financial metaphors to convey the theme of emotional bankruptcy in his work.

Narrator In fiction, the teller of the story. Certain of Fitzgerald's works use first-person narrators—characters who speak in their own voices and who play some part in the story: Nick Carraway in *The Great Gatsby,*

Cecelia Brady in *The Love of the Last Tycoon,* Andy in "The Last of the Belles." Most of Fitzgerald's fiction employs a third-person point of view in which the author reports characters' thoughts and actions. See **Point of View.**

Naturalism Literary movement built on the belief that human beings' characters, actions, and ultimate destinies are determined by external forces beyond their control rather than by the qualities of their own characters. Fitzgerald briefly experimented with naturalism in his novelette "May Day" and his novel *The Beautiful and Damned.*

Novelette A work that is longer than a short story but shorter than a novel. The form typically allows for more extensive development of character and action than does the short story. Fitzgerald wrote three novelettes: "May Day," "The Diamond as Big as the Ritz," and "The Rich Boy."

Page Proofs The final stage of typeset proofs, which include page numbers and other features of the printed book, such as running heads. Because page proofs are expensive to reset, authors normally are discouraged from making substantive changes in their texts at this stage. Fitzgerald, however, sometimes rewrote or revised in page proofs.

Point of View The perspective from which an author presents the actions of his narrative. These perspectives include: 1) the first-person point of view, in which a character in the novel or story—Nick Carraway in *The Great Gatsby,* for example—functions as narrator and limits the story to what he observes or learns; and 2) the third-person point of view, in which the author reports the actions and thoughts of the characters. The third-person point of view can be limited or omniscient (all-knowing). Book I of *Tender Is the Night* employs the third-person, but the perspective is, to a large extent, filtered through

Rosemary Hoyt; the other books of the novel use the omniscient-author point of view, as do most of Fitzgerald's stories.

Realism Literary movement that tends to deal with the immediate, discernible world and that often finds its subject in middle-class or upper-middle-class life and manners. Though Fitzgerald frequently portrayed upper-middle-class life, he tended to be more selective and imagistic in his use of details of person, costume, and place than were such other social realists as Sinclair Lewis and John O'Hara. A characteristic—and brilliant—handling of setting appears in the first chapter of *The Great Gatsby* as, in a single line, Nick Carraway suggests the magnificence of the Buchanans' grounds: "The lawn started at the beach and ran toward the front door for a quarter of a mile, jumping over sun-dials and brick walks and burning gardens—finally when it reached the house drifting up the side in bright vines as though from the momentum of its run" (11).

Roman à Clef Literally, a "novel with a key." In a roman à clef, real people and events are only slightly fictionalized, and the work exists largely to expose the actual people and actions. Fitzgerald never wrote a roman à clef, though his stories and novels often have autobiographical or biographical elements.

Romanticism Literary movement that tends to focus upon imagination rather than reason, upon individualism and individual aspiration rather than interests of society in general, and upon striving for the ideal rather than adhering to the actual. Many of Fitzgerald's best heroes embrace Romanticism, notably Amory Blaine and Jay Gatsby.

Setting The locale (or locales) for the action of a narrative, setting normally conveys important information about the characters' social, economic, psychological, or mental conditions. The

European settings of *Tender Is the Night* and "Babylon Revisited" prove exotic but corrupting to Americans; the differing qualities of East Egg and West Egg in *The Great Gatsby* suggest the distinctions between the old wealth of the Buchanans and the new wealth of Gatsby; and the valley of ashes in *The Great Gatsby* emphasizes the Wilsons' social, economic, and emotional poverty.

Setting Copy The final draft—usually a typescript or carbon copy—from which a literary work is set into type. The setting copy for *The Great Gatsby* was a now-lost typescript, but when Fitzgerald rewrote the novel in galley proofs, these proofs became setting copy for a new set of proofs.

Simile A figure of speech that compares two items using the words *like* or *as*. In the first chapter of *The Great Gatsby*, Fitzgerald uses an extended simile to introduce Daisy Buchanan and Jordan Baker: "The only completely stationary object in the room was an enormous couch on which two young women were buoyed up as though upon an anchored balloon. They were both in white and their dresses were rippling and fluttering as if they had just been blown back in after a short flight around the house" (12). In the first paragraph of *Tender Is the Night*, Fitzgerald sets the scene by saying that "when this story begins only the cupolas of a dozen old villas rotted like water lilies" (7) in the five miles between Gausse's hotel and Cannes.

Stream of Consciousness Technique that records the flow of ideas within a character's mind without regard for logical connections. Fitzgerald used stream of consciousness very sparingly but effectively: see Nicole Diver's reverie in Book II, chapter 10, of *Tender Is the Night*.

Style The distinctive way in which a writer expresses himself or herself. Characteristics of Fitzgerald's style include his marked rhythms, brilliant imagery, sensitivity to color, control of mood, wit, and clarity.

Symbol Any object or action that represents something beyond itself. The green light on Daisy's dock in *The Great Gatsby*, for example, is a symbol of Gatsby's aspiration. The title object in "The Ice Palace" symbolizes the hostile Northern environment and values that Southerner Sally Carrol Happer ultimately rejects.

Synaesthesia The merging of two kinds of sense perceptions in a single image: in *The Great Gatsby*, for instance, Fitzgerald refers to "yellow cocktail music" (44), and in *The Beautiful and Damned* he describes a room "foul with yellow sobbing" (309).

Theme In a literary work a central idea that is conveyed through action, characterization, and other devices employed in the work. The *Crack-Up* essays examine a central Fitzgerald theme of emotional bankruptcy, as do *Tender Is the Night* and "Babylon Revisited." Such works as *This Side of Paradise*, *The Great Gatsby*, and "Winter Dreams" explore both the elevating and destructive powers of aspiration.

Typescript A typewritten document. Fitzgerald delivered typescript versions of his work to Scribners or to Harold Ober, his agent for magazine sales. The documents were prepared by typists from Fitzgerald's manuscript, or handwritten, versions. He revised typescripts (and sometimes carbon copies of these typescripts), which were then usually retyped before they were sent to Scribners or Ober.

SELECTED BIBLIOGRAPHICAL, BIOGRAPHICAL, AND CRITICAL STUDIES (INCLUDES WORKS ON ZELDA FITZGERALD)

BIBLIOGRAPHIES AND CATALOGUES

American Literary Scholarship: An Annual, 1963– . Durham, N.C.: Duke University Press, 1965– . Includes chapters on F. Scott Fitzgerald and Ernest Hemingway.

Bruccoli, Matthew J. *F. Scott Fitzgerald: A Descriptive Bibliography,* revised and augmented edition. Pittsburgh: University of Pittsburgh Press, 1987. Primary. Essential tool for Fitzgerald scholarship.

Bryer, Jackson R. *The Critical Reputation of F. Scott Fitzgerald.* Hamden, Conn.: Archon, 1967. Secondary. Basic annotated bibliography of writings about Fitzgerald.

Bryer. *The Critical Reputation of F. Scott Fitzgerald: Supplement One Through 1981.* Hamden, Conn.: Archon, 1984. Secondary. Basic annotated bibliography of writings about Fitzgerald.

Bucker, Park, ed. *Catalogue of the Matthew J. and Arlyn Bruccoli F. Scott Fitzgerald Collection at the Thomas Cooper Library, The University of South Carolina.* Columbia, S.C.: MJB, 1997.

F. Scott Fitzgerald Centenary Exhibition. Columbia: University of South Carolina for the Thomas Cooper Library, 1996. Illustrated exhibition catalogue.

In their time/1920–1940: Fiestas, Moveable Feasts, and "Many Fetes": An Exhibition at the University of Virginia Library, December 1977–March 1978.

Bloomfield Hills, Mich. & Columbia, S.C.: Bruccoli Clark, 1977. Exhibition catalogue.

Stanley, Linda C. *The Foreign Critical Reputation of F. Scott Fitzgerald.* Westport, Conn.: Greenwood, 1980. Secondary.

BIOGRAPHIES AND MEMOIRS
BOOKS

Bruccoli, Matthew J. *Scott and Ernest: The Authority of Failure and the Authority of Success.* New York: Random House, 1978. Revised as *Fitzgerald and Hemingway: A Dangerous Friendship.* New York: Carroll & Graf, 1994.

Bruccoli. *Some Sort of Epic Grandeur.* San Diego: Harcourt Brace Jovanovich, 1981. Revised edition, London: Cardinal, 1991; New York: Carroll & Graf, 1993. The standard biography.

Buttitta, Tony. *After the Good Gay Times.* New York: Viking, 1974; republished as *The Lost Summer.* London: Robson, 1987.

Donaldson, Scott. *Fool for Love.* New York: Congdon & Weed, 1983.

Graham, Sheilah and Gerold Frank. *Beloved Infidel.* New York: Holt, 1958.

Graham. *College of One.* New York: Viking, 1967.

Graham. *The Real F. Scott Fitzgerald: Thirty-Five Years Later.* New York: Grosset & Dunlap, 1976.

Hackl, Lloyd C. *F. Scott Fitzgerald and St. Paul: "Still Home to Me."* Cambridge, Minn.: Adventure Publications, 1996.

Koblas, John J. *F. Scott Fitzgerald in Minnesota: His Homes and Haunts.* St. Paul: Minnesota Historical Society Press, 1978.

Lanahan, Eleanor, ed. *Zelda, An Illustrated Life: The Private World of Zelda Fitzgerald.* New York: Abrams, 1996.

Latham, Aaron. *Crazy Sundays: F. Scott Fitzgerald in Hollywood.* New York: Viking, 1971.

LeVot, André. *F. Scott Fitzgerald.* Paris: Julliard, 1979; translated by William Byron. Garden City, N.Y: Doubleday, 1983.

Mellow, James R. *Invented Lives.* Boston: Houghton Mifflin, 1984.

Meyers, Jeffrey. *Scott Fitzgerald: A Biography.* New York: HarperCollins, 1994.

Milford, Nancy. *Zelda.* New York: Harper & Row, 1970.

Mizener, Arthur. *The Far Side of Paradise.* Boston: Houghton Mifflin, 1951. Revised edition, 1965. First book-length biography.

Mizener. *Scott Fitzgerald and His World.* New York: Putnam, 1972.

Page, David and John Koblas. *F. Scott Fitzgerald in Minnesota: Toward the Summit.* St. Cloud: North Star Press, 1996.

Ring, Frances Kroll. *Against the Current: As I Remember F. Scott Fitzgerald.* San Francisco: Ellis/Creative Arts, 1985. Memoir by Fitzgerald's secretary during his final years in Hollywood.

Smith, Scottie Fitzgerald, Bruccoli, and Joan P. Kerr, eds. *The Romantic Egoists: A Pictorial Autobiography from the Scrapbooks and Albums of F. Scott and Zelda Fitzgerald.* New York: Scribners, 1974. Essential documentary volume.

Turnbull, Andrew. *Scott Fitzgerald.* New York: Scribners, 1962.

Westbrook, Robert. *Intimate Lies: F. Scott Fitzgerald and Sheilah Graham.* New York: HarperCollins, 1995.

BOOK SECTIONS AND ARTICLES

Callaghan, Morley. *That Summer in Paris.* New York: Coward-McCann, 1963. Passim.

Dardis, Tom. "F. Scott Fitzgerald: What Do You Do When There's Nothing to Do?" In his *Some Time in the Sun.* New York: Scribners, 1976.

Donaldson, Scott. "F. Scott Fitzgerald, Princeton '17." *Princeton University Library Chronicle,* 40 (Winter 1979): 119–154.

Fitzgerald, Frances Scott. "Princeton and F. Scott Fitzgerald." *Nassau Literary Magazine,* 100 (1942): 45; reprinted as "Princeton & My Father." *Princeton Alumni Weekly,* 56 (9 March 1956): 8–9.

Hearne, Laura Guthrie. "A Summer with F. Scott Fitzgerald." *Esquire,* 62 (December 1964): 160–165, 232, 236–237, 240, 242, 246, 250, 252, 254–258, 260.

Hemingway, Ernest. "Scott Fitzgerald," "Hawks Do Not Share," "A Matter of Measurements." In his *A Moveable Feast.* New York: Scribners, 1964. Sensational but unreliable portraits of the Fitzgerald-Hemingway relationship.

Lanahan, Frances Fitzgerald. "My Father's Letters: Advice Without Consent." *Esquire,* 64 (October 1965): 95–97. Reprinted as introduction to *Letters to His Daughter,* by F. Scott Fitzgerald, edited by Andrew Turnbull. New York: Scribners, 1965.

Lanahan. Introduction to *Six Tales of the Jazz Age and Other Stories,* by F. Scott Fitzgerald. New York: Scribners, 1960.

Meyers, Jeffrey. "Scott Fitzgerald and Edmund Wilson: A Troubled Friendship." *American Scholar,* 61 (Summer 1992): 375–388.

Miller, Linda Patterson. "'As a Friend You Have Never Failed Me': The Fitzgerald-Murphy Correspondence." *Journal of Modern Literature,* 5 (September 1976): 357–382.

Schulberg, Budd. "Old Scott: The Mask, the Myth, and the Man." *Esquire,* 55 (January 1961): 97–101. Reprinted in *The Four Seasons of Success,* by Schulberg. Garden City, N.Y: Doubleday, 1972.

Smith, Scottie Fitzgerald. "The Colonial Ancestors of Francis Scott Key Fitzgerald." In *Some Sort of Epic Grandeur* by Bruccoli. San Diego: Harcourt Brace Jovanovich, 1981.

Smith. Foreword to *Zelda,* exhibition catalogue. Montgomery: Museum of Fine Arts, 1974. Reprinted as foreword to *Zelda Fitzgerald: The Collected Writings,* edited by Matthew J. Bruccoli. New York: Scribners, 1991.

TELEVISION PRODUCTIONS

"F. Scott Fitzgerald in Hollywood." 1976. Directed by Anthony Page.

"F. Scott Fitzgerald: The Great American Dreamer." A&E, 1997. Written and produced by Deirdre O'Hearn.

"Marked for Glory." 1963. Written and produced by Gwinn Owens.

CRITICAL STUDIES
BOOKS

Allen, Joan M. *Candles and Carnival Lights: The Catholic Sensibility of F. Scott Fitzgerald.* New York: New York University Press, 1978.

Berman, Ronald. *The Great Gatsby and Modern Times.* Urbana: University of Illinois Press, 1994.

Bruccoli, Matthew J. *The Composition of Tender Is the Night.* Pittsburgh: University of Pittsburgh Press, 1963.

Bruccoli. *"The Last of the Novelists": F. Scott Fitzgerald and The Last Tycoon.* Carbondale & Edwardsville: Southern Illinois University Press, 1977.

Bruccoli, with Judith S. Baughman. *Reader's Companion to F. Scott Fitzgerald's Tender Is the Night.* Columbia: University of South Carolina Press, 1996. Notes, chronology, and other material necessary for the study of the novel.

Bruccoli, ed. *F. Scott Fitzgerald's The Great Gatsby: A Documentary Volume. Dictionary of Literary Biography,* vol. 219. Detroit: Bruccoli Clark Layman/ Gale Research, 2000. Useful background material for study of the novel.

Chambers, John B. *The Novels of F. Scott Fitzgerald.* London: Macmillan / New York: St. Martin's Press, 1989.

Crosland, Andrew T. *A Concordance to F. Scott Fitzgerald's The Great Gatsby.* Detroit: Bruccoli Clark/Gale Research, 1975.

Cross, K. G. W. *Scott Fitzgerald.* New York: Grove, 1964.

Dixon, Wheeler W. *The Cinematic Vision of F. Scott Fitzgerald.* Ann Arbor, Mich.: UMI, 1986.

Eble, Kenneth. *F. Scott Fitzgerald.* New York: Twayne, 1963. Revised, 1977.

Fahey, William A. *F. Scott Fitzgerald and the American Dream.* New York: Crowell, 1973.

Higgins, John A. *F. Scott Fitzgerald: A Study of the Stories.* New York: St. John's University Press, 1971.

Hook, Andrew. *F. Scott Fitzgerald.* London & New York: E. Arnold, 1992.

Kuehl, John. *F. Scott Fitzgerald: A Study of the Short Fiction.* Boston: Twayne, 1991.

Lehan, Richard D. *F. Scott Fitzgerald and the Craft of Fiction.* Carbondale: Southern Illinois University Press, 1966.

Lehan. *The Great Gatsby: The Limits of Wonder.* Boston: Twayne, 1990.

Long, Robert Emmet. *The Achieving of The Great Gatsby.* Lewisburg, Pa.: Bucknell University Press, 1979.

Mangum, Bryant. *A Fortune Yet: Money in the Art of F. Scott Fitzgerald's Short Stories*. New York: Garland, 1991.

Matterson, Stephen. *The Great Gatsby and the Critics*. London: Macmillan, 1990.

Miller, James E., Jr. *F. Scott Fitzgerald: His Art and His Technique*. New York: New York University Press, 1964. Revised as *The Fictional Technique of Scott Fitzgerald*. Folcroft, Pa.: Folcroft Press, 1974. An excellent early study.

Parkinson, Kathleen. *F. Scott Fitzgerald: The Great Gatsby*. Harmondsworth, U.K.: Penguin, 1987.

Parkinson. *F. Scott Fitzgerald: Tender Is the Night*. Harmondsworth, U.K.: Penguin, 1986.

Pendleton, Thomas A. *I'm Sorry about the Clock: Chronology, Composition, and Narrative Technique in The Great Gatsby*. Selinsgrove, Pa.: Susquehanna University Press, 1993.

Perosa, Sergio. *The Art of F. Scott Fitzgerald*. Ann Arbor: University of Michigan Press, 1965.

Petry, Alice Hall. *Fitzgerald's Craft of Short Fiction: The Collected Stories*. Ann Arbor, Mich.: UMI, 1989.

Piper, Henry Dan. *F. Scott Fitzgerald: A Critical Portrait*. New York: Holt, Rinehart & Winston, 1965.

Seiters, Dan. *Image Patterns in the Novels of F. Scott Fitzgerald*. Ann Arbor, Mich.: UMI, 1986.

Shain, Charles E. *F. Scott Fitzgerald*. Minneapolis: University of Minnesota Press, 1961.

Sklar, Robert. *F. Scott Fitzgerald: The Last Laocoön*. New York: Oxford University Press, 1967. Intelligent study of Fitzgerald's development as a fiction writer.

Stavola, Thomas J. *Scott Fitzgerald: Crisis in an American Identity*. New York: Barnes & Noble, 1979.

Stern, Milton R. *The Golden Moment: The Novels of F. Scott Fitzgerald*. Urbana: University of Illinois Press, 1970.

Stern. *Tender Is the Night: The Broken Universe*. New York: Twayne, 1994.

Tate, Mary Jo. *F. Scott Fitzgerald A to Z: The Essential Reference to His Life and Work*. New York: Facts on File, 1998. Indispensable encyclopedia.

Way, Brian. *F. Scott Fitzgerald and the Art of Social Fiction*. London: Arnold, 1980; New York: St. Martin's Press, 1980.

Whitley, John S. *F. Scott Fitzgerald: The Great Gatsby*. London: Arnold, 1976.

COLLECTIONS OF ESSAYS

Bloom, Harold, ed. *F. Scott Fitzgerald*. New York: Chelsea House, 1985.

Bloom, ed. *F. Scott Fitzgerald's The Great Gatsby*. New York: Chelsea House, 1986.

Bloom, ed. *Gatsby*. New York: Chelsea House, 1991.

Bruccoli, Matthew J., ed. *New Essays on The Great Gatsby*. Cambridge: Cambridge University Press, 1985.

Bruccoli, ed. *Profile of F. Scott Fitzgerald*. Columbus, Ohio: Merrill, 1971.

Bryer, Jackson R., ed. *F. Scott Fitzgerald: The Critical Reception*. New York: Burt Franklin, 1978. Useful collection of reviews of Fitzgerald's books that appeared between 1920 and 1941.

Bryer, ed. *New Essays on F. Scott Fitzgerald's Neglected Stories*. Columbia: University of Missouri Press, 1996.

Bryer, ed. *The Short Stories of F. Scott Fitzgerald: New Approaches in Criticism*. Madison: University of Wisconsin Press, 1982.

Claridge, Henry, ed. *F. Scott Fitzgerald: Critical Assessments*, 4 vols. Near Robertsbridge, East Sussex, U.K.: Helm Information, 1991. Best single source.

Donaldson, Scott, ed. *Critical Essays on F. Scott Fitzgerald's The Great Gatsby*. Boston: G. K. Hall, 1984.

Eble, Kenneth, ed. *F. Scott Fitzgerald: A Collection of Criticism*. New York: McGraw-Hill, 1973.

F. Scott Fitzgerald at 100. Rockville, Md.: Quill & Brush, 1996. Includes statements on Fitzgerald by Alice Adams, Frederick Busch, Hortense Calisher, Thomas Caplan, Alan Cheuse, Nicholas Delbanco, Don DeLillo, Nelson DeMille, Thomas Flanagan, George Garrett, Herbert Gold, Allan Gurganus, A. R. Gurney, Joe Haldeman, Alfred Kazin, Edmund Keeley, John McPhee, James Alan McPherson, Arthur Miller, Hugh Nissenson, Reynolds Price, E. Annie Proulx, Budd Schulberg, Carolyn See, Anne Rivers Siddons, Elizabeth Spencer, Christopher Tilghman, John Updike, Richard Wilbur, and Larry Woiwode.

Hoffman, Frederick J., ed. *The Great Gatsby: A Study*. New York: Scribners, 1962.

Kazin, Alfred, ed. *F. Scott Fitzgerald: The Man and His Work*. Cleveland: World, 1951.

Kennedy, J. Gerald and Bryer, eds. *French Connections: Hemingway and Fitzgerald Abroad*. New York: St. Martin's Press, 1998.

LaHood, Marvin J., ed. *Tender Is the Night: Essays in Criticism*. Bloomington: Indiana University Press, 1969.

Lee, A. Robert, ed. *Scott Fitzgerald: The Promises of Life*. London: Vision / New York: St. Martin's Press, 1989.

Lockridge, Ernest, ed. *Twentieth Century Interpretations of The Great Gatsby*. Englewood Cliffs, N.J.: Prentice-Hall, 1968.

Mizener, Arthur, ed. *F. Scott Fitzgerald: A Collection of Critical Essays*. Englewood Cliffs, N.J.: Prentice-Hall, 1963.

Piper, Henry Dan, ed. *Fitzgerald's The Great Gatsby: The Novel, The Critics, The Background*. New York: Scribners, 1970. Useful.

Stern, Milton R., ed. *Critical Essays on F. Scott Fitzgerald's Tender Is the Night*. Boston: Hall, 1986.

Tributes. Columbia: Thomas Cooper Society, 1996. Includes statements on Fitzgerald by Jeffrey Archer, Margaret Atwood, Paul Auster, Richard Bausch, Robert Bausch, Thomas Berger, Sydney Blair, Vance Bourjaily, Frederick Busch, Nicholas Delbanco, Don DeLillo, James Dickey, Annie Dillard, Irvin Faust, Leslie A. Fiedler, George Garrett, George V. Higgins, John Iggulden, John Jakes, John le Carré, Norman Mailer, William Maxwell, Budd Schulberg, Charles M. Schulz, Mary Lee Settle, Tony Tanner, and Arnold Wesker.

JOURNALS

Fitzgerald Newsletter (quarterly, 1958–1968). Reprinted, Washington, D.C.: NCR Microcard Editions, 1969. Includes checklists.

Fitzgerald/Hemingway Annual (1969-1979). Washington, D.C.: NCR Microcard Editions, 1969–1973; Englewood, Colo.: Information Handling Services, 1974–1976; Detroit: Gale Research, 1977–1979. Includes checklists.

F. Scott Fitzgerald Collection Notes. Columbia, S.C.: Thomas Cooper Library, University of South Carolina, 1995– .

BOOK SECTIONS AND ARTICLES

Anderson, W. R. "Fitzgerald After *Tender Is the Night*." In *Fitzgerald/Hemingway Annual 1979*.

Arnold, Edwin T. "The Motion Picture as Metaphor in the Works of Fitzgerald." In *Fitzgerald/Hemingway Annual 1977*.

Berryman, John. "F. Scott Fitzgerald." *Kenyon Review*, 8 (Winter 1946): 103–112.

Bewley, Marius. "Scott Fitzgerald's Criticism of America." *Sewanee Review*, 62 (Spring 1954): 223–246. Expanded as "Scott Fitzgerald and the Collapse of the American Dream." In *The Eccentric Design*, by Bewley. New York: Columbia University Press, 1959. Early treatment of a major Fitzgerald theme.

Bicknell, John W. "The Waste Land of F. Scott Fitzgerald." *Virginia Quarterly Review*, 30 (Autumn 1954): 556–572.

Bishop, John Peale. "The Missing All." *Virginia Quarterly Review*, 13 (Winter 1937): 106–121.

Bruccoli, Matthew J. "Getting It Right: The Publishing Process and the Correction of Factual Errors—with Reference to *The Great Gatsby*." In *Essays in Honor of William B. Todd*, compiled by Warner Barnes and Larry Carver. Austin: Harry Ransom Humanities Research Center, The University of Texas, 1991. Revised edition separately published. Columbia, S.C.: Privately printed, 1994.

Bryer, Jackson R. "Four Decades of Fitzgerald Studies: The Best and the Brightest." *Twentieth Century Literature*, 26 (Summer 1980): 247–267.

Bryer. "Style as Memory in *The Great Gatsby*: Notes Toward a New Approach." In *Critical Essays on F. Scott Fitzgerald's The Great Gatsby*, edited by Scott Donaldson. Boston: G. K. Hall, 1984.

Buell, Lawrence. "The Significance of Fantasy in Fitzgerald's Short Fiction." In *The Short Stories of F. Scott Fitzgerald: New Approaches in Criticism*, edited by Bryer. Madison: University of Wisconsin Press, 1982.

Burhans, Clinton S. "Structure and Theme in *This Side of Paradise*." *Journal of English and Germanic Philology*, 68 (October 1969): 605–624.

Callahan, John F. "'France Was a Land': F. Scott Fitzgerald's Expatriate Theme in *Tender Is the Night*." In *French Connections: Hemingway and Fitzgerald Abroad*, edited by J. Gerald Kennedy and Bryer. New York: St. Martin's Press, 1998.

Carrithers, Gale H. "Fitzgerald's Triumph." In *The Great Gatsby: A Study*, edited by Frederick J. Hoffman. New York: Scribners, 1962.

Corso, Joseph. "One Not-Forgotten Summer Night: Sources for Fictional Symbols of American Character in *The Great Gatsby*." In *Fitzgerald/Hemingway Annual 1976*.

Cowley, Malcolm. "F. Scott Fitzgerald: The Romance of Money." *Western Review*, 17 (Summer 1953): 245–255. Treatment of a central Fitzgerald subject.

Cowley. "Fitzgerald: The Double Man." *Saturday Review of Literature*, 34 (24 February 1951): 9–10, 42–44. Very influential study of Fitzgerald's "double vision."

Cowley. "The Scott Fitzgerald Story." *New Republic*, 124 (12 February 1951): 17–20.

Cowley. "Third Act and Epilogue." *New Yorker*, 21 (30 June 1945): 53–54, 57–58.

Donaldson, Scott. "The Crisis of Fitzgerald's 'Crack-Up.'" *Twentieth Century Literature*, 26 (Summer 1980): 171–188.

Donaldson. "Money and Marriage in Fitzgerald's Stories." In *The Short Stories of F. Scott Fitzgerald: New Approaches in Criticism*, edited by Bryer. Madison: University of Wisconsin Press, 1982.

Donaldson. "The Political Development of F. Scott Fitzgerald." *Prospects*, 6 (1981): 313–355.

Donaldson. "Scott Fitzgerald's Romance with the South." *Southern Literary Journal*, 5 (Spring 1973): 3–17.

Dos Passos, John. "Fitzgerald and the Press." *New Republic*, 104 (17 February 1941): 213.

Elias, Amy J. "The Composition and Revision of Fitzgerald's *The Beautiful and*

Damned." *Princeton University Library Chronicle,* 51 (Spring 1990): 245–266.

Emmitt, Robert J. "Love, Death and Resurrection in *The Great Gatsby.*" In *Aeolian Harps,* edited by Donna G. and Douglas C. Fricke. Bowling Green, Ohio: Bowling Green University Press, 1976.

Friedrich, Otto. "Reappraisals—F. Scott Fitzgerald: Money, Money, Money." *American Scholar,* 29 (Summer 1960): 392–405.

Fussell, Edwin S. "Fitzgerald's Brave New World." *ELH,* 19 (December 1952): 291–306.

Garrett, George. "Fire and Freshness: A Matter of Style in *The Great Gatsby.*" In *New Essays on The Great Gatsby,* edited by Bruccoli. Cambridge: Cambridge University Press, 1985.

Geismar, Maxwell. "F. Scott Fitzgerald: Orestes at the Ritz." In his *The Last of the Provincials.* Boston: Houghton Mifflin, 1943.

Gervais, Ronald J. "The Socialist and the Silk Stockings: Fitzgerald's Double Allegiance." *Mosaic,* 15 (June 1982): 79–92.

Good, Dorothy Ballweg. "'A Romance and a Reading List': The Literary References in *This Side of Paradise.*" In *Fitzgerald/Hemingway Annual 1976.*

Goodwin, Donald W. "The Alcoholism of Fitzgerald." *Journal of the American Medical Association,* 212 (6 April 1970): 86–90.

Grenberg, Bruce L. "Fitzgerald's 'Figured Curtain': Personality and History in *Tender Is the Night.*" In *Fitzgerald/Hemingway Annual 1978.*

Harding, D. W. "Scott Fitzgerald." *Scrutiny,* 18 (Winter 1951–1952): 166–174.

Harvey, W. J. "Theme and Texture in *The Great Gatsby.*" *English Studies,* 38, no. 1 (1957): 12–20.

Haywood, Lynn. "Historical Notes for *This Side of Paradise.*" *Resources for American Literary Study,* 10 (Autumn 1980): 191–208.

Holman, C. Hugh. "Fitzgerald's Changes on the Southern Belle: The Tarleton Trilogy." In *The Short Stories of F. Scott Fitzgerald: New Approaches in Criticism,* edited by Bryer. Madison: University of Wisconsin Press, 1982.

Irish, Carol. "The Myth of Success in Fitzgerald's Boyhood." *Studies in American Fiction,* 1 (Autumn 1973): 176–187.

Kenner, Hugh. "The Promised Land." In his *A Homemade World.* New York: Knopf, 1975.

Kuehl, John. "Scott Fitzgerald: Romantic and Realist." *Texas Studies in Literature and Language,* 1 (Autumn 1959): 412–426.

Kuehl. "Scott Fitzgerald's Critical Opinions." *Modern Fiction Studies,* 7 (Spring 1961): 3–18.

Kuehl. "Scott Fitzgerald's Reading." *Princeton University Library Chronicle,* 22 (Winter 1961): 58–89.

Langman, F. H. "Style and Shape in *The Great Gatsby.*" In *Critical Essays on F. Scott Fitzgerald's The Great Gatsby,* edited by Donaldson. Boston: G. K. Hall, 1984.

Lehan, Richard D. "F. Scott Fitzgerald and Romantic Destiny." *Twentieth Century Literature,* 26 (Summer 1980): 137–156.

LeVot, André. "Fitzgerald in Paris." In *Fitzgerald/Hemingway Annual 1973.*

MacKendrick, Paul L. "The Great Gatsby and Trimalchio." *Classical Journal,* 45 (April 1950): 307–314.

Margolies, Alan. "Fitzgerald's Work in the Film Studios." *Princeton University Library Chronicle,* 32 (Winter 1971): 81–110.

Margolies. "The Maturing of F. Scott Fitzgerald." *Twentieth Century Literature,* 43 (Spring 1997): 75–93.

Miller, James E. "Fitzgerald's *Gatsby:* The World as Ash Heap." In *Critical Essays on F. Scott Fitzgerald's The Great Gatsby,* edited by Donaldson. Boston: G. K. Hall, 1984.

Mizener, Arthur. "Scott Fitzgerald and the 1920's." *Minnesota Review,* 1 (Winter 1961): 161–174.

Mizener. "The Voice of Scott Fitzgerald's Prose." *Essays and Studies,* 16 (1963): 56–67.

Morris, Wright. "The Ability to Function: A Reappraisal of Fitzgerald and Hemingway." *New World Writing,* no. 13 (June 1958): 34–51. Reprinted in *The Territory Ahead,* by Morris. New York: Harcourt, Brace, 1958.

Moyer, Kermit W. "*The Great Gatsby:* Fitzgerald's Meditation on American History." In *Fitzgerald/Hemingway Annual 1972.*

O'Hara, John. "On F. Scott Fitzgerald." In *"An Artist Is His Own Fault": John O'Hara on Writers and Writing,* edited by Bruccoli. Carbondale: Southern Illinois University Press, 1977. Generous appraisals by a major contemporary.

Ornstein, Robert. "Scott Fitzgerald's Fable of East and West." *College English,* 18 (December 1956): 139–143.

Podis, Leonard A. "The Unreality of Reality: Metaphor in *The Great Gatsby.*" *Style,* 11 (Winter 1977): 56–72.

Prigozy, Ruth. "Gatsby's Guest List and Fitzgerald's Technique of Naming." In *Fitzgerald/Hemingway Annual 1972.*

Prigozy. "Poor Butterfly: F. Scott Fitzgerald and Popular Music." *Prospects,* 2 (1976): 41–67.

Raleigh, John Henry. "F. Scott Fitzgerald's *The Great Gatsby:* Legendary Bases and Allegorical Significance." *University of Kansas City Review,* 24 (Autumn 1957): 55–58.

Rosenfeld, Paul. "F. Scott Fitzgerald." In his *Men Seen.* New York: Dial, 1925.

Samuels, Charles T. "The Greatness of 'Gatsby.'" *Massachusetts Review,* 7 (Autumn 1966): 783–794.

Sanders, Barbara G. "Structural Imagery in *The Great Gatsby:* Metaphor and Matrix." *Linguistics in Literature,* 1, no. 1 (1975): 53–75.

Savage, D. S. "The Significance of F. Scott Fitzgerald." *Arizona Quarterly,* 8 (Autumn 1952): 197–210.

Schoenwald, Richard L. "F. Scott Fitzgerald as John Keats." *Boston University Studies in English,* 3 (Spring 1957): 12–21.

Scribner, Charles, III. "Celestial Eyes: From Metamorphosis to Masterpiece." *Princeton University Library Chronicle,* 53 (Winter 1992): 140–155. Study of the dust-jacket art for *The Great Gatsby.*

Scrimgeour, Gary J. "Against *The Great Gatsby.*" *Criticism,* 8 (Winter 1966): 75–86.

Stallman, R. W. "Conrad and *The Great Gatsby.*" *Twentieth Century Literature,* 1 (April 1955): 5–12.

Stark, Bruce R. "The Intricate Pattern in *The Great Gatsby.*" In *Fitzgerald/Hemingway Annual 1974.*

Steinbrink, Jeffrey. "'Boats Against the Current': Mortality and the Myth of Renewal in *The Great Gatsby.*" *Twentieth Century Literature,* 26 (Summer 1980): 157–170.

Tanselle, G. Thomas, and Bryer. "*The Great Gatsby:* A Study in Literary Reputation." *New Mexico Quarterly,* 33 (Winter 1963–1964): 409–425.

Thurber, James. "Scott in Thorns." *Reporter,* 4 (17 April 1951): 35–38. Reprinted in *Credos and Curios,* by Thurber. New York: Harper & Row, 1962.

Trilling, Lionel. "F. Scott Fitzgerald." In his *The Liberal Imagination.* New York: Viking, 1950. Brilliant early assessment of Fitzgerald's vision and style.

Trilling. "Fitzgerald Plain." *New Yorker,* 26 (3 February 1951): 90–92.

Troy, William. "Scott Fitzgerald—The Authority of Failure." *Accent,* 6 (Autumn 1945): 56–60.

Van Antwerp, Margaret A., ed. "F. Scott Fitzgerald." *Dictionary of Literary Biography Documentary Series,* vol. 1. Detroit: Bruccoli Clark/Gale Research, 1982.

Watkins, Floyd C. "Fitzgerald's Jay Gatz and Young Ben Franklin." *New England Quarterly,* 27 (June 1954): 249–252.

Weir, Charles, Jr. "'An Invite With Gilded Edges.'" *Virginia Quarterly Review,* 20 (Winter 1944): 100–113.

Wescott, Glenway. "The Moral of Scott Fitzgerald." *New Republic,* 104 (17 February 1941): 213–217.

Wilson, Edmund. "The Literary Spotlight—VI: F. Scott Fitzgerald." *Bookman,* 55 (March 1922): 20–25.

VIDEORECORDINGS

Bruccoli, Matthew J. *An Introduction to F. Scott Fitzgerald's Fiction.* Modern American Literature—Eminent Scholar/Teachers Series. Detroit: Omnigraphics, 1988. Videorecording with lecture guide by Thomas Jackson Rice. Useful.

Bruccoli. *Reading F. Scott Fitzgerald's The Great Gatsby.* Modern American Literature—Eminent Scholar/Teachers Series. Detroit: Omnigraphics, 1988. Videorecording with lecture guide by Thomas Jackson Rice. Useful.

GENERAL REFERENCES

Aldridge, John W. *After the Lost Generation: A Critical Study of the Writers of Two Wars.* New York: McGraw-Hill, 1951.

Allan, Tony. *Americans in Paris.* Chicago: Contemporary Books, 1977.

Allen, Frederick Lewis. *Only Yesterday: An Informal History of the Nineteen-Twenties.* New York: Harper, 1931.

The American Heritage History of the 20's and 30's. New York: American Heritage, 1970.

Baker, Carlos. *Ernest Hemingway: A Life Story.* New York: Scribners, 1969.

Baker, ed. *Ernest Hemingway: Selected Letters, 1917–1961.* New York: Scribners, 1981.

Baughman, Judith S., ed. *American Decades: 1920–1929.* Detroit: Manly/Gale Research, 1995.

Beach, Sylvia. *Shakespeare & Company.* New York: Harcourt, Brace, 1959.

Behr, Edward. *Prohibition: Thirteen Years That Changed America.* New York: Arcade, 1996.

Berg, A. Scott. *Max Perkins: Editor of Genius.* New York: Congdon/Dutton, 1978.

Bondi, Victor, ed. *American Decades: 1930–1939.* Detroit: Manly/Gale Research, 1995.

Brown, Dorothy M. *Setting A Course: American Women in the Twenties.* Boston: Twayne, 1987.

Bruccoli, Matthew J., and Robert W. Trodgon, eds. *American Expatriate Writers: Paris in the Twenties.* Dictionary of Literary Biography Documentary Series 15. Detroit: Bruccoli Clark Layman/Gale, 1997.

Bruccoli, ed., with Trogdon. *The Only Thing That Counts: The Ernest Hemingway/Maxwell Perkins Correspondence.* New York: Scribners, 1996.

Carpenter, Humphrey. *Geniuses Together: American Writers in Paris in the Twenties.* Boston: Houghton Mifflin, 1988.

Coffey, Thomas M. *The Long Thirst: Prohibition in America.* New York: Dell, 1976.

Collier, James L. *The Making of Jazz: A Comprehensive History.* New York: Dell, 1979.

Cowley, Malcolm. *Exile's Return: A Literary Odyssey of the 1920s*. New York: Norton, 1934. Revised, New York: Viking, 1951.

Cowley. *A Second Flowering: Works and Days of the Lost Generation*. New York: Viking, 1973.

Cowley. *Unshaken Friend: A Profile of Maxwell Perkins*. Boulder, Colo.: Roberts Rinehart, 1985.

Cowley and Robert Cowley, eds. *Fitzgerald and the Jazz Age*. New York: Scribners, 1966.

Delaney, John, ed. *The House of Scribner, 1905–1930*. Dictionary of Literary Biography Documentary Series 16. Detroit: Bruccoli Clark Layman/Gale Research, 1997.

Donnelly, Honoria M., with Richard N. Billings. *Sara and Gerald: Villa America and After*. New York: Times Books, 1982.

Dos Passos, John. *The Best Times: An Informal Memoir*. New York: New American Library, 1966.

Elder, Donald. *Ring Lardner: A Biography*. Garden City, N.Y.: Doubleday, 1956.

Fass, Paula. *The Damned and the Beautiful: American Youth in the 1920s*. New York: Oxford University Press, 1977.

French, Warren, ed. *The Thirties: Fiction, Poetry, Drama*. Second edition, De Land, Fla.: Everett/Edwards, 1976.

French, ed. *The Twenties: Fiction, Poetry, Drama*. De Land, Fla.: Everett/Edwards, 1975.

Greenfeld, Howard. *They Came to Paris*. New York: Crown, 1975.

Hansen, Arlen J. *Expatriate Paris: A Cultural and Literary Guide to Paris in the 1920s*. New York: Arcade, 1990.

Hoffman, Frederick J. *The Twenties: American Writing in the Postwar Decade*. New York: Viking, 1955. Revised, New York: Collier, 1962.

Lanahan, Eleanor. *Scottie, the Daughter of . . . : The Life of Frances Scott Fitzgerald Lanahan Smith*. New York: HarperCollins, 1995.

Manchester, William. *Disturber of the Peace: The Life of H. L. Mencken*. New York: Harper, 1951.

Mencken, H. L. *The American Language: A Preliminary Inquiry into the Development of English in the United States*. New York: Knopf, 1919; revised and enlarged, 1921, 1923; corrected, enlarged, and rewritten, 1936. *Supplement I*, 1945. *Supplement II*, 1948.

Mencken. *My Life as Author and Editor*. New York: Knopf, 1992.

Mencken. *Prejudices: First Series*. New York: Knopf, 1919; *Second Series*, 1920; *Third Series*, 1922; *Fourth Series*, 1924; *Fifth Series*, 1926; *Sixth Series*, 1927.

Meyers, Jeffrey. *Edmund Wilson: A Biography*. Boston: Houghton Mifflin, 1995.

Miller, Linda Patterson, ed. *Letters from the Lost Generation: Gerald and Sara Murphy and Friends*. New Brunswick, N.J.: Rutgers University Press, 1991.

Morton, Brian N. *Americans in Paris: An Anecdotal Street Guide*. Ann Arbor, Mich.: Olivia & Hill Press, 1984.

Reynolds, Michael. *Hemingway: The Paris Years*. Oxford & New York: Basil Blackwell, 1989.

Rood, Karen Lane, ed., with foreword by Malcolm Cowley. *American Writers in Paris, 1920–1939*. Dictionary of Literary Biography, Vol. 4. Detroit: Bruccoli Clark/Gale, 1980.

Spindler, Elizabeth Carroll. *John Peale Bishop: A Biography*. Morgantown: West Virginia University Library, 1980.

Stein, Gertrude. *The Autobiography of Alice B. Toklas*. New York: Harcourt, Brace, 1933.

Thomas, Bob. *Thalberg*. Garden City, N.Y.: Doubleday, 1969.

Toll, Seymour I. *A Judge Uncommon: A Life of John Biggs, Jr.* Philadelphia: Legal Communications, 1993.

Tomkins, Calvin. *Living Well Is the Best Revenge.* New York: Viking, 1971.

Wiser, William. *The Crazy Years: Paris in the Twenties.* New York: Atheneum, 1983.

Wheelock, John Hall, ed. *Editor to Author: The Letters of Maxwell Perkins.* New York: Scribners, 1979.

Wickes, George. *Americans in Paris.* Garden City, N.Y.: Doubleday, 1969.

Wilson, Edmund. *The American Earthquake: A Documentary of the Twenties and Thirties.* Garden City, N.Y.: Doubleday, 1958.

Wilson. *Letters on Literature and Politics 1912–1972,* edited by Elena Wilson. New York: Farrar, Straus & Giroux, 1977.

Wilson. *The Shores of Light.* New York: Farrar, Straus & Young, 1952.

Wilson. *The Thirties: From Notebooks and Diaries of the Period.* New York: Farrar, Straus & Giroux, 1980.

Wilson. *The Twenties,* edited by Leon Edel. New York: Farrar, Straus & Giroux, 1975.

Wright, Austin McGiffert. *The American Short Story in the Twenties.* Chicago: University of Chicago Press, 1961.

Yardley, Jonathan. *Ring: A Biography of Ring Lardner.* New York: Random House, 1977.

WEB SITES

F. Scott Fitzgerald Centenary Home Page. <www.csd.edu/fitzgerald/index.html.> This page is the most comprehensive on-line guide to the life and works of F. Scott Fitzgerald. The site includes extensive primary and secondary bibliographies for Fitzgerald as well as a primary bibliography for Zelda Fitzgerald; a brief biography; and a Fitzgerald chronology. Other sections incorporate quotations, essays, and articles by and about Fitzgerald, as well as facts about him. The site provides information on the 1996 centenary celebrations and photographs of persons, places, and events. It includes pictures of items from the Matthew J. and Arlyn Bruccoli Collection of F. Scott Fitzgerald at the University of South Carolina, such as Fitzgerald's briefcase and engraved flask and the dust jackets to his novels and story collections. Visitors to the site can access audio and video clips of Fitzgerald and can download full texts of eleven short stories published before 1923, juvenilia, and apprenticeship writings. Texts are accompanied by original artwork and magazine covers. Fitzgerald's first novel, *This Side of Paradise,* can be accessed via a link to Columbia University's Bartelby.com. The page offers a history of Charles Scribner's Sons and links to the University of South Carolina Press through which recent texts and videos on the life and work of Fitzgerald can be ordered.

Fitzgerald Campfire Chat. <http://killdevilhill.com/fitzgeraldchat/wwwboard.html.> Part of Kill Devil Hill's Great Books, Literary Cafes, and Chatrooms, this site offers the opportunity to chat on-line or post a message about Fitzgerald topics.

Fitzgerald Childhood Home Tour. <www.pioneerplanet.com/archive/fitzgerald/stories/fitztour10.htm> Pioneer Planet offers an excellent way to "visit" the places of F. Scott Fitzgerald's youth. This site provides a general map and master schedule of the on-line tour. Stops include Fitzgerald's birthplace on Laurel Avenue in St. Paul; his first prep school, the St. Paul Academy; and Scott and Zelda Fitzgerald's rented home at 626 Goodrich Avenue, where they lived between November 1921 and June 1922. Although only some stops provide photographs, each includes informative text linking the place to important times, events, and works in Fitzgerald's life.

The Great Gatsby, A Beginner's Guide. <www.geocities.com/BourbonStreet/ 3844/> This page offers a concise biography of Fitzgerald as well as character studies and a discussion of four major themes in *The Great Gatsby*. It presents a brief summary of life in 1920s America and includes a link to a page titled "Flapper Culture and Style," which further defines the Jazz Age era.

The Great Gatsby Guide. <www.msu.edu/ kulbergr~/gatsbyguide.htm> This page includes a brief biography of Fitzgerald, an essay on the major themes of *The Great Gatsby,* chapter summaries, and a simplistic outline of the novel. Descriptions provided for *Gatsby* are useful in assessing character types and understanding each character's role in the novel. The page links to *The Great Gatsby* Trivia Challenge.

Information on Web sites by Lisa Kerr.

SPECIAL COLLECTIONS

Firestone Library, Princeton University: In 1950 Fitzgerald's daughter, Scottie, made a gift of her father's books and papers to Princeton University. The collection now has some three hundred volumes by and about Fitzgerald and books from his personal library, including his own marked copies of *The Great Gatsby* and *Tender Is the Night.* Princeton also holds the manuscript and corrected proofs for *Gatsby,* and manuscripts, typescripts, and proofs for Fitzgerald's other novels, as well as manuscripts, typescripts, and tearsheets for some of his stories, articles, and poems. The collection includes Fitzgerald's letters to and from Zelda Fitzgerald and his letters from such friends and associates as Harold Ober, Ernest Hemingway,

Arnold Gingrich, Ring Lardner, H. L. Mencken, and Edmund Wilson. The collection also has the Fitzgeralds' scrapbooks, photographs, clippings, and memorabilia. In addition, Princeton holds substantial material by and about Zelda Fitzgerald: the typescripts of *Save Me the Waltz, Scandalabra,* and her stories and articles; several of her drawings; her medical records; and much of her surviving correspondence. Princeton is also the repository for other collections crucial to Fitzgerald scholarship: The John Peale Bishop Papers; The Charles Scribner's Sons Archives, which features the correspondence and other records of the publishing house, including the Fitzgerald-Perkins letters; the John Biggs Papers, which chiefly treat Judge Biggs's management of Fitzgerald's estate between 1940 and 1949; and Sheilah Graham's "College of One" collection, 246 volumes, some of which are inscribed and annotated by Fitzgerald.

A description of the F. Scott Fitzgerald Papers and related collections can be accessed on-line at: <http:// libweb2.Princeton.edu/rbsc2/aids/ msslist/maindex.htm>

Thomas Cooper Library, University of South Carolina: The Matthew J. and Arlyn Bruccoli Collection of F. Scott Fitzgerald, which came to the University of South Carolina in 1994, is the most comprehensive working collection for Fitzgerald research. It includes some three thousand items, among them works by Fitzgerald in all their English-language editions and printings; works about Fitzgerald; and more than three hundred volumes of translations. Among the notable proof and manuscript holdings are the only known set of uncorrected galleys for "Trimalchio," which was rewritten as *The Great Gatsby;* the only known galleys for the first serial installment of *Tender Is the Night;*

and revised typescripts for "The Swimmers," "The Count of Darkness," and "The Kingdom in the Dark." The collection is particularly strong in books inscribed to and from Fitzgerald: recipients of Fitzgerald inscriptions include actress Lois Moran and agent Harold Ober; among the books inscribed by their authors to Fitzgerald are *Ulysses* and *A Portrait of the Artist as a Young Man*, by James Joyce; *For Whom the Bell Tolls*, by Ernest Hemingway; *Ash-Wednesday*, by T. S. Eliot; *Prejudices Second Series*, by H. L. Mencken; and *How to Write*, by Gertrude Stein. The collection is rich in material from Fitzgerald's prep-school and Princeton days and in Fitzgerald-related photographs, including one of Hemingway that he inscribed to Fitzgerald. Among the personal possessions assem-

bled here are Fitzgerald's briefcase and engraved flask. The collection also has substantial holdings for authors associated with Fitzgerald: Ring Lardner, Budd Schulberg, Edmund Wilson, and Ernest Hemingway, among others.

SEE:

Park Bucker, ed., *Catalogue of the Matthew J. and Arlyn Bruccoli F. Scott Fitzgerald Collection at the Thomas Cooper Library, The University of South Carolina.* (See under **Bibliographies and Catalogues**.)

F. Scott Fitzgerald Centenary Exhibition. (See under **Bibliographies and Catalogues**.)

A catalogue for the collection can be accessed on-line at: <http://www.sc.edu/research.html>. Select <USCAN>

MASTER INDEX

Benét, Stephen Vincent 127, 130, 192
Benét, William Rose 127
Benny, Jack 102
Benson, Robert Hugh 16
Benson, Sally 143
Bergen, Edgar 102
Berger, Thomas 189
Berlin, Irving 95
"Bernice Bobs Her Hair" (Fitzgerald) 20, 42, 123, 125
Bernice Bobs Her Hair (play) 143
Bernice Bobs Her Hair (television production) 143
Beyond the Horizon (O'Neill) 96, 176
The Big Money (Dos Passos) 100, 174
Biggs, John, Jr. 43, 174
The Birth of a Nation (motion picture) 98
Bishop, John Peale 16, 26, 131–132, 134, 175, 183
Bits of Paradise (Fitzgerald) 104, 107
Black Money (Macdonald) 192
Black, John 124
The Blacker the Berry (Thurman) 99
The Bodley Head Scott Fitzgerald 105
Boni and Liveright 96
Bookman 126, 128
Borland, Hal 128
Boston Evening Transcript 125–126
Boyd, Thomas A. 157, 175, 177
Bracket, Charlie 26
Brass (Charles Norris) 170
Brecht, Bertold 92
Brenon, Herbert 142
The Bridge of San Luis Rey (Wilder) 171
British Broadcasting Corporation (BBC) 143
Brodkin, Herbert 143
Bromfield, Louis 157, 171
Brooke, D. D. 143
Brooke, Rupert 15, 152
Brooklyn Daily Eagle 124, 126–127
Brooks, Richard 142
"Brother, Can You Spare a Dime?" (song) 102
The Brothers Karamazov (Dostoyevsky) 169
Broun, Heywood 96, 125
Bruccoli, Matthew J. 87, 104–107, 142
Brush, Katherine 139
Bryer, Jackson R. 104–105
Buck, Pearl S. 171–172
Burns, George 102
Butcher, Fanny 125

C

Cabell, James Branch 171
Cain, James M. 175
Caldwell, Erskine 100, 158, 174
Call It Sleep (Roth) 100
Callaghan, Morley 157–158, 174
The Cambridge Edition of the Works of F. Scott Fitzgerald 106
Cambridge University Press 34
"The Camel's Back" (Fitzgerald) 142
Camp Sheridan 17
Canby, Henry Seidel 126, 129
Cane (Toomer) 99
Cantor, Eddie 99
Capone, Al 89
Capp, Al 102
Capra, Frank 102
Carnegie, Andrew 54
The Carolinian (Sabatini) 172
Cather, Willa 95, 169, 171, 176
Cerf, Bennett 70, 96
Chamberlain, John 129
Chambers, Robert W. 126–127
Chamson, André 26
Chandler, Raymond 61, 175
Chaplin, Charlie 98
Chesterton, G. K. 16
Chicago Daily News 19, 126, 128
Chicago Daily Tribune 125
Chicago Sunday Tribune 125
The Chorus Girl's Romance (motion picture) 142
Churchill, Winston 15
Clayton, Jack 143
Cobb, Ty 95
College Humor 27
Collier's 41, 98, 163
Color (Cullen) 99
Colum, Mary 181
Columbia Broadcasting System (CBS) 98, 143
Columbia Pictures 142
Conductor 1492 (motion picture) 142
Conrad, Joseph 66, 160, 169, 171, 178
The Constant Nymph (Kennedy) 172
"Contemporary Writers and Their Work, a Series of Autobiographical Letters—F. Scott Fitzgerald" 151
Coolidge, Calvin 87
Cooper, Ilene 143
Coppola, Francis Ford 143
Correspondence of F. Scott Fitzgerald 105
"Cosmopolitan" (screenplay) 34, 140, 142

Mannes, David 26
Marco Millions (O'Neill) 96
Margolies, Alan 104
Marie Antoinette (motion picture) 140–141
Marquis, Don 96
Matthew, T. S. 129
"May Day" (Fitzgerald) 18, 22, 42, 64–65, 119–121, 127, 171
Mayer, Louis B. 137
McCalls 41
McCoy, Horace 175
McKay, Claude 99
McKenzie, Compton 15
Meehan, Elizabeth 142
Mencken, H. L. 42, 95–97, 124, 126–127, 156, 159, 170
Metro-Goldwyn-Mayer 32–33, 42–43, 98, 102, 137–142
Metropolitan Magazine 103
Metropolitan Opera 144
The Mill on the Floss (Eliot) 176
Millar, Kenneth 192
Miller, Caroline 171
Miller, Glenn 102
Miller, Neal 143
Milwaukee Journal 129
Minneapolis Journal 127
Mistinguet 26
Mitchell, Howard M. 142
Mitchell, Margaret 100, 172
Mizener, Arthur 104, 132
Modern Monthly 184
Moffat, Ivan 143
Mok, Michel 31
Montgomery, Alabama 17–18, 28, 34, 151
Moran, Bugs 89
Moran, Lois 136, 138
Moricz, Michael 144
Morton, Jelly Roll 95
A Moveable Feast (Hemingway) 182
Mr. Smith Goes to Washington (motion picture) 102
Murder, Inc. 89
Murphy, Esther 26
Murphy, Gerald 24, 26, 34, 40, 136
Murphy, Sara 24, 26, 136
Murray, Elizabeth 188
Mussolini, Benito 92
"My Generation" (Fitzgerald) 86
"My Lost City" (Fitzgerald) 18, 58
"Myra Meets His Family" (Fitzgerald) 142–143
The Mysterious Stranger (Twain) 171

"The Mystery of the Raymond Mortgage" (Fitzgerald) 14

N

Nabokov, Vladimir 93
Namara, Marguerite 26
The Nassau Literary Magazine 15
Nathan, George Jean 96, 135
Nation 125–126, 129
National Broadcasting Company (NBC) 98, 143
Neil, Adelaide 163
Nellie the Beautiful Cloak Model (Davis) 177
New Deal 90, 92, 101
"A New Leaf" (Fitzgerald) 47
New Republic 61, 129, 131
New York Evening Journal 129
New York Evening Post Literary Review 127
New York Herald 127
New York Herald Tribune Books 127–130
New York Morning World 125
New York Post 31
New York Times 34, 129
New York Times Book Review 125, 128–130
New York Times Book Review and Magazine 126
New York Tribune 125
New York World 96, 127
New Yorker 96, 128
Newman News 15
Newman School 14–15, 24, 37, 159
Nicholas, Louis 130
The Nigger of the "Narcissus" (Conrad) 160
1919 (Dos Passos) 100, 174
Nineteenth Amendment 88
Norris, Charles 170, 173
Norris, Frank 170, 174
Norton, T. Reid 143
Nostromo (Conrad) 169, 171
Notebooks (Butler) 171
The Notebooks of F. Scott Fitzgerald 24, 28, 30, 44, 47, 58, 60, 105, 133, 149, 164–165, 174–175, 183
Now in November (Johnson) 171–172
Nugent, Elliott 142

O

O'Banion Gang 89